Brazil's state-owned enterprises

This book provides the first systematic analysis of the performance of Brazil's large state-owned enterprises. The Brazilian economic system encourages private enterprise, but the government itself owns and operates such critical industries as petrochemicals, steel, electricity, and telecommunications. The Brazilian state has assumed the role of an entrepreneur not for ideological reasons, but as a pragmatic means of speeding up the process of economic growth. Though relatively few in number, the state-owned enterprises have grown rapidly in size and scale of operations relative to private firms.

The author examines the economic and financial performance of these state-owned enterprises in terms of their contribution to economic growth. He concludes that in Brazil they have been effective substitutes for private investment in a number of strategic industries and that their ability to assemble large amounts of capital, to attract skilled managers, and to earn reasonable profits permitted the Brazilian economy to grow more rapidly over the last twenty years than would have been the case in their absence.

Why the Brazilian state-owned enterprises seem to have performed better than many of their counterparts in other developing countries is a question that will interest development specialists all over the world. Trebat argues that much of the performance is due to the size and dynamism of the Brazilian economy, which allowed these capital-intensive enterprises to realize economies of large-scale production not achievable in smaller countries. But the Brazilian government's policies toward its state-owned enterprises have also been important in avoiding poor performance. The results of these policies provide useful lessons for the supervision and control of state-owned enterprises in other developing countries. Trebat concludes that just as satisfactory state-owned enterprise performance permitted rapid growth in Brazil over the last two decades, so will public enterprise performance in the 1980s be a crucial determinant of how well and how quickly Brazil surmounts its current economic crisis.

CAMBRIDGE LATIN AMERICAN STUDIES

GENERAL EDITOR
MALCOLM DEAS

ADVISORY COMMITTEE
WERNER BAER   MARVIN BERNSTEIN
AL STEPAN   BRYAN ROBERTS

45

BRAZIL'S STATE-OWNED ENTERPRISES

For a list of books in this series please turn to page 292.

Brazil's State-Owned Enterprises

A Case Study of the State as Entrepreneur

THOMAS J. TREBAT

CAMBRIDGE UNIVERSITY PRESS

Cambridge
London   New York   New Rochelle
Melbourne   Sydney

Published by the Press Syndicate of the University of Cambridge
The Pitt Building, Trumpington Street, Cambridge CB2 1RP
32 East 57th Street, New York, NY 10022, USA
296 Beaconsfield Parade, Middle Park, Melbourne 3206, Australia

First published 1983

Library of Congress Cataloging in Publication Data
Trebat, Thomas J.
Brazil's state-owned enterprises.
(Cambridge Latin American studies ; 45)
Bibliography: p.
Includes index.
1. Government business enterprises – Brazil.
2. Corporations, Government – Brazil. I. Title.
II. Series.
HD4093.T727   1983   354.8109′2   82–9564
ISBN 0 521 23716 5

Transferred to digital printing 2004

For Margaret,
Gabrielle,
Nicholas,
and Patrick

Contents

Tables and figures

Tables

viii

Figures

Preface

State-owned enterprises have emerged as important instruments of development policy in most of the mixed economies of Latin America and, indeed, throughout the developing world. The entrepreneurial and commercial activities of the state typically extend to such diverse sectors of the economy as national resource development, banking and finance, external trade and commerce, light and heavy manufacturing, as well as transportation and the utilities.

Brazil has experimented widely with state-owned companies: By 1980 more than six hundred public enterprises were operating in many sectors of the economy. More importantly, the government's firms have grown rapidly in both size and scale of operations and now include all but one of the thirty largest enterprises in the country. At the same time, a large private sector has grown and prospered in Brazil, often with close input or output links with the state companies. The mixture of public and private ownership has resulted in the construction, in the short span of thirty years or so, of a highly integrated industrial complex capable of producing an increasingly sophisticated array of goods for domestic and world markets. Brazil recorded an average annual rate of economic growth of about 7% from 1950 through 1980, emerging as the most dynamic economy in the developing world and, with a GDP well in excess of $300 billion, as one of the largest economies in the world. Brazil is hardly a shining success story of contemporary economic development, but its economic strategy has produced an impressive transformation of a once very poor country. The state-owned enterprises, the subject of this book, were close to the heart of this strategy.

Lessons for other developing countries – on what to do and what to avoid – must abound in the rich Brazilian experience with public enterprises. What are the reasons that lead the state to intervene directly as an entrepreneur and producer? What are the limits of state-enterprise activity? What do government-owned firms in a developing country do well? What are their major shortcomings? How do they affect and interact with the private sector? Ultimately, would the economy and society have been better off had the government resorted less to the instrument of public enterprise? More? Not at all? These are questions that have arisen frequently in recent years in Brazil, but also in Mexico, Peru, Chile, Argentina, and Bolivia, to cite just a few other Latin American examples in which state-owned enterprises have been instruments of development policy. Such questions will surely continue to arise as policymakers throughout the developing world continue to experiment with state-owned companies as a means to attack the dilemmas posed by poverty and underdevelopment.

The study of public enterprises in practice has been hindered over the years by a number of pitfalls. One of these has been ideological, that is, the temptation to look upon government corporations as either good or bad per se, whereas, ultimately, each should be judged on the basis of its particular role in the economy. Thus, well-managed state companies could be relatively successful in one setting – say, Brazil – whereas the same types of firms, if poorly managed, could lead to fiscal chaos in, say, Bolivia. The researcher must be careful when observing state enterprises in operation: Generalizations based on one country's experience with state companies may be inaccurate when extended to other countries.

Another pitfall is theoretical: the lack of any convenient theoretical framework in mainstream economics for examining the role of the state in the economy in general and the state as entrepreneur in particular. Conventional, neoclassical economics seems to make too little allowance for the government to intervene in the marketplace to the pervasive extent that it does in Brazil's mixed economy. By the same token, models of resource allocation for centrally planned economies seem to give a more prominent role to the state planning apparatus and state enterprises than is warranted in the case of Brazil, where government planning is not highly developed and where the private enterprise sector is large and dynamic.

The coexistence of an interventionist state with so many elements of a decentralized and market-oriented economic system make Brazil an intriguing laboratory for the study of "state capitalism." The state-owned enterprises in Brazil illustrate well why it is difficult to apply the tools of conventional economics in a state capitalist setting. Government companies in Brazil are not charged with maximizing profits, but because they are expected to be run on a commercial basis, managers cannot ignore profits. The state-owned enterprises are agents of government development policy and, thus, presumably responsive to central planning and direction. But in practice these firms have their own microeconomic objectives, which can make them unwieldy tools of government policy. Thus, government directives to hold down state company prices in order to subsidize industrial users are likely to be resisted by state-enterprise managers seeking to protect the financial stability of their companies.

The state-enterprise sector in Brazil also raises interesting questions concerning the evolution of economic systems. The primary motivation for the creation of state enterprises – in Brazil and in many mixed-economy developing countries – is almost always the desire of policymakers to speed up the pace of the lagging development process. The motivation is only infrequently ideological; in other words, rarely are state enterprises created or existing private enterprises nationalized solely as part of a general move toward socialism. On the contrary, policymakers often allege that state enterprises are needed in order to assure the long-term development of a capitalist system, with its emphasis on individual initiative and private ownership.

The whole issue of the "statization" of the Brazilian economy has been the subject of much debate in Brazil in recent years.[1] Does Brazil's hybrid economic system simply reflect a stage in its longer-term capitalist development, or does substantial government intervention, once deeply rooted in the economic system of a developing country, preordain movement toward more advanced or efficient forms of socialist economic organization? This book grew out of this debate as an attempt to define the major questions more clearly by isolating and scrutinizing one manifestation of state capitalism in Brazil: the large, state-owned enterprises.

This book took much longer to complete than I would ever have thought possible when the research was begun seven years ago. It is a lineal descendant of my doctoral dissertation, submitted to Vanderbilt University in 1978, but the passage of time and the many changes in the Brazilian economy after the mid-1970s made necessary some major modifications in each chapter.

In the course of preparing the thesis and subsequent book, I have accumulated large personal debts of gratitude to many persons and organizations. I am especially grateful for the day-to-day (and year-after-year) support of family and close friends, the encouragement of fellow Brazilianists, and the financial support of several different institutions. But it is also important to acknowledge the many people whose names I will not have space to mention, who helped me in smaller but important ways via the unexpected word of encouragement, the helpful comment at a seminar, the show of concern with the book's progress. Without all of these people, this book would not have been possible.

I was fortunate to have the generous support of a number of institutions during the basic research stage of this work. The assistance provided during my graduate training from the Danforth Foundation, the Fulbright Commission, and the Social Science Research Council is gratefully acknowledged.

A special debt is owed to Werner Baer, not only for his unflinching support and encouragement at literally every stage along the way, but for his scholarly example as a devoted Brazilian specialist. The idea for this book can be traced to his early articles on the role of the state in the Brazilian economy. And the book, whatever its remaining defects, is much better for his patient criticism.

My advisers at the Department of Economics of Vanderbilt

University helped me shape a mountain of facts into a book. While doing his own field research, Samuel Morley was on hand in Brazil to direct my research energies away from numerous dead ends. Back at Vanderbilt, he then patiently saw the original thesis through many drafts, solved many problems, and provided both the prodding and the encouragement to keep me going at critical junctures. William Steel provided invaluable organizational advice, and he and Andrea Maneschi provided many suggestions for an improved product.

At a later stage in my research, I was privileged to have the detailed comments and criticism of Alfred Stepan, another distinguished Brazilianist. His own comparative perspective on state enterprises helped me to appreciate the importance of the Brazilian case, and I have felt free to borrow from his valuable insights on the role of the state in Latin America. Stepan's counsel was a key element in turning this research into a book.

The fieldwork for this book was done in Brazil during 1975–7 and on numerous return visits since that time. IPEA/INPES provided excellent physical facilities during my research and, more importantly, the support of a lively research community. My special thanks go to IPEA's directors at that time, Hamilton Tolosa, Hamilton Nonato, and, especially, Fernando Rezende da Silva, for their early confidence in the outcome of my research project. While at IPEA, I benefited from the criticism received from Wilson Suzigan, Pedro Malan, and Gervasio Castro de Rezende.

The Centro de Estudos Fiscais of the Fundação Getulio Vargas kindly permitted me access to unpublished data on public enterprises. While absolving them from any responsibility for the use and interpretation of the data, I extend my gratitude to Margareth Hanson Costa, director of the Centro de Estudos Fiscais, and her associates for their generous assistance.

Much of the present version of the thesis was written while I was a visiting member of the faculty of the Department of Economics, University of Texas at Austin. I would like to thank members of the department and the administrative staff for their hospitality and encouragement. Association with the

Institute of Latin American Studies at Texas was a superb fringe benefit. I am especially grateful to the director of ILAS, William P. Glade, and to Alfred Saulniers of the Office of Public Sector Studies for their interest and support.

Support and helpful comments came from many others over the years. I would like to thank Richard Newfarmer, a valued critic throughout, as well as Peter Wogart, Steven Topik, Paul Beckerman, Peter Knight, Randal Johnson, Douglas Graham, David Garlow, William Tyler, Dennis Mahar, and Thomas Bruneau. I am grateful as well to the many conference organizers and participants who gave me valuable opportunities to present the preliminary results of this research and to receive helpful criticism. My colleagues in the business world, particularly Lawrence Brainard and John Purcell, have also contributed importantly to my understanding of economic development and the role of the state.

A final, special acknowledgment is needed for the support of my wife, Margaret. She has shared all the many burdens imposed by this research project, and her relief at seeing it finished is exceeded only by my own. I have promised both of us that the next book will not take so long.

All of these people – and many others – have helped see this project through. They deserve a share of the credit, if any, but the responsibility for the final results and their interpretation is mine alone.

Thomas J. Trebat

Stamford, Connecticut
December 1982

1

Introduction

How should one look upon the role of the state in the economies in Latin America? The answer will certainly influence the criteria for success or for failure used in an evaluation of state-enterprise performance. My premise is that cultural traditions in Brazil and in many countries of Latin America support a much more activist economic role for the state in Latin America than in the Western market economies.[1] An important concern in Latin America has been that an increased scope of free-market forces will lead to undesirable results when, as is the case so frequently, the starting point is one of tremendous inequalities in the distribution of income, wealth, and education between various social groups. In Latin America, privileged domestic elites have traditionally monopolized these economic advantages, so one fear has been that these same elites would benefit disproportionately from a capitalist economic system that placed maximum emphasis on the selfish pursuit of material benefits by individuals. A parallel fear has been that a free-market system operating in the global economy would, for analogous reasons, work to concentrate wealth and resources in the hands of a relatively small number of already wealthy nations while working to ensure the permanent impoverishment of more backward economies and societies simply because more developed countries are richer and more technologically advanced from the beginning.

Understanding this basic mistrust of the market system helps the observer realize the reasons for the many forms of Latin American government intervention in both the domestic economy and the external trade sector. If domestic industrialization appeared to be lagging or if resource allocation patterns, left to their own devices, seemed to be concentrating the benefits of rising output in the hands of a few privileged social classes or geographical regions, policymakers in Latin America have often considered it a moral obligation to step in and change things. State intervention in the internal economy has taken the shape of state-enterprise and direct government investment, subsidized government-lending programs for favored sectors and regions, price and interest-rate controls, subsidies, tax credits, and credit controls. In order to change the way in which the internal economy interacts with the world economy, the state has used tariffs, quotas, compulsory import deposits, import-duty concessions, export incentives, foreign exchange controls, and multiple exchange rate practices. Foreign direct investment has been disciplined by controls on dividend remittances and royalties, by outright nationalization, and by requirements to find local partners, to hire local nationals, to match imports with exports, and to carry out research and development activities in the host country.

Although the degree of state intervention has varied significantly in Latin America, both from country to country and within a single country over time, a substantial amount has been the norm. States' modifications of the structure of the economy and alterations of the allocation of resources, in Glade's summary, "have had at their core one essential rationale...Every one of these cases has reflected a dissatisfaction with the decisions that automatically result from the free play of market forces, and every one of them documents an instance in which the social decision was taken to abridge or suspend the market mechanism by organizing resources through the major public institution that stands most independently above the market: the State."[2]

In his search for the philosophical bases of the social role of the state in Latin America, Stepan argues that a body of ideas that can be traced from Aristotle, through Roman law, medieval natural law, and contemporary Catholic social philosophy forms a coherent "organic-statist" approach to the role of the state in society and that this approach has influenced the responses of decision makers in Latin America to economic and social crises.[3] The core ideas of the organic-statist approach include an emphasis on a harmonious political community as "the moral center of the organic-statist vision" and a concept of the *moral obligation* of the state to achieve the common good. The organic-statist tradition therefore makes allowance for a state that is strong and morally compelled to intervene in society, but it also defines limits for such intervention. Stepan identifies a "principle of subsidiarity" implicit in the tradition, which essentially recognizes important roles in society and the economy for actors other than the state. Stepan explains: "Although the state is the most perfect political community, all the component parts (individual, family, private association) have a proper function of their own within the organic whole. Thus each part has a sphere of natural action that the state should not eliminate."[4] An important presumption is that the interventionist state and the decentralized marketplace not only can, but should, coexist.

To sum up, the organic-statist approach is different from, and fundamentally at odds with, both classical liberal and Marxist conceptions of the proper role of the state: "Organic-statist concepts of the priority of the political community and of the state's responsibility for the common good imply strong constraints on laissez-faire market individualism. However, the principle of subsidiarity implies equally strong limitations on the legitimacy of the state to act as the chief owner of the means of production and the chief planner of the economy."[5]

If we accept for the moment that this organic-statist approach has influenced policymakers in Latin America, including in most cases the military in these countries, a possible contradiction arises between the political goals underlying state intervention and the economic constraints within which the interventionist state must operate. Are the state's goals – as morally sound as these may be – really consistent with overall resource availability in the economy? Can the state achieve its goals without seriously disrupting the functioning of a basically decentralized market economy? Stepan states the problem in this way:

[Policymakers in Latin America] commonly commit themselves to an intermediate statist model that is "neither capitalist nor communist," by replacing private initiative with overall public regulation in economic life, at the same time retaining the marketplace as the basic mechanism for distributing goods and services. *They retain a system that is heavily dependent on entrepreneurial initiative and market flows, while to some extent undermining both.*[6]

It is not enough to recognize that Brazilian and other Latin American policymakers have accepted the coherence of an economic model based on harmonious interaction between the state and the private sectors. Does such a model really "work" by promoting stable economic growth and reasonably efficient resource allocation? What are the boundaries beyond which state intervention becomes excessive, thereby endangering these fundamental economic objectives? These have been, and are likely to be during the 1980s, questions of the utmost relevance in Latin America. In recent years, a number of countries have moved clearly away from the organic-statist model. Chile stands out as the most radical case, but Argentina, Uruguay, Peru, and Jamaica, among others, have also taken steps to cut back sharply on the economic role of the state. But even in these economies, it remains strong, certainly by comparison to the Western market economies.

Despite the controversy that state economic intervention has provoked in Latin America, its actual results have rarely been subject to critical and objective study. This has certainly been the case in Brazil, despite the importance there of the public sector.

Evaluation of Brazilian public enterprise

The questions raised by state capitalism involve relations among political and social groups as well as matters of economic growth, and require treatment from a multidisciplinary perspective. Werner Baer and colleagues, in their own reexamination of the economic role of the state in Brazil, were among the first to recognize its unmet challenge to social science analysis.[7] Since then, political scientists, sociologists, and economists have produced a number of valuable studies on state capitalism and state enterprise in Brazil. Of these, important contributions include a series of studies by Sergio Abranches on the state and economic decision making in Brazil that is rich in institutional and historical detail.[8] Abranches and Sulamis

Dain have provided case studies of decision making in state enterprises in steel, mining, and railroads.[9] Building on his own pioneering early work, Luciano Martins has looked closely at the growth of the state in Brazil from a sociological and political perspective, illustrating his points with case studies of decision making in such key public sector institutions as the Economic Development Council.[10] Renato Boschi has been concerned with the whole issue of private sector industrial elites in Brazil and their often complex interaction with the state.[11] Carlos Estevam Martins and colleagues have contributed theoretical clarifications of state capitalism in the context of a developing country with special reference to the case of Brazil.[12] The relations between state, foreign, and local private investors have been the focus of investigation by Peter Evans in a case study of the Brazilian petrochemical industry.[13] Richard Newfarmer has also produced valuable research results in his examination of the electrical industry.[14]

All of this work has only begun the task of analyzing and interpreting the Brazilian experience with state capitalism. This study of the economic performance of Brazilian public enterprise is an attempt to add another dimension and a new body of data to the multidisciplinary effort. As no comparable study had been undertaken previously, the data-gathering difficulties have been formidable and the reader is well advised at the outset to be mindful of the book's inevitable limitations. There is a heavy emphasis on statistical materials relating to state-enterprise operations in Brazil for the period 1965–80. The Brazilian government did not begin publishing comparable data on its own firms until the early 1980s, indeed, did not even have an estimate of the number of firms it owned until a census was completed in 1980.

At this writing, little in the way of official data is available on public enterprises before 1980. The empirical base for this book has been drawn from a large variety of sources, including annual reports, miscellaneous government documents, unpublished business papers, and interviews. Inevitably, the data presented throughout the book will have to be revised as, hopefully, official data for the pre-1980 period become available in the future.[15] But while decimal-point accuracy is not assured, the conclusions reached in most cases from an examination of the available data should be sufficiently robust as to withstand future data revisions.

Another important limitation of this study, even as description of the Brazilian experience alone, relates to the sample of public enterprises used as a basis for most of the empirical chapters. Given the data difficulties, it was impossible to gather lengthy time-series data on the more than 600 state-owned enterprises in Brazil. Thus, the study is strictly limited to just 50 or so state firms, but these include the largest and most important public enterprises, which represent the bulk of the state's total investment. The relative abundance of statistical materials on these large firms taken individually, and their accessibility to the author for first-hand observation and interviews were also important determinants of their inclusion in the sample.

While the necessary qualifications usually appear throughout the text, the reader is advised to note that most references to the quantitative dimensions of Brazilian state companies or "the public enterprise sector" actually relate to this sample of selected, large public enterprises. But once again, while not large, the sample does include the real core of the state-enterprise sector in Brazil.

After reviewing the motives for public enterprise in many developing countries, one observer concluded: "There is no difficulty in recognizing the *need* for a particular public enterprise. The difficulty lies in establishing it, financing it, providing it with personnel, giving it a suitable organizational shape, assuring that it attains the maximum possible efficiency, subjecting it to adequate – but not excessive – controls, etc."[16] These suggest the types of specific issues with which this book is concerned.[17] The emphasis is on the economic aspects of Brazilian state-enterprise performance, but the political and social objectives cannot be ignored. In reference to Latin American public enterprise in general, Glade has noted:

Changed social and economic relations – "a relational output" as it were – figured importantly among the objectives sought as state firms are ordinarily, in greater or lesser degree, engaged in restructuring the institutional fabric which underpins the workings of the market mechanism. Hence, to capture the essence of their functioning, one must perforce examine their actions in fostering political and social realignments no less than those of their operations which figure in the customary income and product accounts...To ignore this aspect of their operations in assessing their performance would be to miss a great deal of the fundamental rationale lying behind their creation in the first place.[18]

The examination of Brazilian enterprises begins with a description in Chapter 2 of the broad role of the public sector in the Brazilian economy that abstracts from the state's directly productive entrepreneurial activities. The intent is to provide an introduction to the "state as regulator" in Brazil and an overview of its important lending and financial activities. These are not treated elsewhere in the course of the study, but are crucial for an understanding of the broader context in which the state enterprises function.

Historical aspects of the evolution of the state enterprise sector are discussed in Chapter 3 with emphasis on the reasons for the creation of the major companies. If we are to evaluate performance, we must begin with an understanding of why they were created in the first place. The structure of Brazilian public enterprise is examined in the light of the experiences of other developing countries and, not surprisingly, reveals many similarities in the types and functions of public companies. Other topics treated in Chapter 3 include the important role of alliances between the military and civilian technocrats in Brazil to the origins of many state enterprises and the respective spheres of action for public and private enterprises in Brazil.

A key aspect of public-enterprise appraisal, treated in Chapter 4, relates to control: How can the government be assured that companies subject to only loose market and fiscal discipline will avoid waste or other departures from their original goals? This is an issue that has not been well resolved in any country, and Brazil has had its serious organizational and institutional problems in attempting to come to grips with the question of state-enterprise accountability. The crux of the matter is that either too much or too little control will prove harmful to enterprise performance, and finding the right point on the autonomy–accountability trade-off curve can be a difficult matter. Success has much to do with the quality of government supervision and the business acumen and political dexterity of state-enterprise managers, points that are also considered in Chapter 4.

Since an underlying objective of all state enterprise is in one way or another to promote faster economic growth, the relationships between public-enterprise performance and Brazil's growth record must be looked at carefully. This task is confronted in Chapter 5. The capital formation and output records of the large public enterprises are assembled (to my knowledge, for the first time) and interpreted in the context of the overall trends in the economy. A case-by-case look at the performance of the state-enterprise sectors selected for closer scrutiny in this study is also included in Chapter 5. An important insight to be gained from the descriptive materials included is the close dependence that has developed in Brazil between the large public enterprises and a constellation of private firms that are either customers or suppliers of these enterprises.

A common perception of state enterprises is that they are practically synonomous with waste and inefficiency. This point is investigated in a detailed manner in Chapter 6 in the course of tracking trends in capital intensity, labor absorption, and rates of return. Brazil has its share of public enterprises that conform closely to the stereotype of a poorly managed, deficit-ridden operation, but the actual profit performance is varied and complex. Many firms have been consistently profitable and, by and large, Brazilian state enterprises compare well in terms of profitability with Brazilian private companies and state enterprises in other developing countries. Profit performance is closely linked to pricing policy, which in turn is dependent on the degree of enterprise autonomy permitted by the central government. Price policies are examined separately in Chapter 7. These turn out to be close to the heart of the relatively good financial performance of Brazilian state companies.

An enduring problem for state enterprises has been to achieve secure access to sound investment financing through some combination of retained profits, government subsidies, and borrowing from the banking system. The lack of secure access hinders rational planning in the enterprise and leads to inadequate rates of output growth. Recourse to inflationary means of investment finance may solve the problem for the state enterprise, but frequently at the cost of aggravating the deficit of the public sector and provoking unsustainably large increases in external indebtedness. The Brazilian public enterprises managed enormous programs of capital formation during the 1960s and 1970s, using a variety of financing patterns ranging from complete self-finance to total dependence on government subsidies. These patterns are described in Chapter 8 and contrasted with systems of investment finance in public enterprises in selected other Latin American countries.

Finally, conclusions and the "lessons" from this case study of the way public enterprise works are offered in Chapter 9. The Brazilian public enterprise experience has not been without many problems, but it is doubtful that Brazil could have recorded such important economic successes in the 1965–80 period without the results achieved by the public sector enterprises. The role of the state companies is now in the 1980s being reexamined in the light of the energy crisis and severe balance of payments constraints. It seems clear at this point that Brazil will have to recast its economic strategy to continue to grow successfully in the rest of this century. It seems equally clear that, once again, the performance of the public companies will be a major determinant of Brazil's economic success.

2

The economic role of the state

"State capitalism" in Brazil refers to the important decision-making role of the public sector in a supposedly free-market economy. The economic role of the Brazilian state can be broken down into two broad categories of functions: the state as a regulator of economic activity and the state as a direct participant in economic activity.[1] The first category would include the classic allocative, stabilizing, and distributive functions of the state implemented through a variety of traditional tools: monetary, credit, and fiscal policies, trade and exchange rate policies, price controls, and so on. As a direct participant in the economy, the Brazilian state is also important as an owner of banks and enterprises. The state as regulator and the state as entrepreneur: Both of these separate, but interrelated roles of the Brazilian public sector grew in importance over the last twenty years. This book is concerned with a particular facet of state capitalism in Brazil, the nonfinancial public enterprises. But we would miss much of the subject's true importance in contemporary Brazil without at least some initial understanding of the broader role of the state as regulator and as an owner of financial institutions. The origins and major outlines of that broader role are the topics of this chapter.

Historical antecedents

Until the gold boom of the eighteenth century, the Brazilian colony was thought by the Portuguese to be of little commercial value. As a result, trade and development in Brazil were unencumbered by state controls, certainly by comparison to the Spanish imperial system prevalent elsewhere in Latin Amer-

10

ica. The relatively open trading environment was mirrored within Brazil by a decentralized system of government. Glade argues that the principal impetus to early settlement and social organization in Brazil came from the private sector rather than the public sector: "The formal structure of public authority [in early colonial Brazil] was comparatively unobtrusive in the total scheme of things; until the [mid-eighteenth century] reforms the apparatus of bureaucratic interventionism, which was so conspicuous in the Spanish realm, was of modest proportions."[2] Thus, while the public sector was certainly not absent from the scene, Brazil's earlier colonial history is distinguishable from those of its Latin American neighbors by a relatively greater commercial orientation and a more vigorous private sector with more highly developed marketing and finance activities.

Active participation of the state in the Brazilian economy can be traced to the tightened Portuguese controls after the discovery of gold in the eighteenth century. The newly discovered wealth led to stricter trade and fiscal controls and greater centralization of colonial government. Later, under the monarchs from the early 1800s through 1889, the modern role of the public sector began to take shape as the state intervened during the coffee boom of the nineteenth century to extend agricultural development and to touch off the process of industrialization. While, as Glade warns, it would be wrong to assume that public sector resources were mobilized on a scale adequate for development or always used to best advantage to promote it, still, "the Brazilian monarchs seem to have been more sensitive than most Latin American governments to the possibilities of using the resources of the public sector to promote development."[3]

Early in the nineteenth century, the royal government advanced economic organization in the colony by founding (in 1808) the first Banco do Brasil, a bank of issue and a deposit bank, and authorizing the formation of the Rio de Janeiro bourse. Nicia Vilela Luz has described these early attempts to use tariff policies, tax exemptions, and fiscal incentives to encourage invention, technology transfer, and the formation of industry, such as textile mills and ironworks.[4]

By the latter half of the nineteenth century, the idea of using tariff policy in order to protect local industry was firmly established in Brazil. But the prime intent of economic policies pursued by the late monarchical government and governments during the First Republic (1889–1930) was to expand the agricultural export economy, not to push industrialization. Topik argues, however, that the state's actions in this preindustrial era did set a precedent for later intervention: "Most of the Government's decisions during the First Republic were reached through *ad hoc* responses to crises rather than developmental planning...[but] through this haphazard, almost involuntary, procedure the First Republic's State set the precedents that have greatly affected the nature of current interventions."[5] The actions taken by the state in the First Republic to encourage development of the agricultural sector included duty exemptions, guaranteed profits, subsidies, direct investments in private companies, and monopoly concessions. The government also lowered transportation rates on state-owned or state-controlled railroads, used price-support programs for agriculture, constructed warehouses and ports, and ran experimental stations. The so-called valorization programs for coffee in the early 1900s, innovative schemes whereby the state (including the government of São Paulo) intervened to prop up the world price of coffee, solidified the central regulatory role of the state in the coffee economy.[6] Thus, even before the rise of Getulio Vargas and the *Estado Novo* in the 1930s, the Brazilian state had established ample precedent for intervention.

Fiscal functions of the Brazilian state

In retrospect, Brazil's modern development has been a shift of economic activity out of agriculture and into industry. Between 1939 and 1978, agriculture's share in national income plummeted from 33% to 11%; during the same period, industry's share rose from less than 20% to 37%[7] (see Table 2.1). While a decrease in the share of the primary sector in national income is normal during economic development, the compression of the agricultural sector was particularly rapid

Table 2.1. *Brazil: sectoral distribution of national income, 1949–78, in percentage*

	1949	1959	1967	1970	1974	1978
Agriculture	24.9	19.2	12.8	10.2	11.2	11.4
Industry	26.0	32.6	32.5	36.3	31.8	37.1
Services (total)	49.1	48.2	54.7	53.5	49.0	51.5
Commerce	12.4	14.4	14.8	15.7	16.3	15.2
Finance	3.8	3.2	5.1	5.8	6.2	9.3
Trans./Comm.	7.0	6.2	6.0	5.2	5.1	5.6
Government	6.8	7.1	9.3	9.2	7.6	8.0
Rents	6.3	7.0	9.1	8.1	6.2	6.2
Other services	12.8	10.3	10.4	9.5	7.6	7.2

Source: Conjuntura Econômica, various issues. As reprinted in Paulo Rabello de Castro, "Repartição setorial da renda: ciclos e tendências," *Conjuntura Econômica* 33 (December 1979): 84.

in Brazil and reflects the extent to which agriculture was exploited to support the process of industrialization.[8]

Industrialization and modernization, stimulated in large measure by conscious government policy, have provoked alterations in the economic functions of the public sector.[9] Urbanization and the consequent increase in the demand for public services have burdened all levels of government while the development process has required, as predicted by fiscal expenditure theory, larger government outlays for capital formation.[10] The growth of public expenditures, most pronounced in the postwar period, has occurred at all levels of government: federal, state, and municipal.[11] Total public expenditures as a percentage of GNP have doubled in the last fifty years, reaching 25% in recent years.[12] As Table 2.2 indicates, the federally controlled *autarquias* (semiautonomous agencies), especially the social security system, have emerged as the major disbursers of public monies.

The principal reasons for expenditure growth were federal social security programs and state-government infrastructure spending, mostly road and energy investments made possible by shared federal funds.[13] Analysis of public sector (except

Table 2.2. *Public sector expenditures in percentage of GNP*

	Federal	*Autarquias*	State municipal	Total public sector
1920	8.2	—	4.3	12.5
1941	10.4	0.7	8.2	19.2
1960	8.1	4.8	10.7	23.5
1973	5.9	9.4	9.3	24.6

Source: For 1920–60, F. Rezende and D. Mahar, "The Growth and Pattern of Public Expenditure in Brazil, 1920–1969," *Public Finance Quarterly* 3 (October 1975), Appendix; for 1973, *Conjuntura Econômica* 29 (June 1975):84–8.

Table 2.3. *Long-term trends in public sector spending as percentage of GDP*

	1949	1959	1965–9	1970–3	1974–8
Consumption	12.0	10.2	10.4	9.8	9.6
Salaries	(6.5)	(5.6)	(7.2)	(7.0)	(6.5)
Other	(5.5)	(4.6)	(3.2)	(2.8)	(3.1)
Transfers and subsidies	3.1	4.3	7.1	8.1	9.5
Transfers	(3.0)	(3.5)	(6.4)	(7.6)	(8.6)
Subsidies	(0.1)	(0.8)	(0.7)	(0.5)	(0.7)
Capital formation	4.4	3.5	4.5	3.9	4.0

Source: Margareth Hanson Costa, "A discutida ampliação da intervenção estatal," *Conjuntura Econômica* 33 (December 1979):90.

public enterprise) spending reveals a postwar decline in the relative importance of consumption and capital formation categories and explosive growth in the share of budget spending going to transfers and subsidies (see Table 2.3).

The apparent decline in the capital formation share is probably attributable to the fact that many investment activities previously carried out by agents of the central government are now performed by public enterprises that were created as a means of administrative decentralization. Fundação Getulio Vargas estimates of investment spending by federally owned

Table 2.4. *Trends in gross fixed capital formation*
of federal public enterprises

	As % of GDP	As % of total capital formation
1949	0.4	3.1
1959	1.5	8.2
1965	2.0	10.9
1970	2.7	11.9
1975	4.3	16.9

Note: Official calculations of the Fundação Getulio Vargas for 185 federally owned enterprises. These figures are not directly comparable to those provided by the author for a sample of large public enterprises in Chapter 4.
Source: Margareth Hanson Costa, "A discutida ampliação da intervenção estatal," *Conjuntura Econômica* 33 (December 1979):91.

public enterprises in selected years (see Table 2.4) suggest that such spending by the decentralized public sector has grown steadily to an additional 4–5% of GDP. Thus, these figures imply that public sector capital formation has actually grown over the long term from about 5% of GDP in 1949 to 9% in recent years.

A long-term view of the revenue side of public sector finances also suggests an increasing role for the state in the Brazilian economy. We must look at two major sources of revenues to gain the proper appreciation of this role: first, the "traditional" revenues composed of direct and indirect taxes – income taxes, taxes on industrialized products, electrical energy, road use, and so on, and, second, a series of special funds ("forced savings") by which resources collected by the government through taxes on various social groups are then channeled into the private sector via loan programs rather than by means of the government budget.

Looking first at the traditional tax base, Brazil has been successful from a long-term standpoint in increasing the resources available to the public sector. From 1949 through the late 1970s, for example, direct taxes more than doubled in

Table 2.5. *Long-term trends in the traditional tax base as percentage of GDP*

	1949	1959	1965–9	1970–3	1974–8
Direct taxes	5.2	5.0	7.4	9.8	12.1
Indirect taxes	10.1	12.2	15.0	14.9	13.5
Gross tax burden	15.3	17.2	22.4	24.7	25.6
Transfers and subsidies	3.1	4.3	7.1	8.1	9.5
Net tax burden	12.2	12.9	15.3	16.6	16.3

Source: Margareth Hanson Costa, "A discutida ampliação da intervenção estatal," *Conjuntura Econômica* 33 (December 1979):90.

percent of GDP while the gross tax burden (direct plus indirect taxes) increased during the same timespan from 15% to 26% of GDP (see Table 2.5), a figure that is relatively high for a developing country.[14]

A more accurate gauge of resources available for general government spending is obtained by netting-out transfers and subsidies to the private sector from the gross tax burden. The resulting net tax burden (see also Table 2.5) shows a clear, but comparatively more modest long-term increase in the tax base from 12% in 1949 to 16% in the late 1970s.

The revenue-gathering capacity of the Brazilian state has been greatly strengthened since the late 1960s by the growth of index-linked "forced savings" funds, of which three – Fundo de Garantia do Tempo de Serviço (FGTS), Programa de Integração Social (PIS), and PASEP – are the most important.[15] These funds were created to serve various social and redistributive purposes, but their importance in the present context is that they have allowed the federal government to tap the incomes of firms and the individuals (including public sector employees) for resources that, while credited to time deposit accounts set up in the name of contributing employees, can be allocated by the government for housing construction and other development purposes. Obviously, these "forced savings" are different from the government's nonrepayable tax receipts. These funds nominally belong to contributing

Table 2.6. *Trends in government-controlled savings,*
in percentages

	1965	1970	1975	1978
Total investment/GNP =				
Total savings/GNP	18.6	22.5	25.7	22.9
Of which:				
Government-controlled savings/GNP	1.9	8.7	12.4	14.5
General government savings	(1.9)	(5.8)	(4.3)	(3.1)
"Forced savings"/GNP	(0.0)	(2.9)	(8.1)	(11.4)
Government-controlled savings/				
total savings	10.2	38.7	48.2	63.3

Source: Conjuntura Econômica 33 (December 1979):66, 69, 73. *Boletim do Banco Central do Brasil,* various issues.

workers who may draw upon their accounts, subject to certain conditions. Savings must receive monetary correction plus interest, so the government's allocative discretion is limited. Yet, the magnitudes of resources assembled through "forced savings" are significant. Funds deposited in the three major programs (FGTS, PIS, PASEP) increased from 2.8% of GDP in 1970 to 11.2% in 1978.[16]

The data assembled on the growth of the main public sector spending and revenue categories can be brought together to estimate the total "surplus" theoretically controlled by general government (*excluding* public enterprise) and available for allocation (see Table 2.6). Including the resources of the forced savings funds, "government savings" by this extended definition increased from just 2% of GNP in 1965 to 15% in 1978, or from 10% of total domestic savings to more than 60%.[17] Of course, this concept of control does not imply that the public sector makes all decisions regarding the allocation of savings to investment.

What may be concluded from this very brief review of the fiscal functions of the Brazilian state? Certainly, a secular tendency is apparent whereby the state has greatly increased its ability to influence resource allocation and the distribution of income. The state, through the exercise of its fiscal functions, exercises a larger influence on economic activity than it did fifteen or more years ago.

The importance of this expanding role of the public sector to the debate on state capitalism goes beyond the observation that the volume of financial resources – and, hence, of normative decision-making authority in the hands of the federal government – has increased. Luciano Martins points out that this "centripetal force" in the political economy of Brazil has a counterpart "centrifugal force," which has been the creation of relatively independent, decentralized agencies charged with actual resource allocation and the carrying out of government decisions.[18] For example, while the federal government has achieved increased control over financial resources, it has also been active in creating and then delegating considerable autonomy to decentralized agencies, including *autarquias*, funds, foundations, and, especially, public enterprises. Margareth Hanson Costa notes that this same process of centralization of resources, combined with decentralization of authority at the federal level, is mirrored at the level of state and municipal governments.[19] These governments have also been active in creating their own decentralized agencies.

What has been taking place in Brazil is, as Martins suggests, that "the mode of expansion of state activities in Brazil leads to the expansion of bureaucracy 'outside' the government sector, i.e., in the orbit of the so-called decentralized administration (quasi-autonomous institutes, funds, and foundations), not to mention the orbit of the government enterprises."[20] Rezende and Castello Branco, in a study of trends in public sector employment in Brazil, provide evidence on the trend toward increased reliance on decentralized agencies to interpret and carry out the state's economic policy.[21] Overall public employment in Brazil more than tripled between 1950 and 1973, rising from 1 million to more than 3.5 million. Growth in employment was particularly rapid in the decentralized agencies (including public enterprises) at all levels of government – federal, state, and municipal. Whereas only 20% of all public employees in Brazil worked in decentralized agencies in 1950, fully 40% were employed in such agencies by 1973.[22] The number of *autarquias* and foundations within the sphere of the federal government expanded from 140 in 1970 to 170 in 1975.[23] Even more dramatic growth occurred in the number of public enterprises subject to federal government jurisdiction: their numbers had grown from 48 in 1960 to 87 in 1969 and to 185 in 1979.[24]

The regulatory role of the state

An important part of the debate on the role of the state in Latin America has involved the penchant of the public sector to use a broad range of regulatory devices (incentives, sanctions, prohibitions, licenses, and so on) to change relative prices and, thus, to manipulate the behavior of private decision makers.[25] In Brazil, many contemporary controls over prices, production, and foreign trade can be traced back to the early decades of the twentieth century, but the post-1964 use of regulations of all types has broadened significantly the economic impact of the state and led to a proliferation of agencies to carry out control policies.[26] An important consequence in the Brazilian economy, as elsewhere in Latin America, has been a rise in discretionary decision making, that is, resource allocation by administrative action rather than in response to market signals. At the same time, the approach to development planning has been "piecemeal," resulting in little effective coordination between the public sector agents that administer the various controls and subsidies.

Brazil has had multiple development goals over the last fifteen years or so. Some of the more important have been to limit imports, diversify exports, reduce oil consumption, develop domestic sources of energy, encourage agricultural development, protect Brazilian-owned firms, and promote the transfer of advanced technology. The government's approach to these goals has been to intervene directly in the marketplace to guide private resource allocation in the socially "correct" directions. For example, income tax credits have been made available to corporations and individuals for investment in the more backward areas of the country, and generous subsidized lines of credit are available for exports and agriculture. Government agencies also intervene to affect private

Table 2.7. *Some examples of the state as regulator*

Regulations	Agencies
Price controls	Conselho Interministerial de Preços (CIP, SEAP)
Investment approvals	Conselho de Desenvolvimento Industrial (CDI)
Export licensing	Carteira de Comércio Exterior (CACEX)
Technology transfer approval	Instituto Nacional de Propriedade Industrial (INPI)
Agricultural credit and subsidies	Banco do Brasil Central Bank
Domestic procurement incentives	FINAME (BNDE)
Export incentives	BEFIEX (Minister of Industry and Commerce, Central Bank)
Coffee exports	Instituto Brasileiro do Café (IBC)
Energy use	Commisão Nacional de Energia (CNE) Programa Nacional do Álcool (PROÁLCOOL)
Research and development loans	FINEP
Regional investment incentives	SUDENE, SUDAM

decisions through their authority to set tariffs, prices, and wages, and to approve all requests for export licenses, import duty exemptions, and purchases of foreign technology. Of course, the need to administer these many functions has spawned the growth of a large number of government agencies. Some of these functions, and the agencies designated to administer them, are described in Table 2.7.

Brazil's extensive fiscal incentive programs illustrate well the regulatory role of the public sector.[27] In addition to the tax credits available to firms for investment in specific regions of the country, incentive programs have been created to promote growth in a large number of economic sectors that at one time or another have ranked high in government development priorities. Favored industries include forestry, fishing, aerospace, shipping, and iron and steel. Still other fiscal incentives have been provided as a means of promoting exports, particularly of manufactures.

Although their effectiveness is open to question, the fiscal incentive programs have involved very substantial public subsidies. Baer and Villela report that 23% of potential corporate income tax revenues in the mid-1970s were diverted to one or another of the regional development schemes.[28] Export subsidies in the form of rebates on value-added and turnover taxes have also resulted in substantial amounts of foregone public sector income. The pervasiveness of these incentive programs is such that probably every firm in Brazil has availed itself of them.[29] The larger corporations commonly maintain a staff of legal experts to keep abreast of the frequently changing legislation on incentives.

The power of the Industrial Development Council (CDI), an agency of the Ministry of Industry and Commerce, illustrates well how the state as regulator influences private decision making in Brazil.[30] The CDI is an interministerial body that convenes to consider major private sector development projects with an eye to assisting selected projects with fiscal incentives. The criteria for approval vary over time in line with the changing priorities of government development plans. Typical criteria would include the project's potential contribution to import substitution or export promotion, its degree of domestic entrepreneurial control, existing installed capacity in the industry in question, and so on.

The relevance here is that the CDI's approval amounts to the government's blessing, and, as such, opens the door to a wide range of fiscal incentives, including tariff exemptions, and subsidized lines of credit administered by public sector agencies. Given the importance of these subsidies in Brazil, CDI approval – or lack thereof – is often the crucial factor in a decision to construct or scrap a private company project.

The state and the financial system

The state's role in Brazil's financial system is an outgrowth of a number of factors: its historically important role in commercial and development banking, policy reforms in the 1960s designed to modernize Brazilian capital markets, and the increasing reliance of policy in the 1970s on subsidized credit programs.[31] The activist, interventionist role of the state is accomplished through an enormous number of financial institutions, but, once again, these are characterized by a relatively low degree of central coordination, a consequence of the state's piecemeal approach toward the financial system. Here and in subsequent chapters dealing with state-owned enterprises producing goods, we must be very careful not to confuse an a priori state ownership of the key actors with highly centralized state control of resource flows. State involvement with the financial system will illustrate the usefulness of this distinction.

The structure of the contemporary financial system was heavily influenced by legislation enacted in the era of liberal (i.e., market-oriented) economic reform of the mid-1960s. Policymakers at that time established (1) a system of indexation (monetary correction) to protect financial transactions from consistently high rates of inflation; (2) new rules and regulations for financial institutions to improve the access of Brazilian firms to financing and capitalization; and (3) a national housing finance system featuring a dominant role for the government in the savings and loan industry.

The major institutions in the financial system include:

National monetary council. Composed of the key members of the economic policy team, the National Monetary Council (Conselho Monetário Nacional) sets all monetary and credit policies, especially the government's intended rates of expansion of money and credit for the coming year, which are then set forth in the so-called monetary budget.

Central bank of Brazil. Formed as a result of the banking reforms of the mid-1960s, the Central Bank (Banco Central do Brasil) implements the normative guidelines of the Monetary Council. Unusual functions of the Brazilian Central Bank include: control of foreign exchange transactions (*all* foreign transactions, whether by banks or brokerage houses must be

authorized by the Central Bank); and administration on behalf of the government of large economic development programs, for example, funds to promote development in the
poorer regions of Brazil. This development function involves
expansion of the monetary base and, as such, is often in
direct contradiction of the Central Bank's stated monetary
goals.

Bank of Brazil. The hub of the financial system, the Bank
of Brazil (Banco do Brasil) is at once the fiscal agent of the
government, by far the largest commercial bank in Brazil, and
the dominant institution in the foreign exchange market. The
bank, which is 51% owned by the government, has 1,000
agencies in Brazil, 43 foreign branches, and (at end-1980)
almost U.S. $50 billion in assets, making it one of the largest
banks in the world. It is difficult to overstate the central role
of the Bank of Brazil in the financial system. It handles about
50% of all foreign exchange transactions and, as the preemi-
nent lender to agriculture, has an even larger share in Brazil's
rapidly expanding rural sector. The bank is consolidating a
position as the major bank for financing all types of Brazilian
exports and, through its broad international network, has a
capacity for international operations that no Brazilian private
bank will match for decades.

Nominally subject to direction by the Monetary Council
and the Central Bank, the Bank of Brazil in fact possesses a
high degree of autonomy due to its size, complexity, and
profitability (e.g., 25%–30% rates of return on equity). As
an agent of development policy, the bank accepts risk and
seeks business that private banking shuns, but it also has
important funding advantages over private banks. For example, it is not subject to the same reserve requirements and,
thus, can get by with a much lower ratio of deposits to loans.
Furthermore, it enjoys unlimited rediscounting facilities with
the Central Bank and uses these to support the many government development funds it administers. This *conta de
movimento* (discount facility) is a major and troublesome
source of money creation in Brazil. However, the enormity of
the Bank of Brazil's development responsibilities, as well as

its substantial political power, have doomed all government efforts over the years to limit the size and adverse impact of this discount facility.

The National Monetary Council, the Central Bank, and the Bank of Brazil have authority over the mixture of public and private financial institutions that comprises the Brazilian financial system. These include commercial banks, specialized housing and savings banks, and large numbers of non-banking institutions such as credit cooperatives, insurance companies, finance companies, stock exchanges, security dealers, and brokerage houses.

Housing finance system. The housing system is dominated by large, public sector institutions designed to capture savings and to channel these into residential construction. The major institutions are the National Housing Bank (BNH) and the Federal Savings Bank (CEF). The BNH channels funds into low-cost housing and basic sanitation and funds itself through the issue of indexed bonds and its administration of a large pension fund (the FGTS), to which most Brazilians and their employers must contribute.

The CEF (the savings bank) finances middle- and upper-income housing and draws its funds from a substantial base of passbook savings accounts. Alone among Brazilian financial institutions, the CEF can issue indexed savings accounts to individuals, instruments that rise in popularity among individual savers in periods of high inflation.

The housing finance system illustrates the segmentation of the Brazilian financial system. Through indexed housing bonds and passbook accounts, the housing system preempts enormous financial resources that are then not available to private banks for lending to industry. This frequently leads to a surfeit of savings in the housing system and extremely high rates of interest for commercial and industrial loans.

National economic development bank. One of the harmful effects of inflation on financial markets is to instill in lenders a strong preference for short-term lending, the better to match loan portfolio yields with the unpredictable and unstable cost of funds. In countries such as Brazil, this has meant a reluctance on the part of commercial banks to provide the long-term project financing essential for development and to deal instead with short-term (i.e., 180–360 day) lines of credit for working capital purposes. In such a setting, the government frequently steps in to husband resources and to provide the missing medium-term lending capability. The National Economic Development Bank (BNDE) has played this role in Brazil.

The traditional role of the BNDE has been to provide loans to support both public and private industrial-sector projects. The degree of subsidy in BNDE loans has varied over time, but interest has been positive in real terms, although consistently below market rates. The BNDE is funded by a combination of tax revenues and public pension funds and, thus, is able to lend profitably even while charging rates of interest below those quoted by Brazil's commercial and investment banks.

The bank has been a key element in the last twenty years of Brazil's economic growth. The BNDE and a constellation of development banks owned by Brazilian states that administer BNDE programs probably provide close to 100% of all project financing originating in cruzeiro resources of Brazilian financial institutions. The rate of capital formation in the 1970s by private, Brazilian-owned companies (multinational companies are not eligible for BNDE loans, few of which go to state enterprises) certainly would have been much lower without BNDE funding. Furthermore, the bank's FINAME (Special Agency for Industrial Finance, or Agencia Especial de Financiamento Industrial) program, which provides low-cost loans to finance domestically produced equipment purchases, has been at the very heart of the growth of the capital goods industry in Brazil over the last fifteen years.

The BNDE's importance as an agent of public sector intervention in the economy goes well beyond its traditional long-term lending role. It also provides working capital credits for Brazilian companies, financial assistance for corporate reorganizations and mergers, and stock and bond underwriting for small and medium-sized companies.

The operations of the BNDE exhibit two dilemmas encountered by a state playing a major role in an economy that is not centrally planned. The first concerns the distinction between public ownership and public control. All financial entities can by default acquire some stake in the companies their loans support and the BNDE has frequently found itself in the position of "taking over" financially troubled private firms. In this way, a legal gray area has been generated through the de facto and unintended conversion of private into state-owned companies.

The second is that the BNDE today to a certain extent undermines the development of private sector institutions and bond markets capable of providing long-term finance. The attractiveness and availability of the BNDE's publicly subsidized credit facilities are such that few Brazilians care to seek scarcer, comparatively more expensive financing from private investment banks. Baer and Villela were able to verify this point in their interviews with a large number of Brazilian businessmen in the late 1970s.[32] Most of those interviewed said that without BNDE support, especially through FINAME, they would not have been able to expand productive capacity in their firms. The interest rates charged by private investment banks were considered exorbitant, and credit facilities from investment banks were not used for any purposes other than short-term working capital.

An overview: Financial market shares

The composition of Brazil's nonmonetary asset holdings (i.e., financial assets other than currency and demand deposits) shows how public sector institutions have come to dominate the financial system. The huge Federal Savings Bank and its associated banks are the only institutions offering monetarily corrected passbook savings accounts to individual savers. These savings deposits were negligible in 1967; in 1981, they accounted for 25% of total financial assets in Brazil (see Table 2.8). Federal government securities (monetarily connected ORTNs [Obrigacoẽs Reajustaveis do Tesouro Nacional, or

Table 2.8. *Trends in Brazil's financial asset holdings,*
in percentages

	1967	1981
Monetary assets		
Currency	14.0	4.6
Demand deposits	59.2	22.0
Nonmonetary assets		
Savings deposits	0.4	25.8
CDs	3.3	13.4
Bills of exchange	9.7	5.5
Housing bonds	1.4	3.2
State and municipal bonds	—	2.8
Fed. govt. securities	12.0	25.2
Total	100.0	100.0

Source: Boletim do Banco Central do Brasil, various issues.

Readjustable Obligations of the National Treasury], for the most part) account for another 25% of total financial assets. When the share of financial assets accounted for by state and municipal bonds, housing bonds, sight deposits in the Bank of Brazil, and so on, are added in, the conclusion is that public sector institutions have benefited the most from the diversification of financial assets in the economy.

The strong role of government-owned institutions in the commercial banking has been noted. Five government banks rank among the twenty largest commercial banks. While the Bank of Brazil is by far the most important, state banks as a whole control almost 50% of deposits in the commercial banks and an even larger share of loans made by commercial banks.[33]

But a better picture is provided by considering the role of the state when all types of financial institutions are considered, not just commercial banks.

The limited role of the private banking sector is evident in the declining market shares of private banks in total loans to the private sector (see Table 2.9). The main reason has been the rise of public sector lending institutions, especially the

Table 2.9. *Loans to the Brazilian private sector: market shares of institutions, in percentages*

	1967	1981
Commercial banks		
Bank of Brazil	25.3	17.1
Commercial banks	49.0	32.0
Other financial institutions		
Finance companies	9.9	5.1
Investment banks	4.6	9.2
National Housing Bank	1.9	3.5
Housing credit companies	1.2	10.3
Federal Savings Bank	3.7	12.0
National Bank for Economic Development	2.5	7.2
All others	1.9	3.6
Total	100.0	100.0

Source: Boletim do Banco Central do Brasil, various issues.

CEF, the BNH, and the BNDE. Private commercial banks in the late 1960s provided 50% of all loans to the private sector. Today, this has dropped to 30%, and even this figure is deceptive, since, increasingly, private financial institutions act as simple retailers of funds passed on by public institutions for special development lending programs.

Conclusion

This chapter has sought to convey the character of the state's involvement in the economy other than in the nonfinancial public enterprises. Little more than a surface description was feasible here, but we should carry forward to future chapters something of the flavor of the broader role of the state in Brazil. The key concepts to keep in mind are the enormous size of the Brazilian public sector measured in budgetary terms, its pervasive role in economic activity through its use of regulations of all types, and its dominant role in the financial system. But state involvement in the economy is not the same as centralized (or even clear or coherent) control of private decision making. The state's role in Brazil results from a piecemeal approach to development planning and is portrayed by a great number of unwieldy and generally autonomous bureaucracies with important goals of their own. Nor is this large state presence synonomous with repression of private sector initiatives. Indeed, many private sector firms and individuals benefit importantly from the state's ability to affect income distribution through its economic role.

These themes have been presented briefly and in broad-brush fashion here. They will be seen on a smaller canvas and under many different lights as attention is turned to the large state-owned enterprises in the remainder of this volume.

3

Origins of public enterprise in Brazil

How did Brazil come to possess such a large and diversified public enterprise sector by the 1980s? Was it the result of particular historical and political circumstances? Or the calculated moves of a determinedly interventionist government? The argument can be made that the creation of public enterprise in Brazil has been almost accidental, that is, the result of historical circumstances, such as a balance of payments crisis, rather than of conscious government policy. Suzigan, for example, observes: "The rise of the State as entrepreneur did not result from any planned action and its ideological motivation does not extend beyond the economic nationalism that was in vogue at the time that some of these sectors were created."[1]

Recent Brazilian governments have certainly made many public statements that any decision to use state-owned enterprises was taken with the greatest reluctance. An official document of the high-level Council for Economic Development in 1976 emphasized: "There will be projects under control of the government enterprises if, in practice, the private sector demonstrates clearly that it either cannot or does not wish to carry them out."

Another point of view, best expressed by representatives of the Brazilian public sector during the often strident debate on *estatização* ("statization") in the mid-1970s, roundly rejected this "accidental" or "circumstantial" explanation of the creation of public enterprises by a regime with a presumed commitment to fostering private initiative. For these business groups, the explanation rested much more heavily on the unbridled exercise of power by autonomous state bureaucrats. State-enterprise managers were taking advantage of their privileged access to capital and closeness to political power to expand their operations at the expense of the private sector.

In the face of this controversy, it is helpful to look at the experience of other countries with public enterprise sectors. This experience suggests that the ability of the public sector to capture savings and allocate resources improves with economic development. At the same time, the process of industrialization creates needs for resources in sectors in which private investment is not forthcoming. Public enterprises are frequently the response of a growing public sector to crises of supply that threaten to retard industrial growth. How did these two factors – a growing public sector and the process of industrialization – affect the growth of public enterprise in Brazil?

Historical and statistical description of Brazilian public enterprises may provide facts that support or contradict a number of general hypotheses regarding the extent and pattern of public ownership in an economy. Six such hypotheses, suggested by similarities in intercountry experiences, are presented in summary fashion.[2] It should be emphasized that these hypotheses are not the only ones that could be suggested, nor are they mutually exclusive. Further, the hypotheses purport to explain the reasons for public ownership in general rather than for a form of ownership such as the public enterprise in particular.

1. *Weak private sector hypothesis.* Many developing economies, including most of those in Latin America, are committed to the abstract model of decentralized economic decision making known as "the market system" or "the free enterprise model." An important reason for this preference is the "demonstration effect" provided by the development experience of the advanced Western economies.

Fundamental to the success of the model is the provision by uncoerced individuals of economic resources such as funds, risk absorption, managerial talent, and (Schumpeterian) entrepreneurship. The experience of many LDCs is that these privately provided resources are so scarce as to stymie the development process. In the face of private inability to act in specific development projects, public intervention, ownership, and control become an attractive alternative.

John Sheahan has stated this point well:

Private enterprise is ready to grow anywhere that it is given favorable conditions, but favorable conditions can be expensive...One common background factor works in favor of the option to try public enterprise as a means to promote faster economic growth. This is simply the fact that it takes a long time to develop an enterprising private sector. When innovation has historically come from outside the country, when networks of trust and credit that are taken for granted in the industrialized countries hardly exist, and when private wealth is concentrated in very few hands, then the capacity to initiate new economic activities is understandably limited.[3]

A particular manifestation of the weakness of the domestic private sector in developing countries is a small, inefficient capital market. Typically, this includes imperfect information networks, discrimination by lenders for noneconomic reasons, and consequent wide dispersion in social rates of return to existing and new investments.[4] An inefficient and (relative to the country's needs) small capital market means that available entrepreneurial skills in the private sector will be wasted unless the state intervenes. Of course, there is the alternative of large infusions of foreign capital and consequent foreign control, but this alternative is often rejected for political reasons.

In short, this hypothesis argues that the state will use resources obtained via taxation, foreign borrowing, inflationary financing, or other means to provide investable funds not forthcoming from the private sector. It will also intervene when the lack of other resources – risk absorption, managerial talent, and so on – are the major obstacles to specific development projects. Public ownership and control – often in the form of public enterprise – of large development projects in various sectors is the result.[5]

2. *Economies of scale hypothesis.* This hypothesis, alternatively characteried as "natural monopolies" or "optimal size of firm," attributes public enterprise to economic causality. Economies of scale arise for two reasons: Over a relevant output range, technical conditions in the production of certain goods imply a decreasing long-run average cost curve for the industry; also, growth of demand justifies higher rates of output for the goods in question. Efficient production requires

a reduction in the number of firms and consequent increases in the scale of operations.

An a priori prediction of the pattern of public output is possible with this hypothesis. Public firms will emerge in those sectors in which scale is important – energy, water supply, and communications are examples – as demand for the output of these sectors increases. Demand may be measured by such indicators of changing market size as increases in urbanization and industrialization or the rate of growth of GNP. In view of the historical experience of many developing countries, a further hypothesis might be that if output in sectors where scale is important is not provided by public firms, it will be provided by foreign firms.

3. *External economies hypothesis.* This third economic hypothesis looks for public ownership in social overhead capital sectors because, in the absence of elaborate indirect incentives, private owners are not rewarded for the external technological or pecuniary economies that these sectors generate. In many countries, public ownership commonly occurs in the construction and operation of bridges and highways, railroads, ports, sanitation systems, and multipurpose dams. Obviously, this hypothesis does overlap somewhat with the preceding one.

4. *Dynamic public managers hypothesis.* It is reasonable to assume that public enterprise managers, as a class, are characterized by approximately the same distributions of energy, ambition, and entrepreneurial talent as those applying to managers of private sector firms. Kindleberger and Herrick argue that the most important advantage of public enterprise in a developing country is its ability to recruit individuals of superior administrative ability.[6] Thus, public enterprise managers might be expected to mirror private sector behavior by taking advantage of opportunities for profitable growth in the scale, complexity, or diversity of the firm's operations. This often results in the creation of new enterprises that extend public ownership.

This hypothesis argues that public enterprises that possess the market power to accumulate profits will employ these resources to grow through such strategies as vertical integration or diversification into new industries. Thus, efficiency (as measured by profitability) leads to growth. It may also be argued that growth is necessary in order to maintain efficiency:

It is possible that only a dynamic firm can hope to maintain a first-rate staff. The activities of an enterprise which sticks to the narrow limits of initial endeavors becomes routinized and thus unattractive to the best talent. Only firms which allow innovations and thus expansion can hope to maintain the best of technicians and administrators...In other words, state capitalism has to grow in order to stay efficient.[7]

To sum up, efficiency leads to growth; growth, in turn, provides the incentive to maintain efficiency. This simple dynamic, a key to growth in the private sector, also accounts for extension of public ownership in the economy.

5. *Natural resource rents hypothesis.* This hypothesis argues that the private control of a monopoly or the fortuitous ownership of a scarce natural resource generates unearned incomes or rents for their owners. The public appropriation and allocation of this rent surplus are important motivations for public ownership of natural-resource sectors, such as petroleum and copper, in many developing countries.

6. *Political–historical hypothesis.* The preceding hypotheses attribute public ownership and public enterprise primarily to economic causality. This last hypothesis argues that public enterprise stems from political and historical factors that have little to do with economics. Therefore, it is difficult to predict a pattern of public ownership, because it will occur randomly across economic sectors.

An example of political motivation for public enterprise is, of course, a societal preference for public rather than private ownership, leading to the creation of public enterprises by decree in different sectors of the economy. In such cases, economic explanations of the rise of public enterprise are likely to be of little value.

An important political determinant of public enterprise might be hostility toward, or distrust of, foreign-owned enterprises operating within the country, especially if these enterprises are owned by nationals of countries that are perceived as being colonialist or imperialist.[8] Other political circumstances would include the nationalization of all foreign property upon the advent of a populist regime, takeover of the industries owned by nationals of a hostile nation in times of war, and the creation of enterprises to engage in "showpiece" investment projects.

Particular historical events leading to the creation of public enterprises may also outweigh economic factors. For example, natural disasters such as earthquakes or depressions may mandate state intervention to avoid collapse of vital services. A massive earthquake aided the Chilean Popular Front to honor an electoral pledge to strengthen the public sector during the 1930s. The Italian experience in public enterprise can be traced to widespread government intervention in faltering enterprises during the Depression. In short, the argument is that public enterprises established for political–historical reasons might be randomly distributed across sectors. Thus, there is really no basis for predicting which sectors of the economy will come under state control.

Obviously, these six hypotheses are not mutually exclusive. While one or another hypothesis will often seem to "fit" better, public firms are usually created for many reasons. The use of the hypotheses is intended to order the following discussion of public enterprises in Brazil and to provide a wider context for evaluating the Brazilian experience.

The historical background

It is symptomatic of the rapid and largely uncoordinated growth of public enterprises in Brazil that the first official census of federally owned companies was not performed until 1980. We still have no precise data for the total number of companies owned by federal, state, and local governments combined, but it can be estimated at about 700 at the end of 1980.[9] Approximately 250 of these are owned by the federal government, 360 by state governments, and 100 by municipalities. As a general rule, though with some important exceptions, the federal government enterprises are much larger and play a much more important role in the national economy than their state and municipal counterparts.

Public enterprises exist under a variety of legal forms in Brazil, the two most important being the *empresa pública*, in which the government (whether federal, state, or local) owns 100% of the company's capital, and the *empresa de economia mista*, in which some private equity participation is also permitted, subject to majority control by the government.[10] Interestingly, the prevailing legislation does not recognize two other increasingly common forms of public ownership and control: the public–private joint venture over which the government exercises control but not majority ownership; and private firms under the effective control of state-owned credit institutions, especially the BNDE.[11]

A distribution of federally owned state enterprises according to their date of creation (based on information provided by the Fundação Getulio Vargas) illustrates not only the growth of public enterprises in the postwar period but also the proliferation of such entities under conservative military governments in the 1960s and 1970s (see Table 3.1). Note that of a total of 251 federally owned public companies, 88 were created during 1970–5. It is estimated that an additional 33 public enterprises were created during 1976–80.

The large majority of state enterprises in Brazil are located in the highly capital-intensive sectors, such as transportation and other economic infrastructure. Indeed, it has been the government's policy to expand its entrepreneurial activities within these sectors but at the same time not to go "upstream," for example, into manufacturing. This policy is set forth clearly in the Second National Development Plan (1975–9):

To the State [shall be attributed] the classical areas of economic infrastructure and public services [energy, transportation, and communications], social development [education, health, and social security], and the sectors previously transformed by law into monopolies of the State [extraction and refining of petroleum]; while to the private sector [shall be attributed] exclusive responsibility for all of the manufacturing industry.

The extent to which the state has adhered to this broad policy guideline is clear from a consideration of the sectoral locations of the 654 public firms identified by the *Visão* survey in 1979 (see Table 3.2). Well over 500 of these firms are located in the "classical infrastructure areas," including 312

Table 3.1. *Distribution of federal public firms by date of creation and economic sector*

Sector	Before 1939	1940–9	1950–9	1960–9	1970–5	1976–80	Total
Mining and manufacturing	2	5	4	14	24	16	65
Transport and communication	4	1	3	8	19	5	40
Electricity	11	1	5	3	6	0	26
Finance	3	2	3	5	11	7	31
Other	46	1	—	9	28	5	89
Total	66	10	15	39	88	33	251

Source: Pre-1970: Centro de Estudos Fiscais, "Atividade empresarial dos governos federal e estadual," *Conjuntura Econômica,* 27 (June 1973):80, Table IV; *Visão, Quem é quem na economia brasileira,* 1980; Margareth Hanson Costa, "A discutida ampliação da intervenção estatal," *Conjuntura Econômica* 33 (December 1979):92. Post-1970: SEST, *Empresas estatais no Brasil e o controle da SEST: antecedentes e experiência de 1980* (Brasília, 1981), Annex 20, pp. 94–120.

Table 3.2. *Distribution of state enterprises by sector and sphere of government, 1979*

Sectors	Federal government	State government	Municipal government	Total
Agriculture and mining	20	11	1	32
Manufacturing	56	33	3	92
Services	122	312	96	530
Utilities	41	51	11	103
Transport, storage, commerce	40	29	8	77
Planning, research, development	7	70	57	134
Technical and administrative services	19	64	16	99
Construction and engineering	8	9	4	21
Banks, insurance	7	89	—	96
Total	198	356	100	654

Note: Estimates differ from those provided by Fundação Getulio Vargas used in Table 3.1.
Source: Visão, Quem é quem na economia brasileira, August 29, 1980, p. 422.

of the 356 enterprises owned by Brazilian states. But a larger story lies hidden behind these numbers. For example, one of the "infrastructure" areas is Planning, Research, Development, activities prima facie within the competence of private enterprise. Fully 134 public enterprises fall within this classification. Another 21 public firms engage in "construction and engineering," again an area, theoretically at least, within the reach of the private sector. Finally, the *Visão* survey located 92 state enterprises operating in manufacturing, presumably the exclusive responsibility of the private sector in Brazil's mixed economy.

To sum up, Brazilian public enterprises engage in activities such as electricity and communications, which in many developed countries are either nationalized or privately owned but extensively regulated. However, many state firms operate in the mining, manufacturing, and finance sectors that are traditionally occupied by the private sector in developed economies. The major events in the creation of public enterprises, treated in more detail elsewhere, are summarized historically in the next sections.[12]

1889–1930: The early modern period

The Brazilian economy remained essentially preindustrial through 1930. As late as 1920, agricultural pursuits absorbed 70% of Brazil's economically active population.[13] Existing industry was concentrated in the lighter branches of manufacturing such as textiles, clothing, and food products, which together accounted for 70% of industrial value-added in 1919.[14]

Public sector intervention in the economy was important to later industrial growth but was unrelated to any coherent plan for economic development or industrialization. Instead, as Topik has argued, the role of the state grew in order to expand the agricultural sector and to preserve good relations with foreign capital.[15] Economic stability was the paramount concern of government. Federal capital formation dropped from 25.6% of total government outlays in 1919 to just 3.7% in 1923, recovering slightly to 4.8% by the end of the decade.[16] Villela and Suzigan argue:

Until 1945 Brazil never had a deliberate industrialization policy...On the contrary, the defense of coffee interests and the various stabilization programs frequently inhibited long-term industrial growth. Often, however, domestic industrial production benefitted from the side effects of these policies, e.g., from the protection offered by frequent exchange-rate devaluation, and from the indiscriminate levying of tariffs on consumer goods, raw materials, and capital goods.[17]

The early impetus to the construction of basic transportation and utilities in Brazil was provided by foreign capital, although the intervention of the state was essential. For example, the railroads were constructed with heavy inflows of British capital, but investors were guaranteed by the state a minimum rate of return on their investment. Foreign capital, primarily Canadian and American, underwrote the first attempts to exploit Brazil's hydroelectric potential.[18]

Public ownership of the railroads dates from the beginning of the twentieth century and is rooted in particular circumstances. The policy of government-guaranteed rates of return on foreign investment in the railroads had resulted in a heavy strain on the government budget. After a point, it became apparent that it would be cheaper to nationalize the foreign lines rather than to continue the profit remittance policy. Large parts of the foreign-owned rail network were purchased. Thereafter, major expansions of the system were undertaken primarily by the public sector. By 1929, 60% of the system was owned by federal and state governments.[19]

The externalities hypothesis and also the weak private sector hypothesis help explain state involvement in ports, shipping, and sanitation systems that developed during this premodern period. A state policy of guaranteed rates of return, similar to that used to stimulate railroad construction, had failed to attract private investment in port facilities. Public ownership and development of ports, especially the port of Rio de Janeiro, became necessary as a means to lower the costs of transport. Some of the shipping companies that were eventually merged into the state-owned Lloyd Brasileiro were first purchased by the government in 1896 in an attempt to improve coastal shipping.[20]

In considering the growth of the state as entrepreneur through 1930, Topik concluded:

The Federal Government by 1930 came to own more than half of the country's railroad mileage, almost all of the national telegraph lines, more than half of the national shipping capacity, the largest commercial bank, the largest savings bank, most of the major ports, and the largest publishing house. Municipal and state governments also owned, though to a much smaller degree, railroads, minor shipping lines, agricultural banks, ports, and public utility companies.[21]

1930–1945: Beginnings of industrialization

It was only during the 1930s that industrialization became a major concern for policymakers. War and depression interrupted normal external supply lines and stimulated the growth of local import-substituting industry. The public sector expanded considerably during the period. A social security system was developed. Overall government spending rose from 15% to 20% of GNP.[22] Ministries of labor, industry and commerce, education, and public health were created. *Autarquias* were set up to control the production and sale of coffee, sugar, pinewood, and other primary products.[23]

While no new public enterprises were created during the thirties, the regulatory powers of the state were strengthened. The control of prices of basic services (water, electricity, gas, and others) and the determination of interest rate ceilings set the stage for later interventions in utilities and the financial sector.[24]

In the early forties, after repeated failures to develop a privately controlled steel industry, the government of Getulio Vargas established the state-owned national steel company, Companhia Siderúrgica Nacional (CSN).[25] The first of a "new breed" of public enterprises, the CSN became a symbol of the government's commitment to economic development as well as the first component of Brazil's contemporary public enterprise sector.

The steel company was rooted in Vargas's vision of "conservative modernization," which Wirth describes as the "ideological touchstone of the *Estado Novo* period."[26] Accordingly, CSN would be run differently from such preexisting firms as the Central do Brasil railroad and the Lloyd Brasileiro shipping line, which "were notorious for being undercapitalized, mismanaged, and politics-ridden."[27]

Vargas took pains to convey his vision of a state-owned enterprise to a skeptical business community. He set up a company with the following characteristics: (1) It would be a *mixed* enterprise, that is, although controlled by the state, CSN would have minority private ownership; (2) it would be independent of direct subsidies from the treasury and its budget would not be subjected to annual scrutiny by the government; (3) it would not be granted a monopoly but would instead be expected eventually to operate efficiently under competitive conditions.

Although designed with the flexibility of a private firm, the mixed enterprise typified by CSN was created as an agent of the federal government. In case of conflict between the firm's private commercial goals and the wider public interest, as determined by the state, it was made clear that commercial goals would have to be sacrificed. Barring such conflict, however, CSN would behave much as would any private firm.[28]

Two primary motivations can be detected, in retrospect, for the creation of CSN: The demonstrated weakness of the private sector to carry out a project of obvious importance to development; and the conviction of key groups within the Brazilian military that a domestic steel industry was important to their emerging concept of national security. These factors would then provide a basis for a "solid alliance" in Brazil between the military and technicians in the public sector, groups that would work together to bring a strong state presence to the steel sector and to other sectors – petroleum, petrochemicals, and nuclear energy – in the decades ahead.[29]

The development of a steel industry had long been linked by planners to the development of Brazil's substantial iron ore resources. Just as in the case of CSN, the Brazilian private sector appeared incapable of providing the financial resources and technical know-how to develop the rich Itabira deposits and the complementary rail and port facilities. But in contrast to the experience in steel, an alternative source of capital existed: foreign investment.[30] When financial resources became available to the government via large international loans, the Companhia Vale do Rio Doce was created in 1942 as an alternative to foreign control of the Itabira deposits. Other public enterprises formed during the period were related to the particular historical circumstance of war-induced shortages in basic industrial materials. Enterprises created included the Companhia de Alcalis, to produce soda ash for the glass industry, and the Fábrica Nacional de Motores, originally intended to manufacture a variety of small engines.[31]

1947–1962: Import substitution industrialization

In common with many Latin American countries, Brazil pursued an economic strategy of industrialization through import substitution. The major economic policies included high tariff walls, foreign exchange controls, a generally overvalued exchange rate, special inducements to foreign capital, government provisions of infrastructure, and subsidized loans to the private sector.

The resulting industrialization led to a growth in industry's share in the economy and a relative decline of agriculture. Within industry, important changes occurred in the commodity distribution of output, with strong relative gains for consumer durables (automobiles, appliances) and producer goods (steel, heavy machinery) at the expense of textiles and food.

The rapid pace of economic development during the 1950s and a rising tide of economic nationalism created an environment favorable to additional experiment with public enterprise. The founding of new firms in petroleum, steel, electrical energy, and long-term finance not only filled out the core of the modern public enterprise sector but consolidated the concept of the state as entrepreneur.

In the early fifties, important public enterprises were organized in two priority areas: petroleum and long-term financing. One of these – Petróleos Brasileiros (PETROBRÁS), the state petroleum monopoly – became a watershed in the development of economic nationalism in Brazil. The new company was formed when the only private sector alternative – foreign investment – was permanently rejected after bitter debate.[32] "The battle for PETROBRÁS" brought together once again an alliance of state technicians and the military.

Both the demonstrated incapacity of private capital markets and the state's intention to provide the low-cost, long-term finance necessary for industrial growth explain the establishment of the BNDE in 1952. While some of the underdevelopment of the financial sector can be attributed to earlier government regulation of banking transactions, the Brazilian experience appears to validate Gerschenkron's observation that the state in most backward economies will assume the responsibility for financial infrastructure.[33]

Once a long-term lending institution under the control of the state had been established (although its funding was initially quite limited), the creation of public enterprises in social overhead sectors, such as energy, transportation, and basic industry, became more common. This spread of public enterprise was not always intentional. For example, in the mid-fifties, the need for expanded steel capacity became apparent. Several large projects combining private capital and state government finance were approved to supply the additional capacity. When the original financing schemes proved inadequate, the federal government, through the BNDE, became the reluctant owner of three steel plants: Usinas Siderúrgicas de Minas Gerais (USIMINAS), Companhia Ferro e Aço de Vitória (COFAVI), and Companhia Siderúrgica Paulista (COSIPA).[34]

The creation of public enterprises in the 1950s to begin harnessing Brazil's vast hydroelectric potential was one of the most important state initiatives in the entire postwar period.[35] Political factors help explain some elements of the increasing public role in the provision of electric power. Many utilities had traditionally been owned by foreign investors and, in part because of popular resentment, had for many years been denied the minimum rate relief they needed to provide both a return on investment and the resources for the expansion of generating, transmission, and distribution capacity. As a result, many foreign-owned utilities ceased to expand and power bottlenecks became common. State-owned firms free of political encumbrances, such as FURNAS and CHEVAP, were created to relieve the developing shortages.

While particular political and historical circumstances were of undoubted importance in explaining the growing role of the public sector in electricity, such a role would almost certainly have developed anyway in view of legislation – promulgated during the 1950s – to submit electrical energy to overall state planning, to set up special funding mechanisms to finance new public enterprises at the state and federal levels, and to set up the state holding company, ELETROBRÁS. Thus, the hypotheses regarding externalities and economies of scale should be seen as important in the creation of such firms as CEMIG, CHESF, CELUSA, and (in 1963) ELETROBRÁS itself. Many operating companies were established by federal and state governments before demand was apparent to spur regional development through the provision of abundant, relatively inexpensive power.

The public control of telecommunications also resulted from the nationalization of large, unpopular foreign firms. Thus, many of the public telecommunications firms, especially the Companhia Telefônica Brasileira (CTB), were the result of political rather than economic reasons. Nevertheless, it may be argued that the subsequent expansion of communications was attributable to the state's desire to stimulate development and would not have taken place under private ownership even if private firms had not been encumbered by rate controls.

1964–1967: Crisis and stabilization

The nucleus of the modern public enterprise sector had been put in place before the ouster of the elected, left-leaning government of João Goulart in March 1964 and its replacement by a conservative and resolutely nonsocialist military regime. The state had already established itself in many key areas of the economy and, more importantly, the concepts of the state as entrepreneur and of cooperation between technocrats and the military on projects of importance to national development had been well established. These precedents were never repudiated or even seriously questioned by the post-1964 governments.

But from a vantage point in the early 1960s, it would have been difficult to predict the evolution of the Brazilian public enterprise sector. Public enterprises grew rapidly in numbers from the mid-1960s through the mid-1970s. More importantly, the post-1964 period saw a tremendous jump in the *scale* of the largest public enterprises. Many of these expanded installed capacity several times over pre-1964 levels and branched out into different fields.

How could this occur under regimes that consistently proclaimed support for strengthening a market-oriented economy in which private enterprise would enjoy broad scope for initiative? And how did it happen that by the mid-1970s some of the severest critics of the role of the state in the Brazilian economy would be precisely those industrial classes who, presumably, had most to gain from the conservative, free-market stance of the military governments? Answers to these questions are closely related to the economic circumstances confronting the military upon assuming office, the stabilization policies they selected, and the nature of public enterprise growth after 1964.

The military government in 1964 inherited a financial crisis, a result of the conflict between Goulart's political objectives and the economy's resource constraints. The crisis comprised an eroding tax base, a large deficit of the public sector, spiraling inflation (100% per annum), a severe foreign exchange shortage, and external debt service difficulties. At the same time, Brazil was experiencing declining rates of GNP growth.

Stabilization was the first priority of the Castello Branco government, because the legitimacy of the antidemocratic regime hinged on its ability to restore economic growth. As is often the diagnosis in Latin America, the decentralized public enterprises were identified as root causes of the public sector deficit. PETROBRÁS and the public utility companies had been constrained to keep prices low during the Goulart regime. The new policy of "corrective inflation" (discussed in Chapter 6) not only reduced the financial burden of the public sector enterprises on the government budget but led to improved self-financing capacity and greater managerial autonomy and flexibility. Both of those would be very important to growth of the sector over the next fifteen years.[36]

Given the military's parallel emphasis on restoring the basis for sound growth in the medium term, a decision was made not to cut back investment activities in the core areas of the productive structure, where public enterprises were already dominant. As a further inducement, international agencies were making available to Brazil funds needed to finance the large infrastructure projects. Thus, while private firms in Brazil during 1964–7 were contending with severe credit restrictions in the name of stabilization, the economic climate for the newly strengthened public enterprises was quite different. Baer observes:

Government investment expenditures were never cut back during the vigorous stabilization years after 1964, as [during the period] the government engaged in some basic sectoral studies (in collaboration with the U.S. Agency for International Development, the World Bank, and the Inter-American Development Bank) designed to guide the expansion of the country's power supply, transportation system, urban infrastructure, and heavy industries – especially steel, mining, and petrochemicals – which were dominated by government enterprises. The time-lag between these studies, negotiations to finance investment, and actual investment activities, came to three or four years and only in the later 1960s were the results of such planning activities felt.[37]

1968–1974: Expansion

Strong rates of economic growth resulted from Brazil's technocratic formula based on financial reform, foreign capital and technology, tax incentives, and expanded purchasing power for the middle class.[38] During the "boom" period, the public sector continued to expand as a mobilizer and allocator of resources through its fiscal functions. In particular, the post-1964 reform and the post-1967 climate of rapid economic expansion set the stage for a remarkable step-up in the state's direct participation in the economy. A large "highwater" mark for the statization process was achieved with the creation during these six years of approximately 231 new public enterprises at the federal and state levels (see Table 3.3).

Table 3.3. *Creation of new state enterprises by sector, 1968–74*

Sector	No.
Manufacturing	42
Mining	12
Agriculture	2
Services	175
Construction	(10)
Transport, storage	(24)
Electricity, gas, water, communications	(108)
Commerce	(5)
Miscellaneous	(28)
Total	231

Source: *Visão, Quem é quem na economia brasileira*, August 1976.

The major causes of state-enterprise expansion were (1) administrative reforms that made it attractive for units within general government to be restructured as public enterprises; (2) increased demand for infrastructure (such as electricity and telecommunications) of which the state was already the sole provider; and (3) diversification and expansion of existing state enterprises (especially PETROBRÁS and Companhia Vale do Rio Doce, or CVRD) into new areas.

The key administrative reform was Decree-Law 200 of 1967. The measure was intended to stimulate better administrative performance in the old federal bureaucracy by providing units of government with greater decision-making autonomy and improved material rewards.[39] A key provision of Decree-Law 200 was to loosen the salary restrictions imposed by civil service regulations. This allowed the bureaucracies, now newly reborn as public enterprises, to offer higher salaries and better benefits in order to recruit and maintain qualified staff. New enterprises were created to replace units of general government engaged in data processing, agricultural and mineral research, urban planning, sanitation, and many other areas. The process accounts for a significant share of the 175 enterprises created in the service sector after 1968 (see Table 3.3).

But important as it may have been from an administrative standpoint, Decree-law 200 did not really extend the state's role in the Brazilian economy.

The post-1968 expansion of state ownership also derived from the growth in scale and national extension of state monopolies in electricity and telecommunications and and other infrastructure areas in which neither the Brazilian private sector nor foreign investment had much interest. Because Brazil's rapid growth required an extension and modernization of electrical generation and transmission facilities, ELETROBRÁS consolidated and extended public control over electricity operations throughout the nation. In telecommunications a similarly structured holding company, TELEBRÁS, presided over the consolidation of small private telephone companies, most operating with antiquated technologies, into large, regionally organized, state-owned communications firms. This policy resulted in a considerable increase in the number of public enterprises. Furthermore, the creation of EMBRATEL to provide a modern intercity system of telecommunications allowed many of these once isolated regional systems to integrate a nationwide and international network for the first time.

Thus, particular historical circumstances (the administrative reforms) are of some help in explaining the large growth in state-owned companies in the late 1960s and 1970s. So, too, are the hypotheses of economies of scale and pecuniary economies, which overlap in explaining the creation of new companies in telecommunications and electricity and of state-owned engineering concerns for the construction of roads, bridges, airports, and urban transit systems. Of course, these services are publicly provided in many countries. Diversification and expansion of existing state firms can help explain the creation of from fifty to sixty firms in mining and manufacturing after 1968. In the 1970s state capital moved to occupy what were called *espaços vazios* ("empty spaces") of the productive structure. The reasons were multiple, but they frequently involved a revival of the alliance between public sector technicians and the military that was so important to the founding of state enterprises in the 1940s and 1950s. For example, EMBRAER, the state-owned producer of small aircraft for commercial and military uses, was created by the Brazilian air force for reasons of "national security." A country of Brazil's dimensions, it was argued, could not afford to depend on imported aircraft and spare parts, nor could it allow the domestic manufacture of such strategic materials to be controlled by foreign companies.

Nuclear power was another important "empty space" filled by state enterprise in the early 1970s. NUCLEBRÁS and numerous subsidiaries were created with strong military support in 1975 to assemble the enormous financial and managerial resources needed for an ambitious Brazilian nuclear program, including domestic production of enriched uranium. Considerations of national security and, to a lesser extent, national prestige were probably the most important factors in starting up a nuclear industry in Brazil. Brazil's abundant hydroelectric capacity made less compelling the argument that nuclear reactors were needed to add to the nation's overall energy supply. While the nuclear program in Brazil has been scaled down, NUCLEBRÁS and its subsidiaries remain important vehicles for the transfer of nuclear technology.

Of the many different modes of state-enterprise expansion in the 1960s and 1970s, the most controversial and significant was the expansion resulting from the creation of subsidiaries (and, on occasion, of third- and fourth-generation subsidiaries) of existing public enterprises. Often this involved the movement of public enterprises "downstream" into less capital-intensive activities where the need for public ownership based on risk and financial constraints was seemingly less applicable. Different types of firms engaged in such expansion, but the greatest attention was received by two firms, PETROBRÁS and CVRD. The creation of subsidiaries by these two firms might be in close accord with the hypothesis of dynamic public enterprise managers.

PETROBRÁS was particularly active in creating subsidiaries by means of branching into activities that went beyond a narrow reading of the company's original charter and included vertical integration into refining, the commercial distribution of refined products, and maritime transport. The distribution subsidiary, PETROBRÁS Distribuidora, competes with foreign firms that were permitted to remain in the business of retailing refined products after the creation of the state oil monopoly.[40]

Diversification into other activities, such as petrochemicals, took PETROBRÁS farther afield. After a reluctant beginning, through its PETROQUISA subsidiary and literally scores of third- and fourth-generation subsidiaries, it is now the major force in the Brazilian petrochemical industry.[41] Its expansion has two main features: first, entrepreneurship as the move into petrochemicals resulted from a strong profit performance in the 1960s and 1970s and the decision to deemphasize risky domestic petroleum exploration. Second, the diversification effort resulted from the belief of authorities that the domestic private sector would not have invested in petrochemicals. Had PETROBRÁS not intervened, the petrochemical industry would have been completely dominated by multinational companies. Carvalho, for example, attributes state expansion into petrochemicals to "the passivity that has characterized many businessmen in Brazil... The government has not been able to force private industry to accept greater responsibility for developing the petrochemical industry, and has found itself obliged to replace it on certain occasions."[42]

The very large number of state-owned or state-controlled petrochemical firms can also be traced to an innovative financing arrangement that combines foreign, state, and private domestic capital.[43] Under this arrangement, state and private Brazilian capital retain control of the firm, but foreign minority participation still permits important technology transfers to occur. The plan has been well received by multinational petrochemical enterprises. Evans argues that foreign firms view state participation in a joint project as a significant risk-reducing factor that compensates for their loss in control.[44]

PETROBRÁS's growth and diversification brought the firm into a broad range of other activities, including fertilizers, international exploration and refining (through its BRASPETRO subsidiary), and international trade (through its INTERBRÁS subsidiary, which actively promotes exports of Brazilian agricultural and manufactured products). PETROBRÁS had been one single domestic company in the mid-1960s. By the early 1980s, it controlled or was the dominant partner in more than seventy other companies – a veritable constellation of subsidiaries and joint ventures (see Figure 3.1).

The Companhia Vale do Rio Doce (CVRD) proved equally adept at transforming a liquid cash position into diversified investments through the organization of subsidiaries and joint ventures. CVRD also illustrates problems encountered when a conglomerate, whether state-owned or not, overextends itself and is forced to cut back on ambitious investment plans when its basic business encounters cyclical problems. Starting from its profitable base in the mining and shipping of iron ore (it is the largest producing and exporting corporation in the world), CVRD through the early 1970s sought broad diversification in the natural-resource sector and moved aggressively through subsidiaries and minority-owned affiliates into bauxite, alumina and aluminum, manganese, phosphates, fertilizers, pulp, paper, and reforestation, and titanium, as well into ancilliary activities such as mineral surveys and natural-resource engineering and planning. A key subsidiary, AMZA, was set up to develop the rich iron ore deposits in Carajas in the north of Brazil. At the height of what critics called its "empire building," CVRD owned twelve major subsidiaries and was an active partner in twelve joint ventures, primarily with foreign capital and related to the development of iron ore deposits and iron ore pellet plants (see Figure 3.2).

In its reach for rapid diversification, CVRD overextended itself. When world iron prices tumbled in 1977, the company did not have the capital necessary to fund its investments. This led to a management shake-up and the company was forced to dismantle or sell to the private sector subsidiaries in aluminum, cellulose, bauxite, and manganese.[45]

1976–1980: Oil adjustment

Despite its status as the largest oil importer in the developing world, Brazil was slow to adjust to the first round of oil price increases in 1973–4. The adverse terms of trade movement signified an enormous transfer of income from Brazil to OPEC,

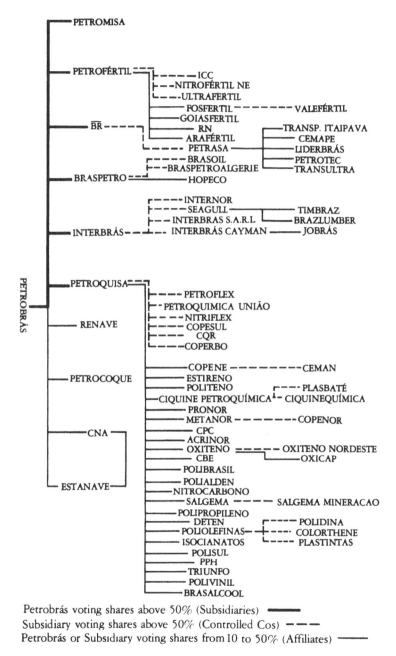

Petrobrás voting shares above 50% (Subsidiaries) ▬▬▬
Subsidiary voting shares above 50% (Controlled Cos) ▬ ▬ ▬
Petrobrás or Subsidiary voting shares from 10 to 50% (Affiliates) ▬▬▬

Figure 3.1. PETROBRÁS system in 1980.

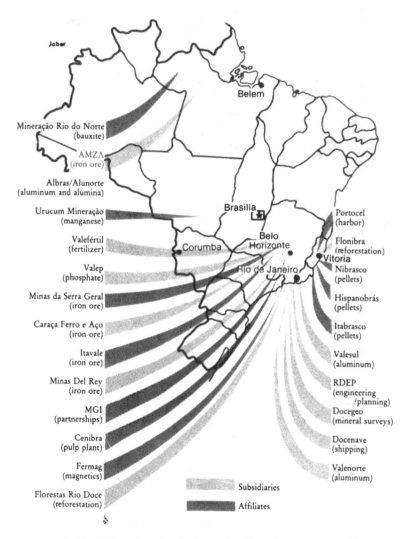

Figure 3.2. CVRD's main subsidiaries and affiliated companies, 1976. (Source: CVRD Annual Report, 1976.)

but Brazilian policymakers still resolved to press ahead with projects envisioned in the Second National Development Plan (1975–9). By 1976, however, the need for downward adjustment in aggregate demand, in general, and public sector investment, in particular, was apparent. Although far from consistent, economic policy gradually became more restrictive through the shock of the second round of oil price hikes in 1978–9 and into the early 1980s. The tightened monetary and credit policies hit hardest at the private sector in the mid-1970s, but as time went on the public enterprise sector as well came under steadily increasing pressures to adjust spending downward. The large state companies were increasingly pinpointed by policymakers as major factors behind excess aggregate demand pressures, which, in turn, were triggering severe balance-of-payments and inflation problems.

In retrospect, then, the era of the rapidly expanding state-enterprise sector in Brazil probably ended about 1975. Effective government restrictions on imports, investment, remuneration, in short, on the size and autonomy of public enterprises came about only gradually (see Chapter 4), however, regardless of a key early move by the Geisel government in 1976 to prohibit the creation of new public enterprises, including subsidiaries of existing enterprises, without presidential review and approval. In fact, a number of new state enterprises were set up in the late 1970s – some examples being the CVRD subsidiaries previously mentioned and a firm known as COBRA, a public enterprise producer of small and medium-sized computers.[46] Yet the long-term trends became clear as the government through the late 1970s repeatedly affirmed its intention to halt the growth in the number of public enterprises. With the advent of the Figuereido government in 1979 came the explicit policy (discussed later) of rolling back the state-owned sector through the denationalization of many companies outside the "classic" public enterprise sectors of the utilities and transport sectors. Thus, by the late 1970s, the public enterprise sector in Brazil had probably reached, and was likely to remain at indefinitely, a plateau in terms of the number of firms and their areas of operation.

Statistical dimensions: a summing up

Brazil's public enterprises are concentrated in the traditional public utilities, transportation, and (mainly by virtue of CVRD) mining. They hold an important stake in key sectors in industry (especially steel and petroleum), but most other manufacturing pursuits in Brazil, particularly the manufacture of consumer and capital goods, are dominated by private enterprise. Furthermore, agriculture is in the hands of the private sector in Brazil as is most of commerce.

Public enterprises accounted for only 7% of the nearly 7,000 firms in Brazil with more than $1MM in capital in 1979 and only 18% of total employment. However, these same public enterprises accounted for 50% of all capital invested in these same 7,000 firms (see Table 3.4). Again, by comparison only to the sample of large firms, the public enterprise share of capital invested in utilities and transport sectors ranged from 85%–95% versus only a 22% share in manufacturing investment.

In general, public enterprises operate in sectors that require large amounts of investment. Although the pace of technological change in some of these sectors is not rapid, in many others government enterprises must contend with sophisticated and rapidly evolving technologies. The government petrochemical industry is one example; the atomic power industry is another. New technologies are also an increasingly important part of the steel, mining, and communications industries.

Trends in sectoral distribution of assets

Little recent change has occurred in the pattern of federal enterprise investment despite the vigorous economic growth of the past decades (see Table 3.5). Shifts in the distribution of federal assets have occurred within, rather than between, the major economic sectors of mining, manufacturing, and the utilities. For example, in manufacturing, investments in petrochemicals (fertilizers, rubber, and a wide range of intermediate goods) increased the proportion of assets in this

Table 3.4. Nonfinancial public enterprises: indicators of relative size, 1979

Sector	No. of public enterprises	Invested capital (Cr$ billion)[a]	Employees	Each sector's % of shares		
				Total firms	Total capital	Total employment
Mining and agriculture	32	76.2	41,000	4.5	34.7	23.7
Manufacturing	92	371.3	178,000	2.5	22.2	5.5
Public utilities	103	679.9	396,000	41.2	86.4	80.8
Transportation	77	492.8	184,000	31.3	94.9	62.0
Power	155	101.2	73,000	10.4	34.8	11.6
Chemicals	48	1721.4	872,000	7.1	49.3	18.0

Notes: The annual Visão survey covers only firms with more than $1MM in capital, about 7,000 firms in the 1980 edition. Thus, this table represents the shares of public enterprise in only the 7,000 largest firms, not the total economy. The Visão figures have been adjusted to eliminate assets held by holding companies. The author believes such institutions should be considered financial institutions.
[a]Patrimônio líquido, or net worth.
Source: Calculated from Visão, Quem é quem na economia brasileira, August 28, 1980.

Table 3.5. *Sectoral shares of assets of federal public enterprises, selected years (percentages)*

Sectors	1966	1970	1974	1979
Mining	7.0	6.3	7.4	4.5
Manufacturing	41.9	43.9	40.4	21.6
Steel	11.3	15.7	11.5	n.a.
Chemicals	30.1	27.5	27.7	n.a.
Petroleum	29.9	25.1	24.7	n.a.
Petrochemicals	0.2	2.4	3.0	n.a.
Diverse	0.4	0.8	1.1	n.a.
Public utilities	48.6	49.3	50.9	68.1
Transports	20.5	10.8	7.4	n.a.
Communications	8.2	17.1	22.6	n.a.
Electricity	19.9	18.4	19.2	n.a.
Diverse	0.0	3.0	4.3	n.a.
All other sectors	2.5	0.5	1.2	5.8
Total	100	100	100	100

Note: Federally owned enterprises only.
Source: Visão, Quem é quem na economia brasileira, 1967, 1971, 1975, 1980.

subsector from almost nil to 3% of the total over the period 1966–74. The share of "diverse" industries increased, but only slightly, with the creation of firms in nuclear technology and aircraft manufacture.

Within public utilities, the neglect of the railroads caused a significant drop in the share of transportation assets in the total. Electricity investments maintained an approximately constant share, and those in telecommunications increased significantly from 8.2% in 1966 to 22.6% in 1974, a result of the growth of EMBRATEL and the federal takeover of telecommunications that began in 1966. Net assets in different public services increased steadily, largely as a result of the administrative reforms mentioned earlier.

Relative size of public enterprises

A major aspect of the controversy over public enterprise in Brazil has concerned the *scale* of public enterprises vis-à-vis

Table 3.6. *Brazil: ownership distribution of the thirty*
largest nonfinancial firms, selected years, 1962–79

Ownership	1962	1967	1971	1974	1979
Public	12	13	17	23	28
Private	18	17	13	7	2

Note: Firms are ranked according to net worth (*patrimônio líquido*).
Source: Frank Brandenburg, *The Development of Latin American Private Enterprise* (Washington, D.C.: National Planning Association, 1964), p. 16; *Visão, Quem é quem na economia brasileira*, 1968, 1972, 1975, 1980.

the private sector. Graham and Mendonça de Barros argue, convincingly, that public enterprises were better able to take advantage of the post-1964 reforms, which improved the functioning of the price system and spurred the development of money and capital markets.[47] Very striking evidence of the *scale* aspects of Brazilian public enterprise is provided by the evolution of Brazil's 30 largest nonfinancial firms since the early 1960s (see Table 3.6). In 1962, state-owned enterprises accounted for just 12 of the largest 30 (ranked by capital). State-enterprise representation grew to 17 in 1971, 23 in 1975, and 28 of the top 30 in 1979. The lone private sector representatives were two foreign-owned auto producers (GM and Volkswagen) and neither of these ranked among the top 20. Growth in activity rather than in the acquisition of private firms explains the emergence of public enterprises, with one exception: the 1978 purchase by ELETROBRÁS of the sole remaining private electric utility of any consequence, the Canadian-owned Light. Public enterprises dominate even the 100 largest firms in Brazil. In the early 1970s, 46 of the largest 100 were public; by the early 1980s, 54 state enterprises were ranked among the largest 100.

These results suggest that a relative handful of public enterprises also dominate the group of government-owned firms. Of the federal public enterprises considered in the 1966 *Visão* survey, the largest ten among them accounted for 96% of assets owned by federal firms. Although this share has fallen in similar surveys in subsequent years, the largest ten still accounted for 67.3% of federal assets in the 1974 survey.[48] This group of "super-firms" would include ELETROBRÁS, PETROBRÁS, RFFSA (railroads), CVRD, FURNAS (electricity), TELESP (telecommunications), CSN, and others. Thus, the debate over "statization" in Brazil concerned not only the *creation* of new public enterprises but also the *growth* in scale of existing public enterprises enjoying (private sector critics alleged) capitalization advantages not available to private firms.

An international perspective

Is the Brazilian pattern any different from the role of state-owned enterprises in other economies? An answer to this question would help us to decide between the more general economic explanations versus the more country-specific historical and political explanations of the rise of public enterprise.

Although a detailed comparison is beyond the scope of this study, even a brief look at the experience with public enterprise in other countries can be instructive. Mexico, Argentina, Chile, and Peru may be considered as representative of Latin American countries with important public enterprise sectors. From among other groups of countries, the case of Italy also offers illuminating similarities and contrasts with that of Brazil. Definitions vary, but in each of these countries a large number of enterprises can be classified as public. Recent estimates put the number of state-owned enterprises at 845 in Mexico and (again, depending on definitions) between 400 and 800 in Argentina.[49] At one point in the early 1970s, the Chilean public enterprise sector included more than 500 firms.[50]

A common characteristic of Latin American public enterprise structure is the concentration of state equity in a relative handful of capital-intensive firms operating in the basic sectors of the economy. In the case of Mexico, of the more than 800 public firms, just 15 large firms account for 90% of the equity of the Mexican state in all public firms.[51] Another survey of Mexican public enterprise revealed that only 5 state enterprises had been responsible for 88% of public investments by the 34 public enterprises in manufacturing.[52]

As in Brazil, the largest public enterprises in other Latin American countries are usually among the largest firms in each country. Even in Chile this pattern of public enterprise dominance holds, despite the doctrinaire pro-private enterprise policies of the post-Allende government. Thus, in 1979, 8 of the largest 10 Chilean firms (in terms of net worth) and 13 of the largest 25 belonged to the state with little prospect that any of these would be transferred soon to the private sector.[53] Although only 16 state enterprises ranked among the top 100 Chilean firms in 1979, this handful still accounted for 71% of total net worth of the 100 largest.

Thus, public enterprise sectors, in Brazil and elsewhere in Latin America, can be divided into two groups: a small core group of very large firms in the utilities and the basic sectors of industry and a numerically much larger collection of smaller firms engaged in a large variety of activities.

By confining attention to the "core group" of large public enterprises in each country, a common pattern of state intervention by industry is readily apparent. Despite the obvious differences between the selected countries in Latin America in terms of size, regime, ideology, and historical evolution, public enterprise monopolies are found to dominate the same key branches of the utilities and industry in each, a pattern that gives weight to the supposition that certain common economic determinants of public enterprise are at work in each country.

Examples of public sector monopolies, or dominant public sector firms, in six sectors in six countries are provided in Table 3.7. The basic sectors selected include long-term finance, petroleum and petrochemicals, steel, electricity, communications, and railroads.

The comparison could be extended to other sectors of the economy. For example, Brazil's reliance on the mixed-enterprise Banco do Brasil not only as a large commercial bank but also as a fiscal agent and agent of specialized credit finds close parallels in Chile (Banco del Estado), Argentina (Banco de la Nación Argentina), and Peru (Banco de la Nación). The use of the CVRD to exploit rich mineral deposits is echoed by

Table 3.7. Examples of public enterprise by economic sector in six countries

Country	Long-term finance	Petroleum/ petrochemicals	Steel	Electricity	Communications	Railroads
				Economic sector		
Mexico	NAFINSA	PEMEX	Altos Hornos	CFE	Telefonos de Mexico	F.F. Nacionales
Argentina	BANADE	YPF	Somisa	SEGBA	ENTEL	Ferrocarriles Argentina
Brazil	BNDE	PETROBRÁS	CSN	ELETROBRÁS	TELEBRÁS	RFFSA
Chile	CORFO	ENAP	CAP	ENDESA	CTC	F. del Estado
Peru	COFIDE	Petroperu	Siderperu	Electroperu	Entelperu	Enafer
Italy	IRI	ENI	FINSIDER	Enel	STETI	Ferrovie dello Estato

Chile's CODELCO (copper), Peru's Mineroperu and Hierroperu (copper and iron ore), Bolivia's COMIBOL, and others. The similarity of cross-national patterns, especially in Latin America, calls attention to common economic and political factors that must have exercised influence over policy decisions in all these countries. Two such factors can be highlighted, although others may also have played a role: (1) the scale, risk, and financial requirement inherent in the basic sectors that the state entered clearly exceeded the resources available in the private sectors of these economies; and (2) the foreign private investment that was often available as an alternative to public enterprise was rejected for political considerations.

Although emphasizing common patterns and causal factors, this brief glance at the experience in other countries nevertheless suggests some important differences in the "reasons for" public enterprise in the basic sectors of the economy and differences also in the growth and extension of public enterprises once established. Some of these are highlighted in the following discussion, although further research is needed.

Significant differences are apparent in the *timing* of state intervention in Latin America even if the ultimate patterns of intervention are broadly similar. In comparative perspective, the Brazilian state did not pioneer in Latin America as an entrepreneur in the basic sectors of the economy. Glade points out that the Chileans in the 1930s were among the first to experiment broadly with state-owned special-purpose credit institutions.[54] The founding of CORFO (in 1939) long predates the establishment of the BNDE. Similarly, the Argentine state had already moved across a broad front into the basic sectors of the economy by the 1940s, well before similar moves in Brazil. On the other hand, direct state intervention in the basic sectors of the economy in Brazil was almost completed before it was even attempted on a large scale by Peru in the late 1960s.

Public enterprise as a means for the state to control the "commanding heights" of the economy played an important role in the creation of many state companies in Peru and

Chile in the 1960s and 1970s as regimes in both countries attempted to implement socialist development strategies. Thus, the Unidad Popular government in Chile moved quickly after its inauguration to establish a "social property area" composed of the large copper mines, the bulk of the commercial banking system, the utilities, petrochemicals, pulp and paper, and other strategic areas.

In Peru, after 1968, the national plan held that "the overcoming of the dependent capitalist model and underdevelopment requires the State to undertake a role of active participation as promoter and leader of national development, through its direct and indirect intervention in economic activity."[55] As a reflection of this policy, the Peruvian regime promoted broad ownership reforms, including the creation and expansion of state enterprise in petroleum, mining, food marketing, and fishing. In contrast, the expansion of the Brazilian state into the basic sectors of the economy was usually justified in pragmatic terms. Rarely has the Brazilian state taken over healthy private firms, preferring instead to expand into the "empty spaces": steel, petroleum, iron ore. Most cases of nationalization of private enterprise in the basic sectors (e.g., telecommunications and electricity) occurred after private firms proved unable to expand plants in line with development needs.[56]

Another characteristic of the state Brazilian public enterprise sector has been its growth by diversification of state firms beyond the confines of their original charters, for example, the rapid expansion of CVRD and PETROBRÁS in the 1970s. Few parallel patterns of enterprise creation are apparent in Latin America. Perhaps the entrepreneurial behavior of Italian state-enterprise managers (e.g., the ENI under Mattei and the IRI) provides the closest analogy. The Brazilian experience, by comparison to that of other countries in Latin America, also stands out for its greater state-enterprise joint ventures with foreign investment. This suggests that public enterprise in Brazil may have been permitted a greater degree of autonomy and flexibility than has been the case in other Latin American countries.

The predominant modes of the creation of public enterprise in Brazil have been through new government investments, spin-offs of units of general government, and diversification using retained earnings of existing enterprises. In general, the pattern is one of orderly growth of the state-enterprise sector from a stable base of operations. This contrasts with the experience of other countries in which the growth of the public enterprise sector was accomplished through absorption of financially troubled private firms that the government for political reasons desired to rescue from bankruptcy. The Argentine public sector grew rapidly in the 1960s and 1970s for precisely these reasons. Italy's public enterprise sector expanded to absorb a large number of bankrupt private firms in the 1930s. Many of the Mexican public enterprises have also resulted from bailouts of foundering private enterprises.

Conclusions

How and why did public enterprise grow in Brazil? What are the implications for the dynamics of public enterprise growth?

The first hypothesis argued that public ownership and control result from the inability of the private sector to supply needed resources (funds, risk absorption, entrepreneurship) at crucial junctures during the development process. The Brazilian experience with public enterprise in ports, shipping, and steel illustrates this hypothesis. For example, it was only after the failure of repeated attempts to interest the private sector that public enterprise was originally created in steel. Other large steel enterprises became public only after private entrepreneurs were unable to put together ambitious financing schemes. In the 1960s and 1970s, new public enterprises were created in technology-intensive "empty spaces" of the productive structure, such as aircraft, petrochemicals, and nuclear energy.

The economies of scale hypothesis attributed public ownership to technical conditions in the production of certain goods and to the growth of the market for those goods. Advancing industrialization in Brazil required increasing investments in activities such as electrical energy, telecommunications, and steel, and the public sector did move into these areas of the economy. This is not to deny the importance of short-run political factors, especially the rate control exercised over private firms, but rather to emphasize the basic economic rationale for takeover in these sectors.

The external economies argument could be used to predict public ownership of transportation networks and other social overhead capital. In Brazil it was found that railroad systems, electrical energy firms, port facilities, shipping lines, and heavy construction firms are a large part of the group of public enterprises. State financial enterprises, especially the National Economic Development Bank, were also created for reasons of externalities, as their operations reduced the cost of long-term finance to Brazilian firms.

The dynamic state managers hypothesis argued that efficient state enterprises that are also commercially successful will expand or diversify their operations. Furthermore, the state will permit this expansion to encourage continued efficiency in its enterprises. Observation of the Brazilian case reveals that a number of commercially successful firms, such as Vale do Rio Doce, PETROBRÁS, and others, have in fact created new subsidiaries, diversified activities, and otherwise expanded the extent of public control. This has resulted in the creation of public enterprises in industries and sectors where the familiar arguments for public ownership based on risk and financial constraints were seemingly less operable, for example, in engineering, research, data processing, construction, tourism, and cellulose.

As other examples, ELETROBRÁS and TELEBRÁS managers have steadily widened the degree of public ownership in their respective industries through organizational reforms, which resulted in many new public enterprises in electricity and telecommunications.

The natural resource rents hypothesis traced public enterprise to public appropriation of surplus in the form of rent. Intervention in the iron and petroleum sectors may be seen as attempts by the state to remove monopoly profits from the grasp of potential foreign investors. Other valuable mineral resources, including bauxite, are also controlled by state enterprises.

The five economic hypotheses set forth at the outset, although not mutually exclusive, have provided a useful context in which to examine the basic structure of public enterprise in Brazil. This structure appears very similar to that of other Latin American countries, a fact that lends support to general economic (rather than political–historical) explanations of the rise of public enterprise. In this "typical" Latin American pattern, the directly productive activity of the state is concentrated in the utilities, transportation, and heavy industry (especially steel and petroleum) where its primary purpose is to support and stimulate relatively lighter manufacturing activities under the control of the private sector.

These remarks do *not* imply that political dynamics or historical circumstances unique to Brazil were unimportant in shaping the structure of the public enterprise sector. On the contrary, at least three important historical or political processes were identified in the Brazilian context: (1) trends toward a decentralization of government decision making (e.g., Decree-Law 200, holding companies), (2) national security concerns, and (3) relations with foreign capital. This last process has been complicated by policy goals that preclude entrance of foreign capital into key sectors, support the takeover of politically unpopular foreign enterprise, and endeavor to attract foreign investment and technology without sacrificing domestic control (e.g., joint ventures).

To sum up, the growth of public enterprise in Brazil has involved an expansion and reorganization of state enterprise in basic industry and an extension – at the margin, as it were – of public ownership into new areas. The structure of the public enterprise sector in Brazil has been stable but not static and unchanging, and it continues to evolve in ways that support and sustain the major policy goals of the Brazilian government. Growth has been, to an important degree, a function of the relative autonomy the state companies have possessed.

Postscript: Privatization?

The end of that remarkable period of rapid and sustainable growth in Brazil from roughly 1967 through 1974 did force policymakers to reexamine the role of the state in the economy. The sharp drop in the rate of creation of public enterprises in the late 1970s was certainly one outward sign of this process of reexamination with an eye to a secular retrenchment in the public sector's share of GNP.

Reducing the size of the public enterprise sector, by "privatizing" selected state-owned firms, seemed to be a means of taking one more step in this direction. Shortly after taking office in 1979, President João Figueiredo recommended to his cabinet a consideration of the measures needed "for the 'privatization' of any state-owned enterprises not strictly necessary to correct market imperfections or to attend to the demands of national security."

To be sure, the Brazilian government's concern for denationalization was devoid of the ideological fervor for the task that was so evident in Chile in the 1970s, but the need to restructure the Brazilian economy made this concern both authentic and durable, albeit easier said than done. Planning Minister Antonio Delfim Netto made clear repeatedly his intention to remove gradually the state as entrepreneur from all sectors where its presence was not essential, that is, where it competed with, or preempted, a role for private enterprises.

How should this concern for privatization be interpreted? The new policy thrust was certainly important in halting the growth of public enterprise after the late 1970s, but it is very unlikely for a number of reasons to result in any significant change in the size and shape of the public enterprise sector as we know it in the 1980s.

One important reason is that the government has no intention of selling, nor does the Brazilian private sector intend to buy, the most important government undertakings in the utilities, transportation, and heavy industry. In terms of capital invested, these firms are 80%–90% of the public enterprise sector. The attitude of the Brazilian government is charged with pragmatism. In looking, for example, at the big three companies of the SIDERBRÁS complex in steel, policymakers see a reasonably well managed and productive group of public enterprises. So why sell these firms and risk disruption of a vital industrial input? And, of course, who in Brazil would be willing or able to purchase the enormous steel concerns? Even if sufficient private capital was available, would entrepreneurs accustomed to a quick return on their investment be attracted to those public firms, such as steel, with chronically low rates of return?

A second reason for some skepticism on the eventual extent of privatization in Brazil hinges on the role of the military in the management of some of the largest companies. PETROBRÁS, for example, as well as NUCLEBRÁS, CSN, EMBRAER, and a host of others, is wrapped in the protective blanket of "national security." The military is unlikely in any foreseeable future to permit the auctioning off of any state firm in which it had a hand either in establishing or running.

Third, Brazilian populist sentiment would also stand firmly in the way of any major changes in the current structure of Brazilian public enterprise. A broad segment of the population, including parts of the military, is strongly suspicious of privatization as a code word for a takeover of key sectors of the economy by multinational enterprises, which are widely believed to be the only entities even remotely capable of purchasing and managing the large state enterprises in Brazil.[57]

So where does this leave privatization? A large number of small firms at the margin of the state-enterprise sector are certainly candidates for sale to the private sector should interested parties be found. These would include (at both the federal and state levels) shipping lines, airlines, sugar refineries, certain small subsidiaries of PETROBRÁS and CVRD and even a few hotels and other odd components of the public enterprise sector. Certainly, these are the only types of firms being considered for sale by the government through the 1980s.[58] Yet all these types of firms taken together represent probably a very small proportion of public enterprise investment in Brazil and, in any case, many are not likely to be sold for the same reason that they will be up for sale: a lack of commercial profitability. And this suggests another topic for treatment in future chapters.

4

The control of public enterprise in Brazil

Public ownership per se will not ensure that state-owned enterprises always act in line with the broader public interest. An inherent problem is that the state-owned company is primarily an agent of government development policy, but it also pursues a set of sometimes conflicting microeconomic objectives. The conflicts between the "macrosocial" and microeconomic objectives of the public enterprise pose institutional problems that would not appear to have been resolved in a completely satisfactory manner in any national setting. In Brazil, they have been a source of controversy over the last two decades.[1] What types of social controls over public enterprises have been created? How well (or poorly) have these operated in practice? What forms of control might emerge in the future?

Control over public enterprises in Brazil has been a matter of relations between individual public enterprises and the central government as represented by a supervisory ministry. This *ministerial model* of control has demonstrated weaknesses that have resulted in either poor control of the public enterprise sector, causing public firms to overlook broad social objectives, or excessive control that has prevented them from paying attention to proper business goals. Yet these ministerial controls have been the only controls functioning since Brazil's closed political system removed from the scene other potentially important agents of social control over public enterprises, for example, a legislature, political parties, consumer groups, and labor unions.

An argument developed in this chapter is that the overall condition of the Brazilian economy has been a determinant of the quality and intensity of ministerial controls. This is because the expenditure policies and general economic performance of the public enterprise sector have an important impact on the rates of inflation and GNP growth, the money and credit markets, the balance of payments, and the level of external debt. The state-enterprise sector in Brazil has had an adverse impact on key economic variables, particularly the rate of inflation and the balance of payments, either when it had too little autonomy, as it did before 1964, or too much autonomy, as may have been the case by the mid-1970s. In both cases, the poor performance of the public enterprises has led to a realignment of relations between them and the ministries concerned, but to date Brazil has not succeeded in developing the stable model of social control that is necessary. Before looking at the Brazilian case in detail, a framework for the analysis of the control problem will be developed in the next section, drawing on international experience.

A framework for control

Control is understood as the effective regulation of decisions affecting the policies and economic resources of public enterprises, for example, pricing, budgets, investment programs, access to credit markets, employment, procurement, and so on. Effective regulation implies that the controlling agent (i.e., the government) is able to impose sanctions in the event of poor enterprise performance. Any system of state control must come to grips with the diversity of firms within the public enterprise sector. Left to their own devices, some firms will require substantial "outside" (e.g., central government) guidance and support, while others will require little, and still others (the majority, perhaps) will fall somewhere in between.

The main factors determining the need for and the feasibility of external supervision would include:[2] (1) *The market structure of the firm.* Does the firm have a monopoly, or must it deal with "market disciplines" because of the need to compete with private firms? (2) *The degree of public ownership and management.* Is the enterprise wholly owned by the government and, if not, is the government a majority or minority participant? (3) *The degree to which the firm is dependent on public subsidy to meet current or capital expenditures.* Obviously, the higher the degree of public subsidy, the greater the need for and the feasibility of external control. On this basis, at least four types of enterprises can be identified:

1. Public monopolies with a high degree of dependence on public subsidies. These firms will ordinarily require close supervision. Examples include the railroads and other transportation companies.
2. Firms with minority public ownership, operating in competitive markets with little dependence on either operating or investment subsidies. External supervision requirements in these cases are generally minimal. Examples of such companies in Brazil are the public–private joint ventures in petrochemicals and mining and private firms that became state owned by "accident," i.e., as a result of bankruptcy proceedings.
3. State companies in monopoly or oligopoly market settings and some partial dependence on public subsidy. Some public supervision will be needed to prevent waste and to guide investment decisions. Most public utilities and the steel companies in Brazil fall within this category.
4. Public monopolies with little dependence on public subsidy. Again, some degree of external supervision will be required. PETROBRÁS, CVRD and its subsidiaries, the BNDE, and the National Housing Bank (BNH) are examples.

The control problems discussed in this chapter concern primarily the last two categories, that is, the large state companies that can earn, in theory, sufficient revenues to cover current costs and, in some cases, high profits as well. These firms account for the great bulk of the state's total investment in the public enterprise sector.

The complexity of the control setting in Brazil is conveyed in Figure 4.1. The controlling "government" speaks with many voices, and this fragmentation of authority to influence goals, policies, and managerial decisions often results in the transmittal of mixed signals to the enterprise. The list of government agents able to influence decision making in the public enterprise includes: (1) the Secretariat of Planning (SEPLAN), with authority to set general plan goals and sectoral output goals within which public enterprises must operate; (2) a new (late 1979) budgetary agency, the Special Secretariat for the Control of State Enterprises (SEST), a unit of SEPLAN with broad powers over most aspects of public enterprise budgets; (3) the Ministry of Finance; (4) the Central Bank, which oversees the borrowing policies of these firms, including bor-

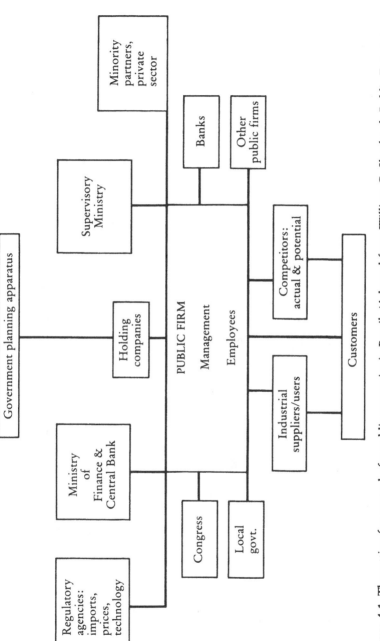

Figure 4.1. The setting for control of a public enterprise in Brazil. (Adapted from William G. Shepherd, *Public Enterprise: Economic Analysis of Theory and Practice.* Lexington, Mass.: Heath, 1976.)

rowing abroad; (5) the sectoral ministry to which the public enterprise is attached (e.g., the Ministry of Mines and Energy); (6) numerous regulatory agencies dealing with such matters as price controls, foreign exchange controls, tariffs, and technology agreements; and (7) in some sectors, a holding company that must try to coordinate the set of signals from this welter of control agencies into coherent instructions to the enterprise.

The typical public enterprise is also subject to pressures from Congress and from a large number of potentially powerful special-interest groups that place legitimate demands on public enterprises in the course of ordinary commercial transactions. These groups include banks, other public firms that sell to or buy from the public enterprise, other supplier firms (including multinational firms), labor unions, and minority partners. Much hard research is still needed on how the interplay of these various agents affects the goals and performance of the public enterprise.[3] This chapter will focus more narrowly on relations between control agents in the central government and the public enterprise.

The setting for control

The basic model of social control over public enterprise in Brazil has been a *sectoral ministry* model whereby instructions, incentives, and sanctions are provided by the particular ministry to which each Brazilian public enterprise is legally subordinated. Thus, CVRD, in theory, is guided by the Ministry of Mines and Energy, USIMINAS by the Ministry of Industry and Commerce, Empresa Brasileira de Telecomunicações (EMBRATEL) by the Ministry of Communications, and so on. This sectoral ministry model is used in many countries. Hanson maintains that it is only through ministerial controls that enterprises can be made to operate in ways consistent with overall public policy. "The alternatives," he argues, "are either no control at all or control by bodies with no political responsibility – both of which may be ruled out as harmful and/or impractical."[4] This system in Brazil may be giving way to one in which a single ministry or budgetary authority (e.g., SEST) develops broad financial and other responsibilities over state companies regardless of the sectors of the economy in which the enterprise operates. But before examining how these ministerial controls have evolved and how well they have worked, it is helpful to consider the nonministerial types of controls attempted in Brazil and important changes that have occurred in the overall setting of control.

International experience suggests that the existence of a legislature and political parties can exercise important influences on public enterprise performance. Yet few countries (Britain may be an exception) have found a successful means to incorporate the legislative branch of government into a system of public enterprise control. Again, Hanson observes that where an elected legislature actively participates in the political process, interference is common in the operation of the state enterprises: the firms are subject to closer scrutiny and may be required to justify their operations at frequent intervals.[5] Where no legislature exists, or where the legislature is a puppet of a powerful executive, government enterprises are often given a freer rein.[6]

No matter what type of political system exists, however, abuses of political enterprises by government officials for political reasons have been frequently observed. Such abuse is the practice on the part of political in-groups to reward cronies with management positions in public firms even though the beneficiaries of this largesse may have no management experience. When ruling elites alternate in power frequently, corruption in management flourishes and managerial continuity is undermined. Frank, observing public enterprise in Africa, notes: "If political rivalry is fierce, it may be desirable to limit the role of public enterprise unless its political autonomy can be assured in some way."[7]

The Brazilian Congress has been unable to develop a role in public enterprise supervision. Reflecting the hostile attitudes of the post-1964 military governments toward an independent-minded Congress, the 1967 Constitution placed all responsibility for the allocation and expenditure of public funds in the hands of the executive branch while at the same time denying the legislature the power either to alter the amount or the purpose of the funds being requested. In practice, Congress acted as a rubber stamp on most expenditure bills presented for its consideration, especially those involving the priority development projects of the government.[8] The 1967 Constitution did, however, provide the Congress with some minor authority to monitor the expenditure of funds and the conduct of operations in the state companies. For example, Congress was empowered to set up investigatory committees for fact-finding purposes, but this function was not effectively exercised and no senior state enterprise manager was ever called to account before Congress. Congress had the additional authority to commission the Tribunal de Contas da União (Government Accounts Tribunal) to inspect the balance sheets of state-owned enterprises and to report generally on the honesty and legality of their operations.[9] In practice, most public enterprises did not recognize the obligation to submit accounts for inspection until more specific legislation to this effect was drafted in 1975. But even after 1975, the tribunal had difficulty in obtaining the requisite balance sheet information and, in any case, remained woefully understaffed to perform anything but the most superficial inspection.[10]

Thus, Congress has played little or no role in determining the policy orientation of public enterprises. Through the early 1980s, no thorough reviews of public enterprise policies or practices had occurred or any evidence of mismanagement or corruption made known. The type of legislative oversight used in Brazil may be very similar to that of other developing countries, but it contrasts, for example, with the very important role of Parliament in guiding British nationalized industries in the public interest.[11] The role (or lack thereof) of Congress calls attention to the general wall of secrecy that enveloped the key decisions of many state companies in the authoritarian Brazil of the 1960s and 1970s. On top of the understandable reluctance of any firm voluntarily to release information on its decision-making processes, state-enterprise managers in Brazil's authoritarian setting had no precedent based on the behavior of other units of government to furnish information on their activities and opportunity costs, including the social trade-offs that underlie any investment decision. Thus, state companies felt little compulsion to justify major and highly controversial expenditures, e.g., the Tubarão steelworks, the nuclear power plants, and the petrochemical complex in Bahia (where it seemed to suffer from serious locational disadvantages). These types of key decisions were made with minimal public debate and often came wrapped in the impenetrable blanket of "national security."

The system of ministerial control

Control over the public enterprise sector in most countries is primarily a responsibility of the central government. International experience points to several institutional control patterns, including one in which a special ministry coordinates and supervises public enterprises, sets goals and budgets, and takes any needed corrective measures. The best example of a special public enterprise ministry is Italy's Ministry of State Holdings, but Mexico has experimented along these lines with a unit of the Ministry of Programming and Budgeting. When no special supervisory unit exists, control responsibilities rest with a sectoral ministry. While the sectoral ministry model dominates in Brazil, institutional reforms in the late 1970s and early 1980s (especially the creation of SEST) might eventually centralize responsibilities for supervision in a new ministry.

How did the system of ministerial control in Brazil manage the trade-off between the need for public accountability, on the one hand, and the state firm's need for a reasonable degree of autonomy and flexibility, on the other? What have been the factors operating in Brazil leading to greater (or lesser) degree of governmental control over the main public enterprises?

Factors increasing autonomy

Certain structural advantages and tactics are available to each side (i.e., government and enterprise) in the "bilateral game" of control. These may be set down in abstract fashion before considering the Brazilian experience in detail. Public enterprises appear to have a number of strategies at hand to increase the degree of autonomy they enjoy. The list is not exhaustive, but would include the following factors:

1. Public enterprises can seek to be as independent as possible from treasury financing of current operating costs and investment requirements. Strategies involve managerial efforts not only to generate profits, but to increase and retain profits within the firm, if necessary by the use of monopoly pricing powers. After observing the successful autonomy-seeking strategies of IRI and ENI in Italy, Posner and Woolf observed: "While much obviously depends on the energy and ambition of the leading executives, it can be stated fairly confidently as a general law that the degree of autonomy achieved by an [enterprise] increases in direct proportion to the profits it makes. The higher the profits, the greater the possibility of self-financing, virtually outside the control of the minister."[12] If recourse to outside funds is required, the autonomy-maximizing public enterprise should seek sources of financing outside the purview of budgetary authorities. Such "tamper-proof" sources of external funds include the proceeds of special consumption taxes (e.g., on gasoline), which cannot be diverted easily by central administration to other uses. Another strategy to obtain funding without dependence on central government decisions is to gain access to private long-term credit markets.

2. Public firms may seek to build a better and more permanent managerial staff than that available to the supervisory ministry. Since most public enterprises (in Brazil and elsewhere) are not subject to restrictive civil service rules and regulations on salaries and promotions, a well-paid staff can be recruited. A competent staff can develop, over time, a reputation for professionalism that discourages interference by less-well-trained civil servants in the ministry.

3. Large state enterprises often enjoy inherent advantages because of their size, their importance to the national economy, and their political connections. Ministries are frequently not strong enough to impose policies on the reluctant management of a powerful public enterprise. Frequently in Latin

America, the management of a key public enterprise is appointed directly by the president of the republic and can remain inaccessible to the ministerial staff. Should serious conflicts arise between the ministry and the enterprise, management can go over the head of the ministry directly to the office of the president. "Incongruity of status" limits the possibilities of a harmonious relationship between enormous and politically powerful enterprises, such as Petroleos Mexicanos (PEMEX) in Mexico or Petroleos de Venezuela (PETROVEN) in Venezuela, and the staff of the ministry that is technically entrusted with supervisory authority over the enterprise.[13] Boneo notes: "If there are relations between enterprises and ministries, it is between ministers and enterprise presidents...Although in many Latin American countries there can be, from time to time, powerful sector *ministers*, rarely are there powerful ministries."[14] His remarks hold equally well for companies such as PETROBRÁS and CVRD in Brazil and ENI in Italy under Mattei.

4. The public enterprises have the ability to control information on their activities and decision-making processes. Even when legislation is enacted to prevent public firms from concealing financial data, such data is rarely useful to ministerial supervisory officials in determining the range of social choices open to the enterprises and what alternative courses of action might have been taken.

5. An additional stratagem for increasing autonomy is the public firm's ability to perform deliberately poorly and to create political difficulties for public officials entrusted with their supervision. For example, a public enterprise experiencing severe budgetary restriction can ease cash-flow problems by delaying payments to suppliers, falling behind in its loan obligations to banks, providing poor service to customers, and so on. These types of actions can bring to bear pressures on the government from many powerful quarters to increase the resources available to the public firm.

Factors increasing accountability

The major strategies available to the government in its attempt to impose a greater degree of accountability on state firms are in many ways the obverse of the state company's autonomy-seeking strategies. They include the following:

1. The government should be able to control directly the flow of *external* public resources to the firm, including operating subsidies, capital increases, low interest loans from public development banks, and the granting of state guarantees for borrowing abroad.

2. Governments can exercise important controls over resources *internal* to the firm by strict controls over budgets, including salaries, equipment purchases, and imports. In addition, the central administration can influence the volume of resources available to the firm – and, hence, its degree of autonomy – by interfering with pricing policies of the state enterprises through price controls. This is a means by which the government can limit the discretion of potentially profitable firms. Alternatively, the government can insist that enterprises surrender all profits to the treasury rather than retain them for subsequent reinvestment. Other potential controls on internal resources of the public firm derive from government's authority to impose special taxes and tariffs that affect the public enterprise sector.

3. A key means of controlling public enterprise rests in the government's legislative authority to set guidelines for the public enterprise, especially in the sphere of investment policies, and to issue directives on operating procedures and requirements for reporting of physical and financial data.

4. Sanctions, including the demotion or removal of management personnel, reprimands, budget cuts, and so on, may be used to correct behavior not in the public interest.

With this brief introduction to possible strategies in the bilateral monopoly game, the unfolding of the accountability problem in Brazil may be reviewed.

Trends in autonomy: 1964–80

From 1964 through 1975–6, the factors increasing state-enterprise autonomy generally dominated in the bilateral game. The turning point at the beginning of this period of greater autonomy was the balance of payments and inflation crisis that Brazil experienced in 1963–4. Authorities identified the large deficits of the decentralized public sector as a major factor contributing to the weakened state of public finances and the rapid growth in the money supply. In order to restore the financial integrity of the public enterprises, the government enacted reforms to improve their autonomy and to make them "more like private firms." The trend toward greater public enterprise autonomy continued through the early 1970s. By the mid-1970s however, and again in response to inflation and balance of payments problems, the government came to realize that the greatly enlarged public enterprise sector was too unresponsive to central direction. It therefore put in motion a series of counterreforms to check the autonomy of the state companies.

To understand the contemporary system of public enterprise control in Brazil, one must perforce begin with the original conceptions of how modern public enterprise was intended to behave. Several important concepts can be traced back to the 1940s and 1950s when the modern public enterprise sector began to take shape. One of these is the notion that while public enterprise managers should remain mindful of the social objectives that led to the creation of the company in the first place, for the most part the company's affairs should be conducted with the same degree of business acumen displayed by firms in the private sector. None of the large public enterprises was set up with the specific charge to maximize profits (or minimize costs), but the public enterprises were to be run in a way that would avoid financial dependence on the National Treasury.

A related underlying assumption in the Brazilian approach to public enterprise control was that since the state companies were to be run "as if" private, then no need should exist to create specific agencies in the public sector for the purpose of overseeing them. Indeed, the presumption was that the state companies would be judged by their results, that is, by their ability to be run in such a way as to minimize, or eliminate entirely, financial dependence on the government. Thus, Brazilian regimes from the time of Vargas through the 1980s made no strong efforts to ascertain that, for example, the budgetary plans of state companies reflected a proper concern for costs, that investment plans were rational, or that the financial surpluses of the companies were as large as they should be.

This initial lack of concern with building strong institutional control links between the central government and the public enterprises is understandable in historical context. After all, through the 1950s, at least, the actual number of state companies was still quite limited and, in any case, the specific sectoral ministries were expected to perform the necessary supervisory duties. This contrasts sharply with the experience in Italy, where a substantial number of the state companies were subject from early on to the guidance and oversight of specific sectoral holding companies, all of which, in turn, were subject to the guidance of the IRI, the "holding of holdings."

Judith Tendler conveyed well the original conception of public enterprise in Brazil in a pioneering study of state entrepreneurship in Brazil's electricity sector.[15] Getulio Vargas had a clear idea of the types of jobs that public enterprise managers could do well. In the case of electricity, for example, Vargas considered state enterprise best suited to the generating end of the productive process, an activity that was quite "skill intensive and project-oriented" in contrast to the retail distribution of electric power (which until very recently in Brazil was entrusted to private firms), with its emphasis on skills in finances and customer relations. These types of activities presented more opportunities for corruption and were more likely to drag the public enterprise into the political arena. Electric-power generation "offered the least opportunity to misbehave, by virtue of its greater facility for inspection and control; and it offered the least latitude for autonomous decision-making by virtue of its high degree of mechanization, limited requirements for personnel, and simplicity of operation."[16]

This same concern on the part of government officials to create in the state companies an environment attractive to the highly trained engineer was also present when public enterprises were organized in other key sectors, for example, petrochemicals, steel, mining, and telecommunications. The emphasis in each case was to challenge public enterprise with the implementation and subsequent administration of large development projects – work that by its nature would not become highly routinized.

The Brazilian idea was that the individual attracted to the public enterprise would be looking for the best professional outlet, the chance to participate in projects requiring skilled engineers and of obvious importance to the national development effort. The working environment of a public enterprise was meant to be different from that of the "typical" government agency dominated by the routine of paperwork, subject to constant political meddling, inefficient, and frequently tainted by corruption and dishonesty.

Abranches and Dain have called attention to the early, highly idealistic concern for staffing the public enterprises with properly motivated individuals. For example, one of the early directors of the CVRD reflected on the origins of the company in the following way:

It was established that the heroic remedy for the success of the state companies would be the unwavering adoption of the need to administer them with a mentality equal to that which is employed in the management of private firms, not permitting that the state-owned companies be transformed into nests of parasites or [overstaffed bureaucracies] and much less into sources of personal enrichment.[17]

The same attitude is encountered repeatedly in the origins of the Brazilian public enterprises. For example, Otavio Marcondez Ferraz, an early and highly respected president of ELETROBRÁS, summed up his management approach to the recently formed company in this 1964 speech:

I am here to work and to create an environment in which all will go about their tasks with honesty, efficiency, and enthusiasm...Our goals are to sweep away the technical and economic distortions of the sector, to implant realistic rate-making procedures, to manage ELETROBRÁS and its subsidiaries like private firms by respecting public money as we respect private money...It is only in this way that we will be able to set Brazil again on the path toward progress, social peace, and respect in the eyes of all nations.[18]

Thus, the concept that Brazilian public enterprises be run as nearly like private firms as possible was well established before 1964. The purpose of this concern was twofold: first, to ensure that public enterprise behaved properly with a minimum of external supervision; and, second and most critical from the viewpoint of the state company managers, to buffer the public enterprises from the political winds that were bound to swirl as development proceeded. In this latter regard, the close association between the Brazilian military and such major companies as PETROBRÁS and CSN was also a means to protect the long-term development goals of the company from falling hostage to the short-term concerns of politicians. Luciano Martins, a careful observer of the origins of such large state firms as CSN, the BNDE and PETROBRÁS, speaks directly to this point: "Some of these firms were created under political conditions such that they were assured considerable autonomy from the outset. The purpose of this was: (1) to guarantee their survival if faced with any change in the (unstable) coalition of political forces from which they arose; and (2) to preserve them from government clientelism. This historical inheritance has served certainly to feed in the enterprises...an idea of autonomy *par droit de naissance*, a certification notarized in some cases by the seal of "national security."[19]

But if the concepts of the state-enterprise autonomy and "as if private" behavior were established before 1964, they were strongly reaffirmed by the technocratic approach to development policy that characterized the post-1964 governments. For example, Decree-Law 200 of 1967, the modern juridical statute that governs the functioning of public enterprise, states explicitly: "It will be assured to the public enterprises and mixed economy societies operating conditions identical to those of the private sector, it being the duty of these firms to be in harmony with the general plan of the Government while under ministerial supervision."[20] So a considerable degree of supervised autonomy has been an important tradition in the development of the Brazilian public enterprises. In practice, however, wide variations have occurred in the degree of autonomy of the companies, with cyclical movements in autonomy touched off by changes in government policy toward its decentralized agencies. The record since 1964 is reviewed in the next section.

Despite the general principles for the guidance of public enterprises in Brazil, it has not always been possible for the state companies to act "as if" private. The early 1960s brought on a weakening in the financial integrity and autonomy of many public sector enterprises. Brazil's high rates of inflation and government price controls affected private firms as well, but were particularly severe for the large, capital-intensive firms of the public sector, such as those in transport and steel. Government attempts to counter rising unemployment resulted in a swelling of the payrolls of the public sector firms. Furthermore, the public enterprises were used increasingly as political bases of support for the Goulart government. PETROBRÁS, in particular, was drawn directly into the political arena as company funds were diverted to support pro-Goulart political forces and its employees were mobilized to furnish support at progovernment political rallies.[21]

Their large operating deficits were symptomatic of the difficulties faced by the public enterprises. They contributed heavily to the overall deficit of the public sector and required inflationary financing. The overall public sector deficit rose from 1.9% of GDP in 1958 to 4.2% in 1963, almost three-quarters of which could be traced to subsidies to state enterprises.[22] Most of these subsidies went to the transport sectors (chiefly the railroads), but the CSN and other public firms were also dependent to a degree on the National Treasury.

Financial autonomy

A central concern of the economic policy team of the conservative Castello Branco government, which took over from Goulart in 1964, was to reduce the government deficit. In part, this meant restoring the financial integrity of the public enterprises and removing these firms from the political arena.[23] The new government took measures to strengthen the autonomy of the public enterprise sector and, thus, to achieve both its stabilization goals and to use the public enterprises more effectively in the development effort. Reductions in excess personnel were achieved over a period of time. State-enterprise managers closely linked to the Goulart government, who had been appointed for their political rather than their managerial skills, were gradually replaced by more business-minded technocrats. The most important reforms affecting the state companies, however, were in the financial area. A more liberal pricing environment was established, even though consequent adjustments in public sector prices and tariffs ("corrective inflation") led to short-term increases in inflation. Public firms were exempted from income taxes and allowed to defer payment of other tax obligations. They also gained greater access to credit from the Bank of Brazil and to sources of long-term capitalization.

In all, Coutinho and Reichstul could later point to measures such as these as having prepared the way for the "metamorphosis" of many state enterprises into "typically capitalistic firms" in the late 1960s and 1970s.[24] In retrospect, the metamorphosis that occurred is best understood by focusing on two autonomy-increasing factors: a strengthened self-financing capability and the recruitment of a well-qualified managerial staff.

Financial integrity

Price-setting freedom and increased flexibility in the rate-setting environment for regulated firms. While looser price controls did not apply to all public firms at all times (e.g., the steel firms experienced price controls through the late 1960s), prices in most public enterprises remained constant or even increased in real terms. As a result, many large public enterprises were able not only to cover costs in this period, but to accumulate profits that could be used to finance investment and to loosen the ties of financial dependence on the treasury.

Earmarked tax resources. In a number of sectors, special taxes on the sales prices of public enterprise goods and services allowed the state companies to accumulate additional resources for investment. Examples of such earmarked taxes include: the Sole Tax on electricity use (ELETROBRÁS and subsidiaries);the federal telecommunications tax (TELEBRÁS and subsidiaries); and the Sole Tax on lubricants and fuels (PETROBRÁS). In addition, a share of federal income tax revenues was earmarked for use by the BNDE and, later, PIS/PASEP funds were added to the bank's loanable resources. The importance of these funds is best appreciated by considering the permanent dependence on the federal government (for operating subsidies or investment) of those public firms that did *not* have access to such resources, the best examples being the steel and railroad companies.

Access to long-term foreign capital. The capital-intensive public enterprises provided just the suitable types of projects to match the lending capabilities of the World Bank, the Inter-American Development Bank, and other multilateral lenders, and Brazil became a major borrower from these institutions in the 1960s and 1970s. But for the state companies, an even more important source of funds came to be borrowing from foreign private banks. Through the 1970s firms such as PETROBRÁS, ELETROBRÁS, SIDERBRÁS, and CVRD borrowed frequently under their own names in the eurocurrency markets.

The pattern of state-enterprise investment finance reveals that the major public enterprises had achieved a degree of independence from direct public subsidy by the mid-1970s (see Table 4.1). For the group of large public enterprises, treasury subsidies provided only 10% of investment requirements. Resources internal to the firms (profits plus depreciation) accounted for 50%. Earmarked tax revenues provided an additional 12%. Except for accounting conventions, these revenues could be added to retained earnings and considered as a type of profits. If this is done, the estimated share of internally generated resources in 1974–5 investment finance rises to 63%. Even with regard to borrowed resources, a pattern of relative resource autonomy is suggested by the 1974–5 pattern of financing. Of the 25% of external investment funding provided by banks, only 8% was provided by the government-owned BNDE. Twice as much financing – 17% – was arranged via public enterprise borrowings in eurocurrency markets and from official international lending

Table 4.1. *Estimated sources of finance for public enterprise investment, 1974–5 (excluding railroads), in percentages*

Profits, depreciation	50.5
Specific tax revenues	12.3
Treasury subsidies	10.2
Private equity	1.8
Long-term debt	25.2
Domestic	(8.3)
Foreign	(16.9)
Total	100.0

Note: Annual percentage shares of finance in 1974 and 1975 contributed by each source were weighted by the amount of investment in each year to obtain the figures reported above. Investment expenditures were deflated, using a wholesale price index.
Source: Annual reports of public firms in mining, steel, petrochemicals, electricity, and telecommunications.

agencies, such as the World Bank. Small amounts of equity capital raised in Brazil from the private sector completed the financing pattern.

On balance, these figures do suggest a strong financial position for the state companies, but relative autonomy from central government finance did *not* mean a lack of discipline. Obviously, this pattern of finance suggests the working – strong in some sectors – of "market disciplines." In order to achieve and preserve a degree of autonomy from central government, public enterprises were faced with the need to generate profits, and borrowing funds abroad brought with it the need to assure orderly debt servicing so as to preserve the firm's credit rating. Above all, the state firms faced the need to use their resources in support of investment projects that would provide an adequate rate of return in the future.

State-enterprise managers: The emerging profile

What type of managerial corps did the large public enterprise succeed in attracting? Were they able to recruit and maintain

Table 4.2. *Distribution of university degree courses completed by high-level civil servants and public enterprise managers (n = 97), in percentages*

	Engineering	Economics & business	Law	Military academy	Other
Civil servants	39.4	45.5	12.1	—	3.0
Public enterprise managers	56.3	7.8	4.7	23.4	7.8
Total	50.5	20.6	7.2	15.5	6.2

Source: Luciano Martins, "A expansão recente do Estado no Brasil," Rio de Janeiro: IUPERJ, 1976 (mimeograph), p. 192.

first-rate technicians and administrators who could then operate the firm efficiently with a minimum of external supervision? Or was the system of managerial selection primarily a matter of political favoritism with relatively little concern for the technical abilities of the managers or for the social consequences of incompetent state-enterprise management?

Detailed empirical studies of the management of Brazilian public firms are not available, but there is enough information on the characteristics of the "typical" managers or technocrats of a large Brazilian public enterprise in the 1970s to give a partial answer. By far the best work in this field has been done by Luciano Martins, and much of what follows is based on the results of his extensive interviews with about 100 state-enterprise managers and civil service officials.[25] In answer to the question: "Who are the state-enterprise managers?" in many cases, Martins's findings confirm and fill out my own impressions, and those of other observers.

Education. The "typical" state-enterprise manager is a college graduate with a degree from one of the larger and (in Brazil) more prestigious public universities in Rio and São Paulo. The manager's degree tends to be in engineering or science, rather than in business or law. The dominance of the engineering or technical background is surprising, for example, 80% of the managers interviewed by Martins had degrees in a technical field (see Table 4.2).[26] In my experience, it was common to find even financial directors of large public enterprises with educational backgrounds in engineering. Engineering is a traditional course of study in Brazil, but the data seem to suggest that the large industrial projects and major construction works carried out by many Brazilian state firms offered attractive career opportunities for technically trained individuals. Furthermore, the Brazilian public enterprises were staffed with relatively well-educated individuals.

A large number of managers appears to have complemented a formal educational background with practical experiences or advanced study outside Brazil. A growing handful have Ph.D.s or other advanced degrees from major U.S. or European universities. But far more common is the case of a manager who has been sent abroad by his employer during the course of his career to complete, say, a training program in a foreign government institution or private company, typically in the United States or Europe. Martins's results suggest that possibly 80%–90% of high-level managers have had at some time or another training abroad in a foreign company.[27] Presumably, these experiences resulted in a significant transfer of technical and administrative skills to the Brazilian public firms.

Work experience. While it is now increasingly common to find middle-level technocrats and administrators who began their careers in a public enterprise, those holding senior executive positions in the 1970s by and large did not. A large proportion (40% in Martins's study) were in fact career government employees who transferred at some point to the public enterprise sector from the civil service bureaucracy. A small minority (see the next section) came from the ranks of the Brazilian military. Still another minority joined the ranks of public enterprise management after acquiring business experience in the private sector.

What emerges from this evidence is that few managers have long-standing experience in private business to help them fashion an approach to public service management. They tend to be former employees of the ministries entrusted with the supervision of public enterprise or, indeed, employees of government agencies that were turned into public enterprises by civil service reforms in the 1960s.

Relations with the military. A popular image in Latin American countries run by military regimes is that of a public enterprise sector overloaded with bored generals and colonels anxious to hold down high-paying jobs for which they are ill prepared. The stereotype is not completely inappropriate for Brazil. Certainly, former military personnel are employed in high-level positions in the public enterprises, but the military manager is not a common phenomenon, and the impact of his presence on the efficiency of the large state enterprises is not clear.

Martins could identify as former military officers only 16 of 66 high-level state-enterprise managers.[28] Hard data is not available, but it is probable that even those few are likely to have been concentrated in a few public enterprises with traditional and understandable links to the military. This would include public firms originally founded by the armed forces in the interests of national security. The National Steel Company (CSN) is one such example, and its top executives are usually, though not always, retired military officers. PETROBRÁS is another example of a state enterprise founded for national security purposes and to this day is often headed by military personnel. General Ernesto Geisel was serving as president of PETROBRÁS in 1973 when tapped for the presidency of Brazil by the military high command. Other enterprises in which military managers are common include the state railways and the large telecommunications companies.

While the role and importance of the military in certain key enterprises is important, civilians still dominate in the middle and upper ranks of management in these firms. Furthermore, many Brazilian public enterprises, for example, CVRD and most firms in the electricity sector, have rarely if ever had military managers in senior executive positions and would appear to have little in the way of direct contact with the armed forces.

Cases have occurred in which the military has used certain of the public enterprises either as a dumping ground for high-ranking officers who did not quite make it to the top of their respective military services or as a means to reward retired generals with a substantial income beyond their military pensions. Yet these cases do appear to be the exception rather than the rule, at least in the large public firms. In any event, the practice of placing unqualified former military in public enterprise management would appear to be far less common in Brazil than in, say, Bolivia or Argentina. A final point is that a background in the Brazilian military service has often provided individuals with skills in technical areas or in the administration of complex organizations – skills likely to be put to good use in public enterprise management.

Earnings. Brazilian state-enterprise managers generally earn incomes which are at least on a par with and probably better than the average compensation of their counterparts in the private sector. It is difficult to estimate the total compensation package for state-enterprise managers since this includes such nonsalary benefits as bonuses, profit sharing, and retirement plans. It is also hard to quantify such frequently encountered benefit plans as guaranteed pay raises for time of service. By comparison to their private sector counterparts, state-enterprise managers probably enjoy greater job security by virtue of the lower risk that their employer will go bankrupt or that poor decision-making on their part will lead to dismissal.

In terms of straight salary, many higher-level executives of public firms were probably earning annual salaries on the order of U.S. $50,000–60,000 in the early 1980s. Assuming that bonuses added another 15%–30% to the base salary, the state sector executives were undoubtedly well paid by comparison to average salaries for managers in the private sector.

They were certainly well paid by comparison to high-level officials in the state bureaucracy. Martins estimated that by the mid-1970s, state-enterprise managers received approximately twice as much as highly placed employees of the regular government apparatus.[29] This helps explain the previously mentioned migration of managers out of the civil service and into public enterprise positions. The differential in state enterprise salaries over those in the rest of the public sector has been a sore point. In 1980, for example, President João Figueiredo attempted to put a cap on the growth of public enterprise salaries with a well-publicized presidential decree henceforth constraining all salaries paid in the state enterprises to be less than his own, or under about U.S. $80,000 annually. The ultimate effectiveness of the decree, the wisdom of which is subject to debate, is not as important as the fact to which it calls attention: the top-level managers in Brazilian state enterprises tend to be well-paid.

Attitudes toward bureaucracy. Ironically, public enterprise managers appear to share a common disdain for the typical public bureaucracy. They tend to look upon themselves as a different type of public servant altogether. Thus, in a country in which the government has developed a deservedly poor reputation in the eyes of its citizenry for elaborately prepared plans that are never implemented, it has been a source of great pride over the years to ELETROBRÁS and its subsidiaries that not only could they make plans, but they could carry them out as well.

Two findings by Martins are particularly interesting. He asked 66 state-enterprise managers where they could envision employment if they left their present positions in the public enterprise. The order of preference expressed by the managers was: (1) another public enterprise; (2) a private Brazilian-owned enterprise; and (3) the government.[30] Martins also asked for opinions or attitudes on which forms of ownership (private Brazilian-owned, or public–private joint venture, or public enterprise) could do most in the future to "accelerate industrial development." More than 75% of the managers believed that *either* private enterprise (Brazilian-owned rather than foreign) *or* joint-venture public–private companies would be the most efficient ownership form in the Brazilian context. Only 15% argued that development objectives could best be accomplished by increased use of public enterprise!

To sum up, a competent managerial staff is a key to increasing the autonomy of a public enterprise. High-quality management reduces the risk of outside meddling in the business of the enterprise and reduces the need for close government supervision. Without overstating the case, and mindful of many exceptions to the rule, the large Brazilian state enterprises appear to have been successful in recruiting and maintaining a capable group of managers. The evidence, incomplete as it is, suggests that the "typical" state-enterprise manager in Brazil was well educated in technical fields, disdainful of government bureaucracy, knowledgeable of private enterprise methods, and relatively well paid, at least in the Brazilian context. We will see below that not all large public sector industries (e.g., the railroads) were able to assemble strong managerial teams. But at least we can hypothesize that the lack of competent management was not generally an obstacle to the expansion of public enterprise in Brazil. More hard research is needed on the profile of the state-enterprise manager, but this may show that management was a key factor in stimulating the growth of the state companies.

An overview of the ministerial control system

The largest Brazilian public enterprises had achieved an important degree of autonomy by the mid-1970s, but the degree of autonomy varied significantly both between firms in different economic sectors and, at times, between firms in a single sector. Some of the reasons for greater or lesser autonomy are treated in the following case studies, which also illuminate some of the more relevant institutional details of the state-enterprise control system.

Low autonomy: Federal railway system

From many economic and social points of view, the Federal Railway System is probably the least successful of the large public enterprises in Brazil. In part, the railway's difficulties are problems that afflict railroads worldwide: competition with highways, antiquated capital equipment, large amounts of uneconomic track, and excess employment. But from the viewpoint of public enterprise control, the case of the Federal Railway System may be taken to illustrate the relationship between poor government guidance and poor results from public enterprise.

A lack of secure access to investment finance has been a major problem for the railway. Even after rail transport gained a higher priority in government investment plans after the first oil crisis in 1973, no secure source of external funds was ever made available to fund the ambitious expansion of rail service described in the 1974 Railroad Development Plan. Forced to borrow money at commercial rates to finance the investment program, the railway soon reached the limits of indebtedness capacity and the development plan was eventually abandoned.

The railroad's difficulties with investment finance were compounded by a parallel inability to control its internal resources. Forced to operate many money-losing lines, including suburban passenger service, while receiving rate adjustments below the rate of inflation, the railway became dependent on treasury subsidies to meet ordinary operating expenses. Further, the environment of the company has created obstacles to attracting and maintaining a well-qualified staff. The atmosphere is highly bureaucratic, and interference by the Ministry of Transportation in decision making has left little autonomy at the firm level. The firm's dismal performance record and inability to bring about any significant capital improvements have made morale a problem for management. Political considerations, rather than efficiency, have often been the prime determinants of the allocation of the railway's scarce investment resources. In short, the performance of the railway system has been poor, and the environment within the firm has been bureaucratic and unchallenging. It is a clear case of poor external supervision and insufficient internal autonomy.[31]

Steel and the utilities: The holding company format

Even under the best of circumstances, it is difficult for state firms in sectors such as steel, electricity, and telecommunications to escape an important degree of dependence on the central government. Rates of return in these sectors tend to be low and capital requirements high so that enterprises will not ordinarily be able to accomplish expansion of physical infrastructure without the strong support of the government. Within these constraints, however, Brazilian state-owned companies in electricity, steel, and telecommunications did manage to increase their autonomy, at least through the mid-1970s, by organizational reforms in each sector, including the creation of a holding company structure.

The sectoral holding company is not a Brazilian innovation. In fact, several of the Brazilian sectoral holdings were modeled after those grouped under the IRI in Italy. For example, SIDERBRÁS, the Brazilian holding company for the state steel companies, was inspired by the Italian FINSIDER model. The holding company model in Brazil does not work uniformly well in all economic sectors. ELETROBRÁS is, by a wide margin, the most effective holding company and the electricity firms are probably more autonomous than state companies operating under the aegis of the less successful SIDERBRÁS or of TELEBRÁS in telecommunications. Yet for public firms in each of these sectors the holding company format has altered the nature of the autonomy–accountability trade-off by introducing a buffer between the sectoral ministry and the firms. Furthermore, while the holding company model has acted to increase the autonomy of firms, it has also ensured the preservation of accountability and a degree of central control. The cases of steel, electricity, and telecommunications provide good examples.

The key characteristic of organizational reform in each of these capital-intensive industries has been a centralization of decision-making power at the subministerial level – in effect, creating new and more flexible control agents between the ministry and the operating company. The most important functions handled by these intermediate bodies relate to rate setting, long-range investment strategy, and investment finance. Steel is a typical case. The structure of public decision agents (as of 1975) directly or indirectly involved in setting or implementing sectoral policy is set out in Figure 4.2.

The decision-making structure of public steel institutions reflects an integrated approach to sectoral planning in which all government agents are linked in a chain of command. Thus, policies affecting, say, the steel or electricity sectors, can be developed in the context of overall macroeconomic policy, but operating firms in this organizational setting are still several decision levels removed from the highest planning

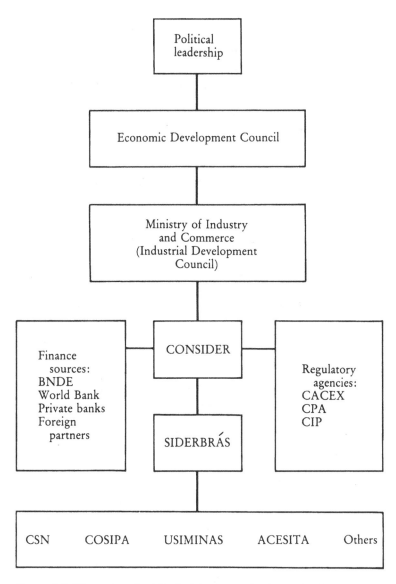

Figure 4.2. Hierarchy of public decision agents in the steel industry, 1975.

levels and insulated against the threat of direct intervention in their operations. The firms receive government instructions regarding pricing and expansion goals, for example, only after these have been filtered through several intermediate decision levels. And the operating firms remain relatively autonomous in matters relating to technology, personnel, cash management, and marketing.

The most important intermediate bodies in the case of steel include CONSIDER, which is an interministerial decision-making council for coordinating all federal policy relating to the steel industry, and SIDERBRÁS, the holding company founded in 1973.[32] Close institutional parallels are found in other sectors: the National Department of Waters and Electrical Energy (DNAEE) and ELETROBRÁS in electricity, the National Department of Telecommunications (DENTEL) and TELEBRÁS in telecommunications.

In all three sectors, these intermediate bodies came to fill a vacuum that had been created by the inability of the government ministry to supervise large, complex, and far-flung public enterprise operations. The case of electricity provides a good example. The supervisory powers of the Ministry of Mines and Energy with respect to ELETROBRÁS and its subsidiaries are inherently limited by the ministry's legislative obligations to oversee public enterprises in a number of industries in addition to electric power – including minerals, petroleum, petrochemicals, and nuclear energy (see Figure 4.3). The Minister of Industry and Commerce, nominally charged with supervision of state steel companies, is similarly burdened with diverse supervisory functions.[33]

The organizational advantages provided by the intermediate bodies merit consideration. The normative council in steel, CONSIDER, has acted to prevent conflicting decisions by public regulatory agencies from obstructing steel policy, for example by negotiating agreements with the price control board (CIP), the tariff policy council (CPA), and the foreign exchange control board (CACEX) on a range of matters affecting the steel industry. The intervention of CONSIDER has also been important in arranging borrowing facilities from the National Economic Development Bank (BNDE) and several international lending institutions.

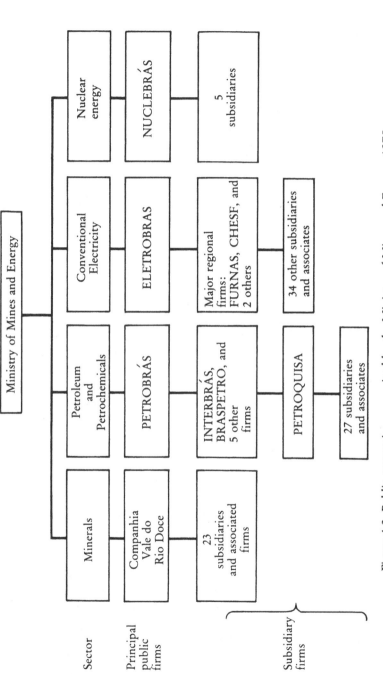

Figure 4.3. Public enterprises supervised by the Ministry of Mines and Energy, 1975.

The powers of normative councils in electricity (DNAEE) and telecommunications (DENTEL) are less central, but still worth noting. These bodies must give formal approval for rate increases, but they do so in a mechanical fashion in accord with complicated rate-of-return regulations affecting utilities in Brazil, which effectively amounts to little control over rate setting at all. The rate-setting agencies may have a built-in bias to look favorably on requests for increases in rates. The political role of the regulatory agencies (e.g., DNAEE, CONSIDER) is directly related to the health of the enterprises they supervise. Thus, successful financial performance and a satisfactory rate of capital formation by the enterprises affect directly the status of the regulatory agencies. In addition, these agencies are often staffed by former employees of the operating companies or by persons desiring to assume positions in the management of the public enterprise. Furthermore, no public regulatory hearings are held to determine the fairness of requests for rate increases, nor does any open inspection of enterprise accounts by regulatory authorities take place to guard against rate-base padding and unwarranted cost inflation.

The control systems in steel, electricity, and telecommunications revolve around relations between the holding company and the operating firms. The authority of the holding companies derives from their legislative mandates not only to hold the government's equity participation, but also to standardize operating and administrative procedures in subsidiaries, to provide initial approval of expansion projects requiring external funds, and to allocate external public funds to the firms. The exercise of these functions puts the holding company in the potentially powerful position of a managerial and technical consultant and a banker to its subsidiaries.

In practice, the ability of the holding company to control subsidiaries functions better in some sectors than in others. ELETROBRÁS is the best example of how the holding company format can serve both to control public enterprises and to insulate them from more direct central control. The key to ELETROBRÁS's success in the 1970s was its ability to gain access to and control over "safe" sources of external resources.

Table 4.3. *ELETROBRÁS, financial resources, 1977*

	Cr$ million	% of total
Internal	12,622	36.4
Amortization payments	(3,141)	(9.1)
Dividends, interest	(4,377)	(27.0)
Other	(104)	(0.3)
External	22,078	63.6
Tax on electric energy	(1,345)	(3.9)
Budget allocation	(465)	(1.3)
Depreciation funds	(6,769)	(19.5)
Compulsory loan	(4,366)	(12.6)
Foreign loans	(5,542)	(15.9)
All other	(3,609)	(10.4)
Total	39,700	100.00

Source: ELETROBRÁS, 1977 report.

This control gave ELETROBRÁS considerable independence from the Ministry of Mines and Energy and more authority over the operating electricity firms as well, because it became the most important creditor to its subsidiary firms in the power sector. Neither TELEBRÁS nor SIDERBRÁS have managed to gain the financial power of ELETROBRÁS and, thus, the holding format has not been as successful in these two sectors.

More than one-third of ELETROBRÁS's resources derive from its investments in power companies in Brazil, including both wholly owned subsidiaries and associated companies in which ELETROBRÁS holds less than 50% of total stockholder equity (see Table 4.3). The bulk of its external resources is "safe" in that it is provided by taxes and compulsory "loans" from power consumers, special depreciation funds formed at the company level but managed by ELETROBRÁS, and the proceeds of foreign loans raised directly by ELETROBRÁS on its own behalf and then passed on to operating power companies. Ordinary budget allocations – funds allocated to ELETROBRÁS by the federal government for use in the power sector – formed only 1% of total resources allocated by ELETROBRÁS in the late 1970s.

By contrast, most of SIDERBRÁS's and TELEBRÁS's resources are allocated via the government budget. Thus, the power of these holding companies, both of which can still be considered as in the early stage of development, is weaker with respect not only to the supervisory ministry, but also to their subsidiaries since the holding companies are not important external sources of capital.

To sum up, organizational reforms in each of these three sectors – electricity, steel, and telecommunications – provided a way to lessen the traditional dependence of highly capital-intensive firms on government guidance while maintaining control links. The holding company structure allows planning functions and control over investable funds to be centered in organizations, such as ELETROBRÁS, that are removed from day-to-day operations and more able to concentrate on long-range strategy. The holding company is also able to monitor firms for their ability to execute global plans, to act as an internal capital market by pooling and switching funds among subsidiaries, and to provide technical and managerial expertise to its operating subsidiaries. While exercising control over state companies, the holding companies also serve as buffers between ministries and public enterprises, helping to preserve enterprise autonomy.

High levels of autonomy: CVRD and PETROBRÁS

While the economic and political environment in Brazil encouraged greater autonomy for most state companies in the 1960s and 1970s, few of the public firms could match the degree of autonomy attained by CVRD, the state-owned iron ore company, and PETROBRÁS. Profitability was the key to a high degree of autonomy in both cases. Large profits allowed both firms to stay free of dependence on government subsidies and to invest and diversify according to criteria devised by company management rather than those imposed by the Ministry of Mines and Energy. Yet the fact that both firms have been highly profitable should not obscure many important differences between them and the nature and durability of the autonomy that each enjoyed. While both firms

deal in natural resources there are important differences in the
extent of their resource bases, market structures, and political
visibility within Brazil. CVRD operates in a highly competitive market setting: the world market for high-quality,
oceanborne iron ore. The company has a vast mineral base,
both for its core iron ore business and its diversification into
other mining ventures. The bulk of its resources derives primarily from exports. Its managerial staff has developed a reputation for technical competence and relatively little involvement
in national politics. PETROBRÁS possesses a legal monopoly over petroleum exploration and refining in Brazil. Its
major problem has been Brazil's poor hydrocarbon resources,
so that over the years the company has become primarily an
importer, refiner, and distributor of foreign oil for domestic
consumption. Its export earnings are negligible. While its staff
also has developed a reputation for technical competence, the
company often throughout its history has become embroiled
in domestic political issues.

The case of CVRD. From its formation during the 1940s
through the early 1980s, CVRD has grown to become the
largest exporter of oceanborne iron ore in the world and has
achieved a record of profitability interrupted only occasionally by falls in world iron ore prices.[34] In retrospect, the
history of the company to date shows two important trends:
the capture of a dominant position in the world iron ore trade
in the 1950s and 1960s; and the diversification of activities
within Brazil plus an increase in its share of the world iron ore
market in the 1970s. The export nature of CVRD's activities
and the risk inherent in the oceanborne iron ore business help
to explain the company's traditionally high degree of autonomy. Brazil's chronic balance of payments constraints have
prompted the government to allow CVRD wide latitude for
increasing its exports of iron ore while discouraging outside
intervention in CVRD activities. As an exporter to nonaffili-
ated steel mills overseas, CVRD has had to deal with fluctuations in world ore prices and the search for long-term markets
for its output. These business risks have forced the company
not only to pay close attention to its cost structure relative to

exporters in other countries, but to moderate its heavy dependence on earnings from iron ore by an aggressive policy of diversification into other natural resources in Brazil. The successful pursuit of both these goals has required and encouraged a substantial degree of managerial autonomy.[35]

Competitive pressures led in the 1950s and 1960s to vertical integration by CVRD into shipping and international marketing and involved continual modernization of its infrastructure in rails, mining equipment, and ports. In the view of company management, such moves would ensure CVRD's position as a low-cost, reliable producer for overseas customers whose steel operations depended upon prompt delivery of consistently high-quality ore. Abranches and Dain describe how early managers stressed the importance that CVRD as a state enterprise be perceived in the world market as independent of possibly abrupt changes in regime and regime policies in Brazil.[36] That they succeeded is shown by the fact that CVRD was able to continue normal activities despite political turmoil, including an abrupt change in regime, in the early 1960s. The relatively low level of political involvement of CVRD contrasts with the high visibility of PETROBRÁS, which was heavily involved in the political upheaval surrounding the overthrow of Goulart.

After the late 1960s, its position in the world ore trade assured, CVRD made major moves to diversify into a broad-based natural resource conglomerate. Obtaining the requisite ministerial approval was not difficult in view of CVRD's tradition of autonomy and the fact that its new projects invariably were linked to the prospect of increased exports. Furthermore, the company's diversification moves offered an attractive means for Brazil to develop its natural resource bases while at the same time arranging for technology transfers – many of CVRD's projects were joint ventures with experienced foreign companies. Besides, CVRD was asking the government for little in the way of public subsidy, because its own resources were adequate to meet most of its investment needs. The diversification efforts also made good business sense in that they took advantage of the vast infrastructure in roads, rails, and ports that the company had constructed over the years. In numerous cases, CVRD's foreign partners assured markets abroad for the output of the new ventures, for example, Japanese participation in the ALBRÁS bauxite, alumina, and aluminum operations, with much of the output destined for Japan.

To sum up, the elements of CVRD autonomy were its relative simplicity of management objectives (i.e., increased exports), the company's need to survive in competitive markets, and, above all, its profitability. For the most part, relations between the Ministry of Mines and Energy and CVRD have been loose and unstructured. An exception came, however, in the late 1970s when a downturn in world steel production depressed iron ore prices and wiped out the company's profits for a brief period. Coming at the height of CVRD's expansion and diversification efforts, this made the company subject to public criticism and government intervention.

Responding in part to the firm's financial difficulties, the Minister of Mines and Energy intervened to change the president of CVRD and other members of the management team. The new and technically well-qualified management simply pared off some diversification projects that were straining CVRD's resources, and when ore prices had moved up again in the late 1970s CVRD regained its strong financial performance and its position as a highly autonomous state enterprise.

The case of PETROBRÁS. PETROBRÁS is another example of a state-owned enterprise that achieved a high degree of autonomy during the 1960s and 1970s. The company is, technically, subject to the jurisdiction of the Ministry of Mines and Energy and the National Petroleum Council, but in practice the control links have been very loose. PETROBRÁS's historical ties to the army, its high profits, and its good management reputation have meant over the years that government intervention into the affairs of the company has only been possible with the direct involvement of the Office of the President. The company's financial and managerial skills have propelled diversification into petrochemicals, shipping, international trading, and international oil exploration. In the process, PETROBRÁS has become the largest enterprise in Brazil and one of the largest in the world. In Brazil, PETROBRÁS, even more than CVRD, has been the best illustration of a state-owned enterprise that is a power unto itself.

But PETROBRÁS's size, nationalistic symbolism, and high public visibility, have also served to draw the firm into politics in ways that have restricted its ability to pursue purely commercial goals. And, unlike CVRD, PETROBRÁS has not had a rich natural resource base to draw upon. Large oil reserves in Brazil might have given the state oil monopoly a clear role to play but, instead, the company has had to redefine its purpose and mission over time – another reason why it has been drawn frequently into the national spotlight.[37]

Founded amid much controversy in the 1950s, PETROBRÁS became deeply enmeshed in Brazilian politics after 1960 when the labor unions representing its 40,000 employees became an important part of Goulart's political base. Anxious to placate labor supporters, Goulart shifted PETROBRÁS managers frequently, at times appointing to company leadership individuals who had neither the requisite technical skills nor any demonstrated administrative ability. Decision making within the company responded to political motivations, as when PETROBRÁS proceeded with the much publicized, but probably unnecessary and expensive nationalization of small private refineries. The general economic performance of the company suffered during the early 1960s. Exploratory activities slowed; production levels declined; key departments within the firm were at odds with one another; long-run planning functions were virtually abandoned. The company's financial integrity was threatened amid allegations of widespread corruption. The picture that Smith paints of PETROBRÁS before 1964 suggests very little autonomy indeed. He argues that PETROBRÁS was "under the dominance of demagogic politicians who used chauvinism for selfish ends,"[38] "a political football,"[39] "tied inextricably to the government in a position of obvious dependence."[40]

Yet the next fifteen years or so would tell a quite different story as the company changed directions and managed to achieve a high degree of profitability and autonomy. A first priority of the new military government in 1964 was to depoliticize PETROBRÁS. The power of the labor unions, never deeply rooted, was broken by military legislation prohibiting strikes and removing union leaders. Those managers closely linked by political allegiance to Goulart were removed, imprisoned, or forced into exile. But what is surprising in retrospect is how little surgery the military performed on the organization of PETROBRÁS and how quickly the company recovered from the turmoil of the early 1960s. Smith reports that thorough investigations of PETROBRÁS by more than thirty official committees led to only a handful of firings and, while special efforts were made to identify fraud, no major charges of corruption were made against the former managers. As far as PETROBRÁS was concerned, the most important moves of the military government were to increase the relative power of the existing technocratic groups within the company and to lessen some of the prior financial constraints through price increases on refined products and the removal of subsidies on crude imports.

Importantly, after the mid-1960s PETROBRÁS's managers were given a relatively free hand to redefine the company's purpose in more commercial terms. This amounted to a new business philosophy that clearly deemphasized domestic petroleum exploration, in view of Brazil's poor oil prospects, and instead concentrated on importing crude oil and preparing for the more lucrative "downstream" activities of refining and distribution. Ultimately, PETROBRÁS's improved profitability resulting from this strategy became a means for the firm to diversify into the wide field of petrochemicals.

Through the early 1970s, PETROBRÁS maintained a high degree of decision-making autonomy. In its concern for profits, expansion, and diversification, the company was criticized frequently by private business groups in Brazil for behaving too much like a private firm, for example, for concentrating on its profits rather than on a low price for petrochemicals. Its high level of political support, however, relieved the firm of any pressures to alter its goals.

Much of this began to change when the dimensions of Brazil's long-term petroleum dilemma became clearer after 1974 and PETROBRÁS's lack of emphasis on domestic exploration came to be seen in a harsher light. Brazil's energy crisis made the company vulnerable to widespread criticism that it had become too concerned with simple commercial profitability. Indeed, domestic crude production had leveled off at 200,000 barrels per day since the mid-1960s, and had even begun to decline. Meanwhile the volume of imported crude oil was approaching 1 million barrels per day, making Brazil by far the largest oil importer in the developing world.

Thus, a longer-run implication of the energy crisis was to reduce managerial discretion in PETROBRÁS by forcing the company to concentrate its investments in petroleum exploration. As the prospects of striking large oil deposits are not encouraging, the energy crisis also presaged a declining role for PETROBRÁS in the longer-term supply of energy. Brazil's energy plans now call for the accelerated development of energy sources such as hydroelectricity, alcohol from sugar cane, coal, and nuclear power, in which PETROBRÁS plays no role. Petroleum will remain an important primary energy source, but the development of these alternative energy sources will reduce Brazil's relative dependence on it, and PETRO-BRÁS's central role in Brazilian energy supply will probably diminish.

The dispute in the mid-1970s about the role of foreign oil companies in oil exploration in Brazil served to underline the new limits on PETROBRÁS's autonomy. In the wake of the first round of OPEC oil price increases in 1973–4, one option open to policymakers was to invite foreign oil companies to develop leased offshore areas in Brazil entirely at their own risk. If commercial amounts of oil were discovered, these would be turned over to PETROBRÁS for further development, with payment to the foreign company either in oil or in cash.

PETROBRÁS management was deeply opposed to the entire concept of risk contracts. After all, the company had been created in 1953 as a means to preserve Brazil's oil resources from the grasp of foreign oil trusts, and the nationalist tradition still permeated the ranks of management. Furthermore, the decision to proceed with the risk contracts implicitly questioned the ability of the company to carry out the necessary hydrocarbon development by itself and thus was a blow to the prestige of a proud organization.

The decision to go ahead with the risk contracts was made in 1975 by President Ernesto Geisel, himself a former president of PETROBRÁS, but the actual negotiation of the service contracts with the foreign companies was entrusted to the reluctant management of PETROBRÁS. The hostility in the company to the whole idea was evident in the subsequent long delays in drawing up the terms of the first contracts, PETROBRÁS's refusal to communicate details of the contracts to the National Petroleum Council, and its insistence on such stringent terms in the original contracts that of the forty companies that had originally expressed interest in oil exploration in Brazil, only five eventually signed contracts, an embarrassingly low number. The original terms imposed by PETROBRÁS were unattractive to most interested companies: they involved high initial fees; no duty exemption on imported equipment, all of which reverted to PETROBRÁS upon expiration; and, in case of drilling success, payment in cash instead of the crude oil that most companies preferred. PETROBRÁS's reluctant approach to the risk contract issue prompted at least one Brazilian newspaper to complain that company technicians were deliberately sabotaging the risk contracts by engaging in "unpatriotic, conscious, organized obstruction."[41]

Ultimately, the company yielded to government pressures to liberalize the terms and conditions of the risk contracts so as to attract additional foreign investment in exploration. By the early 1980s, forty-nine contracts had been signed with some fifteen foreign companies, although no significant drilling success had yet occurred. The risk contract episode symbolized a change that has occurred in PETROBRÁS's managerial autonomy. While remaining highly profitable and, thus, retaining a certain degree of autonomy, the company's stature as a symbol of economic nationalism has been altered. Furthermore, the need to discover and develop additional oil reserves is now of such paramount national importance that PETROBRÁS's ability to set and pursue its own entrepreneurial goals will be more circumscribed in the future than it has been in the past. Yet the case of PETROBRÁS does suggest the ability of a large, well-run, and profitable state company to develop and maintain a high degree of political independence from the central government.

Reforming the ministerial system

To sum up, the system of control that emerged in Brazil through the mid-1970s involved, primarily, control by a sectoral ministry that in many cases, though not all, had resulted in a substantial degree of autonomy for the public enterprises. This relative autonomy was reflected in the ability of many companies to finance projects, to recruit and maintain high-quality management, and to develop more efficient internal decision-making structures. But, in retrospect, the relative autonomy of state companies was also due to the absence of serious macroeconomic imbalances in the Brazilian economy that would have forced government policymakers to exercise more effective central control over public enterprises. From the mid-1960s through the mid-1970s, Brazil experienced stable and even declining rates of inflation, high rates of employment growth, stable interest rates, and ample foreign exchange liquidity.

These ideal macroeconomic conditions began to deteriorate after 1975 and it was from that point on that the costs of a lack of central command over the public enterprise sector became increasingly evident. Through the late 1970s, there began to emerge in Brazil the institutions that would give the central government much greater power to control the spending of state companies, and to make key decisions relating to investments, prices, and personnel. By the early 1980s, Brazil had a full-fledged central budgetary authority with broad powers to influence decision making in state firms.

The main motivation for increased central control over the public enterprise sector was the belated recognition by the Brazilian government that its own companies exercised a large and independent influence on total spending in the economy and, hence, on the key macroeconomic variables – including domestic interest rates, the rate of inflation, the level of international reserves and external debt, and total employment. Beginning in 1975, a policy decision was made to begin coordinating state-enterprise decisions more closely with the government's fiscal policies. One of the first control moves was to require, in 1976, that all federal firms (whether wholly or majority-owned) submit annually their investment budgets and the estimated sources of investment finance for prior approval by the Secretariat of Planning. Until that time, this very basic system of information had not been available to the central government. Eventually the information on investment and financing plans would be merged into a system of overall control of state-company budgets.

Other centrally imposed restrictions in the late 1970s began to place important limits on state-company autonomy. These included tighter price controls on many companies, which led to a decrease in self-financing capability and, ultimately, to a cutback in investment plans, a trend that was accelerated by across-the-board cuts in investment budgets. Other central controls on the public companies were limits on their access to domestic money markets, increased restrictions on borrowing in foreign capital markets, limits on permissible salary increases for state-enterprise managers, and the prohibition of the creation of any new state companies except by express decree of the president of Brazil.

The controls on public enterprise became gradually tighter through the late 1970s, but as some of the government's objectives in imposing controls were contradictory, many of these were applied in an on-again, off-again fashion that undercut their effectiveness. For example, prohibitions on state-company borrowing abroad complicated the Central Bank's management of international reserve levels and led to a lifting of the borrowing controls. Attempts to hold down the prices of state-owned enterprise goods and services forced the firms to borrow more in domestic and foreign credit markets. Given the size of these companies in the economy, such borrowing pressured domestic interest rates upward, caused Brazil's external debt to increase, and burdened the firms with rising financial costs. Again, attempts to limit the impact of state-enterprise liquid assets on money market interest rates by forcing company treasurers to invest surplus cash in government long-term bonds proved counterproductive when the firms subsequently encountered cash flow difficulties; regulations to control management salaries in state enterprises were announced, but could not be strictly enforced; restrictions on state-company investment were rescinded when the cutbacks provoked loud complaints from domestic capital goods producers who depended heavily on public enterprise equipment orders.

Still other on-again, off-again measures of control introduced during the late 1970s included requirements for state companies to report on all goods to be purchased abroad, requirements to remit the government's dividends to a common fund rather than to retain them within the firm as had been the custom, prohibitions on investing in short-term money market instruments, and the temporary freezing of cruzeiro proceeds of external borrowings in short-term government securities for the first 90 days.

Most of the clamps on public enterprise autonomy were intended to serve legitimate macroeconomic control purposes, but many were designed without proper consideration of their medium-term impact on public enterprise performance. The need was evident to center the macroeconomic control functions in some type of agency that could apply restrictions on the state-enterprise sector, but in a way consistent with the parallel need to maintain a coherent planning environment in the firms. Such a central control agency, SEST, initially a unit of the Secretariat of Planning, was created in 1979 and given broad budgetary authority over all federally owned firms.[42] SEST's legislative control extended to many areas of state-enterprise activities that previously had been regulated either sporadically or not at all, including imports, salaries, capital increases, borrowing, and the disposition of dividends. In addition, SEST received authority to oversee managerial performance in public firms with an eye to encouraging increased operating efficiency. SEST would only be successful in curbing politically powerful state enterprises if it enjoyed strong political backing of its own. Planning Minister Delfim Neto, the dominant figure in recent Brazilian economic policymaking, moved to provide this support, emphasizing his backing for the historical control effort by appointing Nelson Mortada, a highly regarded top aide of Delfim, to be the first secretary of SEST.

SEST's ability to control public enterprise also derived both from its increasingly detailed knowledge of state-company operations and, hence, of the likely impact on the firms of centrally imposed control measures. The information problem was crucial to better control. When it began operations, in late 1979, SEST did not know even how many public firms existed in Brazil. By the early 1980s its growing authority was evident, and top government officials considered SEST a major step forward in the conduct of fiscal policy.[43] SEST achieved sustained cutbacks in state-enterprise investment and imports, controlled price increases, disciplined external borrowings, and enforced a hiring freeze. While SEST will probably continue to develop into a more powerful superholding, early in its existence it was already able to force companies as powerful as ELETROBRÁS and CVRD to stay within predetermined budgets.[44]

What was the significance of the creation of SEST? It came at the end of a period of increasingly tighter control in Brazil of the "state as regulator" over the "state as entrepreneur," a period touched off by Brazil's problems of macroeconomic stability after 1975. Thus, SEST, and the ad hoc system of controls it replaced, came to recognize the need to bring the increasingly large state companies within the discipline of a centrally determined fiscal and monetary policy. SEST also represented an attempt to restore better balance to the autonomy–accountability trade-off, which had previously tended to favor the state companies. Prior to the late 1970s, the public enterprises had escaped meaningful control by the executive branch of government. By the early 1980s, the government had finally managed to assemble the information base that would allow it to exercise such control in the future.

Questions must remain about the longer-term effectiveness of a state-enterprise control agency, such as SEST. Will it be a means to harness the enormous state-enterprise sector for concerted action and much improved government economic policy? Will it develop into a Brazilian superholding, along the lines of Italy's IRI? Finally, will it be able to increase the central control of public enterprise in Brazil through controls on budgets, managerial performance, and so on, without undermining the minimum degree of autonomy needed for satisfactory state-enterprise performance in the 1980s and 1990s?

5

Relationships with economic growth

By most standard measures, the fifteen-year period between 1965 and 1980 witnessed as thorough – even revolutionary – a change in the structure of the Brazilian economy as any in the country's history. It was a period during which GDP expanded by 8.5% per annum, real per capita income doubled, and the output of the industrial sector practically quadrupled. All of the usual indicators of economic progress – steel production, electricity generation, auto-vehicle production, paved highways, energy consumption, imports, exports, and so on – reflect the feverish pace of economic activity in these fifteen years.

By the early 1980s, Brazil had established itself as the dominant economy in Latin America and, arguably but plausibly, the largest and most important economy in the Third World. If the status of world power still eluded it, Brazil had achieved an undeniably important position in the world economy. Almost every multinational corporation of any standing had operations in Brazil. Every large bank in the world had on its books loans to Brazil equal to a substantial proportion of its capital. Increasingly, Brazilian manufactured goods ranging from frozen orange juice to computers were penetrating world markets, large and small.

The definitive story of Brazil's economic growth from 1965 to 1980 would contain important chapters dealing with stabilization in 1965–7, rapid economic expansion through 1973, the first oil shock and the transition to slower growth from 1973 on, and – while its inception is hard to pinpoint – the gathering crisis and the restructuring of the Brazilian economy in the 1980s. It would be the story of the birth, youth, old age, and death, of one economic model and the emergence of a new pattern of growth. This is not the place to recount the story in detail. But Brazil's large state-owned enterprises were central actors in the old economic model and will be, I argue, equally as important to the eventual success of the new one. The growth and transformation of these public enterprises in 1965–80 provide us with windows through which to observe and reflect upon the wider process of growth and transformation that occurred in the Brazilian economy. What did the large state-owned firms contribute to national output and capital formation in 1965–80? What does an industry-by-industry view tell us about the growth performance of the major public firms? What were the major lessons of this performance and what do they augur for the future of the Brazilian economy?

Industrialization policies and state enterprises

Rapid industrialization was the principal policy goal of the numerous postwar governments in Brazil and the economic performance of the public enterprises must be seen in this light. Public enterprise has been considered in Brazil as a shortcut to industrialization – an expediency forced upon policymakers by the absence of a well-financed domestic private sector and by Brazil's reluctance to allow transnational corporations into certain strategic sectors. Thus, in looking at the public enterprise sector critically, the major questions relate to the ability of these firms to channel resources into the industrial sector, to put physical capital in place, and to increase output in order to prevent or alleviate bottlenecks in industry.

Brazilian policy has been oriented toward placing public enterprises in sectors producing social overhead capital (dams, roads, and the like) and basic industrial inputs (e.g., petrochemicals, steel). These are sectors characterized by high forward or high combined forward and backward linkages with other sectors of the economy. Furthermore, Brazil's public enterprises tend to be located in sectors in which internal economies of scale are potentially very important: expanded output will mean lower unit costs and, consequently, lower input costs for user industries which, in Brazil, will be mostly owned by the private sector. Because of these complex input–output relations with the entire industrial structure, the investment and output performance of the public enterprise sector has been crucial to the government's industrialization program.

Brazil was clearly successful in channeling increasing investment into all types of productive activity in the postwar period. While an increasing investment–GDP ratio is normal for a country undergoing the sort of rapid growth that Brazil has experienced since the 1940s, Brazilian investment spending through 1975 was unusually high. Chenery and Syrquin, for example, observed a range in the investment–GDP ratio of from 14% to 20% in a cross-sectional study of large developing countries; for large manufacturing countries, the observed range was from 10% to 23%.[1] Brazil from 1965 to 1975 managed to devote 25% of annual spending to gross fixed investment.[2] After 1975, the investment ratio began to decline as the oil crisis forced a more restrictive set of economic policies and business confidence began to wane. By the late 1970s, gross investment amounted to only 20%–22% of GDP. Yet the main point holds: Brazil in the postwar period achieved a substantial investment effort.

The role of the Brazilian state in stimulating this increase in investment has been twofold: first, through a maze of regulations and incentives that reduced the cost of capital and, thus, encouraged private investment; and, second, by direct government investment, either through fiscal programs contained in the budget or through the state-owned enterprises. While our concern here is with the public enterprises, mention must be made of the types of measures used in Brazil to encourage private investment.[3] A partial inventory of these policies would include exchange rate policies and tariffs designed to protect domestic industries, tax credits for exporters and agriculturists, subsidized loans to the capital goods industry by the BNDE, and liberal rules for profit remittances, royalty, and technology payments for transnational corporations with operations in Brazil. An early example of the often close involvement of government and private enterprise in Brazil was the *grupos executivos* (executive groups) of the import substitution industrialization heyday in the 1950s. These groups were formed by leading industrialists and key government planning officials with the purpose of planning for the expansion and financing of projects in nascent industries that would be dominated by private enterprise, such as automobiles, chemicals, shipbuilding, and capital machinery and equipment. More contemporary examples are provided by the cooperation in the 1970s between government planners, state enterprises, and private industrialists to launch aerospace and computer industries in Brazil.[4]

Suzigan has provided a useful catalogue of some of the more recent industrial incentive policies. These include: (1) "nationalization indexes" established to encourage higher proportions of domestic components and finished goods; the carrots offered were various tax or credit incentives for products achieving a prescribed minimum of "nationalization"; (2) "participation agreements" whereby the government enters into often protracted negotiations with manufacturers' associations such as Associação Brasileira para o Desenvolvimento da Indústria de Base (ABDIB) or Associação Brasileira das Indústrias de Máquinas e Ferramentas (ABIMAQ) to determine what percentage of major industrial projects would be supplied by domestic industry and what percentage by imports; (3) sectoral incentive programs to encourage a flow of private investment into priority sectors (examples of industries designated as priorities from time to time include steel, nonferrous metals, petrochemicals, paper and cellulose, fertilizers and soil correctives, and many others); (4) requirements that government enterprises direct a large part of their capital goods purchases to domestic industries; (5) programs to aid small and medium-sized firms and firms majority-owned by Brazilians; (6) regional development programs; and (7) tax rebates for exporters.[5]

The array of incentives for private industrial investment has been matched by the growth of public bureaucracies to administer the industrial programs. Whether or not these programs, separately or jointly, achieved their stated goals is not the prime concern of this study. What is important for the

reader to realize is the vastly reduced scope by the late 1970s
and early 1980s for the play of pure price signals in determining the allocation of private investment in Brazil. Profitable
investments in Brazil depended to a high degree upon the
ability of the investor to take advantage of one government
incentive program or another. Such government policies in a
labor-surplus economy acted to reduce the price of capital for
private investors and to encourage capital use rather than the
creation of employment. More importantly, the plethora of
incentive programs allowed the government a very important
control of private as well as direct government investment in
Brazil. This made the government a much more important
factor in capital formation than a study of the fiscal budget
and the public enterprise sector would reveal.

Public enterprise investment and growth

Public enterprise investment should be distinguished from
government investment in production of "public goods," of
which the national defense, public education, hospitals, and
housing are examples. In Brazil, this type of investment spending is performed by units of government proper (rather than
state enterprises) and is often referred to as autonomous investment since it results primarily from a process of political
rather than strictly economic decision making. While most
certainly not without important political motivation, state-
enterprise investment is much more the result of ordinary
business decisions on the part of state-enterprise managers
and in this sense may be referred to as having endogenous
components. An investment in plant and equipment at the
state-enterprise level will be made if an effective demand for
additional output exists and if this demand will result in an
adequate rate of return on the investment in incremental capacity. This implies that state-enterprise investment in Brazil
is more closely linked to capital accumulation in the private
sector, that is, to the process of industrialization itself, including the development of a domestic capital goods industry. As
with any investment, state-enterprise investment affects economic activity in two ways: by increasing income via the

Table 5.1. *Sectoral allocation of public enterprise investment,
1947–79, in percentages*

	1947	1956	1965	1966–9	1970–5	1976–9
Steel	34	16	46	4	9	13
Mining	10	8	6	4	6	4
Petroleum & petrochemicals	1	52	20	19	21	23
Telecommunications	—	—	—	6	9	10
Electrical energy	—	5	13	55	43	40
Railroads[a]	39	12	10	12	12	10
Not classified	16	7	5	—	—	—
Total	100	100	100	100	100	100

[a]For 1947–65, this category also includes other types of transportation
enterprises.
Sources: For 1947–65, Arnaldo Werneck, "As atividades empresariais do
governo federal," p. 105; for 1966–75, Thomas Trebat, "An Evaluation of
the Economic Performance of Public Enterprise in Brazil," Appendix C,
Table 43; for 1976–9, annual reports of major firms in each sector.

ordinary multiplier relation (dampened, of course, by any
"leakages" from the domestic spending stream, such as imports); and by providing the increased capacity to produce
the additional goods and services that will be required at
higher income levels.

The history of public enterprise expansion in Brazil was
described in Chapter 3. This history is reflected in a changing
pattern of sectoral allocation of state-enterprise investment
(see Table 5.1).

During the postwar period, sectoral priorities have shifted
from petrochemicals in the 1960s, to electrical energy in the
1960s, to steel and all types of energy infrastructure in the
1970s. The aggregate investment figures behind these sectoral
patterns reveal an increasingly important role for public enterprise investment in gross fixed capital formation in Brazil.
A breakdown of total gross fixed capital formation in Brazil
according to public sector and private sector investment spending is provided in Tables 5.2 and 5.3. The public sector component is further disaggregated as to whether the investment

Table 5.2. *Estimated breakdown of public and private gross fixed capital formation, 1949–79, Cr$000 (current)*

Year	Government budget	Large public enterprises	Private sector [a]	Total
1949	10,000	1,017	21,183	32,200
1959	84,800	35,249	307,051	427,100
1965	2,018,100	1,102,723	4,991,577	8,112,400
1966	2,539,300	1,746,626	8,237,074	12,523,000
1967	3,822,200	2,723,678	10,121,022	16,666,900
1968	5,058,500	3,658,530	17,334,670	25,991,700
1969	8,125,500	4,452,544	23,227,460	35,805,500
1970	8,583,400	7,407,937	30,398,570	46,389,900
1971	11,061,000	10,904,400	41,343,100	63,308,500
1972	13,457,800	15,169,068	54,628,730	83,255,600
1973	18,997,900	22,142,237	73,562,160	114,701,300
1974	28,714,500	35,419,846	110,235,850	174,369,900
1975	43,349,900	52,674,045	159,878,650	255,902,600
1976	65,642,600	92,811,000	211,710,900	370,164,500
1977	90,487,100	130,963,100	294,428,000	515,878,200
1978	123,796,600	178,911,400	463,979,600	766,687,600
1979	147,419,000	272,269,500	824,989,500	1,244,678,000

[a] Private sector figures adjusted to exclude large public enterprises. Recall that in the Brazilian national accounts public enterprise investment is included in the category of private investment.
Sources: Conjuntura Econômica 31 (July 1977):91; public enterprise investment for 1949 and 1959, Arnaldo Werneck, "As atividades empresariais do governo federal no Brasil," *Revista Brasileira de Economia* 23 (1969):99; public enterprise investment for 1965–79 is built up from annual balance sheet figures of firms in steel, mining, petrochemicals, telecommunications, electricity, and railroads.

was carried out by units of the central government (and, hence, captured in annual budget data) or by the decentralized public enterprises.

The derivation of those estimates is important since, in accord with international practice, public enterprise accounts are not reported separately in Brazil's national accounts, but rather are included in those of the private sector. The estimates of state-company investment were obtained by subtracting gross fixed investment in selected large public enterprises

Table 5.3. *Investment shares of the public sector (government and large public enterprises) and the private sector, 1947–79 (in percentages of total gross fixed capital formation)*

Years	Public sector			Private sector	Total
	Government budget	Large public enterprises	Total		
1949	31.1	3.2	34.3	65.7	100
1959	19.9	8.3	28.2	71.8	100
1965	24.9	13.6	38.5	61.5	100
1970	18.5	16.0	34.5	65.5	100
1975	16.5	20.3	36.8	63.2	100
1979	12.0	22.0	34.0	66.0	100

Source: Table 5.2.

from the private investment component of total domestic expenditure (see Table 5.2). This procedure inflates the investment share of the private sector by attributing to it the investment of a large number of (mostly small) public enterprises whose accounts were not examined in this study. However, comparisons of public enterprise investment estimates for 1970 and 1975 with unpublished benchmark data on investment spending by all public enterprises in these two years suggest that the estimates provided in Tables 5.2 and 5.3 do not seriously underestimate actual state-company investment spending.[6]

A first impression on the basis of Table 5.3 is that the overall public sector/private sector division of investment has remained approximately constant in the postwar period. The public sector share fluctuated around 35% with a private sector share of about 65%. Behind these seemingly minor fluctuations, of course, lies a story of cyclical growth patterns in Brazil (a point to be investigated shortly), but a focus on the long-term trends makes it clear that public and private spending grew in an approximately balanced fashion in Brazil after 1949. This fact may come as a surprise in view of the obvious growth of the state in Brazil during the same period (see Table 5.3).

Overall, the public sector has been less affected by downturns in business activity, and has provided a floor to investment spending in the economy. The best example of the countercyclical nature of state investment, a point developed in more detail later, occurs between 1959 and 1965. Public investment expanded from 28% of total capital formation in 1954 to 38.5% in 1965. The severe industrial slowdown of the period could have been much sharper but for the strength in public investment as reflected in the rising investment share of public sector. Public investment also fell off more rapidly than private investment during the late 1970s as the government took measures to cut significantly the capital spending of federal, state, and local government in response to growing balance of payments difficulties.

These exceptions also help call attention to the general rule of a fairly balanced expansion of public and private investment in Brazil during the postwar period. But an important change did occur in the public enterprise/central government breakdown of public sector investment spending. The public enterprise share expands throughout the period while that of central government (federal, state, local) steadily diminishes in percent of GDP. Large public enterprises accounted for 3% of total investment in 1949, 20% in 1975, and from 22% to 25% in the late 1970s, reflecting the expanding role of public enterprise in Brazil. Central government contributed 31% of investment in 1949, but only 12% in 1979.

What are the important lessons behind this shift in the mode (rather than in the overall size) of public sector intervention? Obviously, the commitment of postwar Brazilian governments to industrialization and, more specifically, to industrial and infrastructural projects capable, at some point, of paying their own way was important. But the shifting public sector investment shares also reflect the nature of the Brazilian economic model: a relative deemphasis of the role of government investment in redistributing wealth. The central government share of capital formation includes not only public buildings, defense installations, roads, and the like, but more purely social expenditures, such as hospitals, schools, housing, and recreational areas. These types of social investments fell far behind spending on economic infrastructure and basic industry in Brazil.

In a macroeconomic sense, the payoff to public investment is increased output upon maturation of the investment. What has been the overall output performance of Brazilian public enterprise? And how does the share of national output provided by public enterprises compare with the investment shares of these firms?

Indicators of the output (real value-added) obtained from investment in public sector industries trace a generally strong performance. For the most part, these industries have important input–output links with industry, so it is reasonable to expect output in each of these sectors to have grown roughly in line with the rate of industrial expansion in Brazil and probably more rapidly, since many older privately owned industries have not participated fully in the rapid growth of Brazil since the mid-1960s.

The record indicates high rates of output growth in the public enterprise sector, both in comparison to industry as a whole and in absolute terms. This is particularly true of the 1966–75 period of rapid economic growth in Brazil. Real value-added in the large public enterprises increased 3.7 times (an annual rate of 14%) from 1966 to 1975 compared with 2.4 times in industry as a whole, so that publicly provided goods and services increased substantially as a share of GDP during the boom period (see Table 5.4).

Each of the public enterprise sectors included in this study grew faster than Brazilian industry as a whole, with particularly large increases in output occurring in electricity, mining, and telecommunications. Within the public enterprise sector, petrochemicals, rails, and steel have grown somewhat more slowly, but generally in excess of the industry average. The state-owned steel enterprises during 1970–5 provided what is perhaps the only example of a state-sector "bottleneck"; growth in this high-linkage sector was less than growth in industry as a whole.

The evolution of value-added in large Brazilian public enterprises and private industry in Brazil is shown in Table 5.5. From 1949 to 1978, the ratio of public to private value-added

Table 5.4. Index numbers of real value added, 1964–75, (1966 = 100)

	CVRD	Petro-chemicals	Rail-roads	Elec-tricity	Steel	Tele-com-munica-tions	Total public enter-prises	Rate of growth (%)	Real product in industry	Rate of growth of industrial output (%)
1964	30	30	—	—	46	—	—			
1965	27	96	—	75	113	—	79		89	
1966	100	100	100	100	100	100	100	(26.5)	100	(11.7)
1967	93	110	82	124	124	105	110	(10.0)	103	(3.0)
1968	91	131	115	167	152	123	134	(21.8)	119	(15.5)
1969	163	161	110	139	170	154	156	(16.4)	132	(10.8)
1970	208	158	178	268	198	167	183	(17.3)	146	(11.1)
1971	222	168	135	308	234	219	200	(9.3)	163	(11.2)
1972	261	183	196	375	257	292	231	(15.5)	185	(13.8)
1973	392	247	186	401	283	365	288	(24.7)	213	(15.0)
1974	465	287	237	501	291	405	334	(16.0)	230	(8.2)
1975	468	323	271	564	307	475	371	(11.1)	240	(4.2)

Sources: Public enterprise value-added in current cruzeiros is from Trebat, "An Evaluation," nominal value-added deflated with own-price indexes in Chapter 7. See also Trebat, "An Evaluation," Appendix B, for explanation of data base. Real product in industry, *Conjuntura Econômica* 3 (March 1976):89.

Table 5.5. *Value added in public enterprises and in private industry and ratios of public to private value added and investment, 1949–78, in percentages and Cr$ million (current values)*

	Public enterprise value-added	Private industry value-added[a]	Public to private value-added	Public to private investment
1949	2.74	55.37	4.95	4.9
1955	11.61	220.77	5.26	7.1
1959	46.78	615.97	7.59	11.6
1965	1,141.09	10,813.92	10.55	22.1
1970	7,775.04	53,841.41	14.44	24.4
1975	54,396.51	280,458.20	19.40	33.0
1978	150,762.08	894,499.14	16.85	33.0

Note: Value-added is defined as gross value of sales minus the costs of raw materials, outside services, indirect taxes, depreciation, and miscellaneous expenditures.
[a]Adjusted to exclude values corresponding to the large public enterprises.
Sources: Public enterprise value-added for 1949–65, Werneck, "As atividades empresariais do governo federal," p. 101; for 1970–8, calculated on the basis of receipt and expenditure data assembled by the author for the public enterprises listed in Appendix A in steel, mining, petrochemicals, electricity, telecommunications, and railroads (see Trebat, "An Evaluation," Appendix B for explanation and also Appendix C, Table 43). Private industry value-added, *Conjuntura Econômica* 33 (December 1979):79; public to private investment, Table 4.2.

in industry increased from 5% to almost 17%, a threefold increase; during the same period, the public enterprise/private enterprise investment ratio increased almost sevenfold, from 5% in 1949 to 33% in 1978. The divergence in relative shares is not, in itself, an indicator of misallocation in view of the rapid growth in public enterprise investment toward the end of this period and the normal lag between investment and output in capital-intensive industries. What is important is the fact that, in pursuit of development goals of the Brazilian state, the public enterprise sector has significantly expanded its shares of national output and investment relative to the private sector. But, granted that the public enterprise sector has grown strongly, was such growth complementary to or competitive with the growth of private industry?

The cyclical role of public enterprise investment

What has been the role of the state enterprise and, more specifically, state-enterprise investment in the cyclical movements of the Brazilian economy? The next sections deal with the major eras of recent growth, providing time frames within which the apparent relationships between public enterprise investment and investment by the private sector can then be examined.[7]

1956–1962: Big push

The period from 1949 to 1962, particularly 1956–62, saw the backbone put into Brazil's modern industrial sector: the automobile industry and many other industries producing capital goods. While the core of the modern public enterprise sector had taken shape over the preceding decades, the investment impact of the public firms was still very limited by the mid-1950s and the state enterprises accounted for only 3% of total investment (less than 0.4% of GDP) in 1956. This figure had declined somewhat since the early 1950s, with the completion of two very important projects, the first petrochemical complex at Cubatão, São Paulo, and the major expansion of the CSN steelworks. By the end of 1962, however, public enterprise investment had expanded to 13.4% of total investment, or almost 5% of GDP.

It was during this important six-year period that the state-enterprise sector began to affect the productive structure in significant ways. State enterprises were the vehicles chosen to carry out key aspects of Kubitschek's *Plano de Metas* (Target Plan). Steel capacity was significantly increased through the construction of COSIPA and USIMINAS; the large PETRO-BRÁS refinery at Caxias in Rio de Janeiro was completed; and the enormous hydraulic potential of river systems in the Center-South was tapped through the power projects of Centrais Eletricas de Minas Gerais (CEMIG), Furnas Centrais Eletricas

(FURNAS), and Companhia Hidroeletrica do São Francisco (CHESF).

The rapid expansion of both capacity and output of the public enterprise sector in the late 1950s was matched by important increases in complementary private sector investment (including large amounts of foreign investment) in automobiles, auto parts, and many other "modern" and relatively capital-intensive activities. Coutinho and Reichstul have pointed out the great importance of the forging of important input–output links between the large public enterprises and the core of the modern industrial sector that occurred during the 1950s.[8] In effect, through their investment, the large state enterprises not only established themselves as providers of cheap intermediate inputs to Brazilian industry, but also as important sources of demand for goods and services produced by domestic industry. Henceforth, state-enterprise demand for the output of private industry, including construction materials, vehicles, and sophisticated capital equipment, would become an increasingly important determinant of investment decision making in the Brazilian economy. This cyclical role began to appear during the years of crisis and stabilization in the mid-1960s.

1963–1967: Cooling off

Brazil experienced mounting inflationary pressures and balance of payments disequilibria in the early 1960s. These economic difficulties then overlapped the political crisis of 1963–4 and were countered by an orthodox stabilization program emphasizing the control of aggregate demand and financial reforms to improve the functioning of money and credit markets. These measures led to a gradual reduction in inflation and a sharp fall-off in the rate of growth of GDP.

The state-enterprise sector had already, prior to 1963, assumed a substantial share of total investment spending. Thus, its role was, potentially, very important to the extent that investment elsewhere in the economy (notably in civil construction and the incipient capital goods industry) was now linked to investment decisions in the state sector. A clear macroeconomic trend was a fall in the rate of capital formation during these economically and politically troubled years. Investment spending as a percentage of GDP declined from 22% in 1962 to 16% in 1965 and remained at a low level through 1967. The investment of the state-owned enterprises began to decline sharply after 1961, thus preceding somewhat the sharp fall-off in overall investment.

In part, the decline in the investment spending of the state enterprises reflected the fact that many firms (e.g., in steel and petrochemicals) had constructed substantial excess capacity. But the firms also were deterred from further expansion by price controls that sapped profitability and by the political disintegration of the era, which limited long-range planning.

In all, the investment of state enterprises declined from a peak 2.5% of GDP in 1961 to 1.5% in 1964 before recovering to 3% by 1967. Coutinho and Reichstul emphasize the recessionary impact of this sharp reversal in the rate of growth of state-enterprise investment:

Certainly, the effect of this reversal was transmitted with a lag to the [capital goods and construction sectors], but after 1962 the decline hit these sectors, constraining their sales and expansion plans. The interdependence between these sectors and the state enterprise sector amplified the decelerating effect and reinforced the decline in investment in consumer durable goods.[9]

In contrast to the procyclical movement of state-enterprise investment, ordinary government investment remained stable at 4%–5% of GDP throughout the crisis period (see Table 5.6).

1968–1973: Rapid expansion

Brazil managed to achieve reasonable price stability, strong growth in investment, and a large expansion in GDP during the boom period of 1968–73. Investment grew from 19% of GDP in 1967 to 28% in 1973. Double-digit industrial growth occurred each year during the six years from 1968 to 1973 at an annual average rate in excess of 13%, so industrial output more than doubled during the period as a whole. Once again, a strong procyclical movement of state-enterprise investment can be identified.

Table 5.6. *Government, state-enterprise, and private sector investment in percentage of GDP, 1954–79*

	Investment	Government investment	State-enterprise[a] investment	Private investment
1954	16.8	3.3	0.7	12.8
1955	18.4	2.8	0.6	15.0
1956	20.2	2.7	0.4	17.1
1957	21.9	3.9	0.9	17.1
1958	23.3	4.7	1.2	17.4
1959	23.8	4.1	1.8	17.9
1960	22.8	4.7	2.4	15.7
1961	22.3	4.3	2.5	15.6
1962	22.1	4.5	2.4	15.2
1963	20.5	4.1	2.0	14.4
1964	19.8	4.2	1.5	14.1
1965	16.1	4.4	2.5	9.2
1966	17.6	4.0	2.8	10.8
1967	17.6	4.5	3.1	10.0
1968	19.8	4.1	3.0	12.7
1969	19.8	5.6	2.8	11.4
1970	21.0	4.7	3.6	12.7
1971	22.0	4.5	3.9	13.6
1972	24.4	4.6	4.2	15.6
1973	26.5	3.8	4.4	18.3
1974	24.2	4.0	4.9	15.3
1975	25.4	4.3	5.2	15.9
1976	23.7	4.2	6.0	13.5
1977	22.2	3.9	5.6	12.7
1978	22.0	3.5	5.1	13.4
1979	21.5	2.6	4.7	14.2

[a]The reader is reminded that the state enterprises included here after 1965 are only the largest public firms. Thus, the post-1965 investment for this group is understated while that attributed to the private sector is overstated.
Sources: National Accounts Data, Fundação Getulio Vargas; state-enterprise investment: See sources, Table 5.2.

Public enterprise investment increased by almost 19% each year between 1966 and 1973, rising from 2.8% of GDP to 4.4%. The investment effort of the state-enterprise sector in the late 1960s was paced by expansion in electricity and

Table 5.7. *Real rates of growth of public enterprise investment and output in industry and construction, 1966–73*

	Public enterprise investment	Industrial product	Construction industry
1966	11.9	9.8	2.4
1967	24.4	3.0	6.2
1968	3.4	13.3	10.2
1969	12.4	12.1	16.6
1970	24.4	10.4	3.1
1971	27.1	14.3	12.5
1972	19.1	13.4	8.6
1973	27.5	15.8	15.1

Source: Output for industry and construction, *Conjuntura Econômica* 33 (December 1979); public enterprise investment, see Table 5.2. Deflator: wholesale price index.

petrochemicals, which accounted for 75% of total investment spending. In the early 1970s, the investment effort became more broadly based with major new projects in steel, telecommunications, and other state sectors. This heightened investment activity preceded the surge in private sector investment that took place after 1970 (see Table 5.6). It is also strongly associated with the simultaneous rates of expansion in civil construction and in manufacturing, additional evidence of the strengthening multiplier and interindustry links between the state-enterprise sector and the rest of the Brazilian economy (see Table 5.7).

To sum up, the evidence suggests an increasingly strong procyclical role for public enterprise throughout the boom period. As late as 1973, public enterprise investment expanded by 28% in real terms as numerous public enterprise industries expanded their main lines of business and diversified into new areas. In addition, through the ordinary multiplier and through increasingly important interindustry links, the growth of state sector was clearly important in stimulating the parallel growth of industrial outputs and construction activity. By the end of 1973 (and perhaps earlier), the public enterprise sector had matured into a key element of the Brazilian model of economic growth and was an important determinant of cyclical movements in the Brazilian economy. These links were strengthened in the latter part of the 1970s by a greater emphasis across all sectors on domestic procurement of machinery and equipment.

1974–1980: Overheating and crisis

The end of the Brazilian "miracle" can be traced to the drastic changes in relative energy prices after 1973 that called into question the postwar structure of the economy. Relatively inexpensive fossil fuel has been one of the underlying parameters of the entire industrialization effort, an effort symbolized by the great São Paulo automobile manufacturing complex. Development of the automobile and truck essentially allowed a low-income developing country to bypass the railroad era and to climb to middle-income status with a transportation system heavily dependent on the modern highway. Beyond this, the sudden – and permanent – deterioration in external terms of trade signified once and for all the obsolescence of Brazil's dependence on relatively cheap (publicly subsidized) capital for industrial investment and the relative lack of development of export potential in agriculture and manufactured exports.

While the idea of restructuring the economy to emphasize agriculture, exports, and reduced dependence on imported oil was accepted readily enough by post-1974 Brazilian governments, in fact the necessary determination to reorder industrial policy was lacking. For example, the first major government response to the energy crisis was to reaffirm a commitment to the so-called Second National Development Plan which, in outline, was conceived before the permanence of the change in relative energy prices had been fully realized. Thus, the plan emphasized large investments and rapid rates of growth in most of the existing sectors of the economy. Implicit in the plan was the belief that Brazil's future growth and the alleviation of chronic foreign exchange shortages depended upon a more self-sufficient industrialization. Accordingly, it emphasized increased domestic production and, hence, reduced imports of basic industrial inputs such as steel, petrochemicals, pulp and paper, and capital goods.

The Brazilian economic record from 1974 through 1980 was one of continued rapid economic growth, but at the cost of increasing instability in domestic prices and the balance of payments (see Table 5.8). Real GDP grew by an average of 7% during this period, an annual gain of 4% in per capita terms. Annual growth in industrial production advanced by rates ranging from 6% to almost 11%. Yet the cost of such rapid expansion proved high. The rate of increase in consumer prices more than doubled – from 34% in 1974 to 86% in 1980 and to 100% in 1981. Weighed down by petroleum imports, the balance of trade remained stubbornly in deficit and the current account of the balance of payments rose by 1980 to a deficit of U.S.$12.1 billion. Accordingly, Brazil's external debt mushroomed from U.S.$17.2 billion in 1974 to U.S.$54.4 billion at the end of 1980. Most importantly, the volume of petroleum imports grew by 45% between 1974 and 1979. In all, by the early 1980s, Brazil's payments abroad for oil imports and the servicing of its external debt were absorbing more than 100% of its total export earnings.

What was the role of public enterprise in this era of increasing difficulty for the Brazilian economy? An examination of the output performance of the six major public enterprise sectors suggests growth roughly in line with the overall advance of GDP in Brazil. Thus, physical output in steel, electricity, rail freight, and telecommunications grew by annual rates ranging from 6% to more than 20% during the late 1970s (see Table 5.9). In terms of investment performance, as well, the late 1970s was a period of expansion of the public enterprise sector. Public enterprise investment expanded from 4.4% of GDP in 1973 to a peak of 6% in 1976 (see again Table 5.6). After 1976, public enterprise investment was cut back, especially in those sectors, such as telecommunications and railroads, with relatively low levels of enterprise autonomy. Yet other sectors, especially steel, petroleum, and electricity, continued to engage in large investment projects, and public enterprise remained near 5% of GDP throughout the 1970s. Thus, the public enterprise sector on the whole provided a strong procyclical stimulus to the economy during

Table 5.8. *Indicators of Brazilian economic performance, 1974–80*

	1974	1975	1976	1977	1978	1979	1980
Real GDP (% increase)	9.8	5.6	9.0	4.7	6.0	6.4	8.5
Industrial output (% increase)	9.8	6.2	10.7	3.9	8.1	6.9	8.3
Consumer prices (% increase)	33.8	31.2	44.8	43.1	38.1	76.0	86.3
Petroleum imports ('000 barrels per day)	694	718	822	816	901	1003	929
Balance of payments (U.S. $ millions)							
Balance of trade	–4,690	–3,540	–2,255	–99	–1,024	–2,840	–2,829
Current account deficit	–7,122	–6,700	–6,017	–4,037	–6,990	10,742	–12,100
Total external debt (U.S. $ million)	17,166	21,171	25,985	32,037	43,511	49,904	54,400

Sources: Central Bank of Brazil; Fundação Getulio Vargas.

Table 5.9. *Index numbers of physical output of selected public enterprise products, 1960–79 (1966 = 100)*

	Flat steel	Iron ore	Domestic crude oil	Elec-tricity	Rail freight	Tele-communications
1960	33	47	70	n.a.	64	n.a.
1965	74	98	81	92	96	n.a.
1970	132	241	141	145	155	n.a.
1975	183	523	148	288	303	100
1976	203	527	143	328	361	n.a.
1977	281	477	138	368	388	n.a.
1978	310	536	133	411	439	n.a.
1979	361	655	138	464	544	247

Sources: Equivalent ingot tons of flat steel products for 1960–64 are from Companhia Siderúrgica Nacional, *Relatório Anual da Diretoria,* 1960–64; for 1965–75 from Instituto Brasileiro de Siderúrgia, *Anuário Estatístico da Indústria Siderúrgica Brasileira*; for 1976–9, annual rates of growth in output at the three largest state-owned steel companies – CSN, COSIPA, USIMINAS – as reported in annual company reports, 1976–9. Iron ore production in tons, Companhia Vale do Rio Doce, *Relatório Anual*, various years, 1960–79. Domestic crude oil production in cubic meters, *Conjuntura Econômica* 30 (March 1976):87; also, PETROBRÁS, *Annual Reports*, 1976–9. Electric power consumption in GWh, Centrais Eletricas Brasileiras, S.A. (ELETROBRÁS), *Relatório Anual*, 1979. Rail freight, excluding animal freight, in billions of ton-kilometers, *Conjuntura Econômica* 30 (March 1976):165; for 1976–9, increases are for Rede Ferroviaria Federal, S.A. only, as reported in annual reports. Local telephone calls completed in Greater São Paulo area. Telecommunicações de São Paulo, S.A. (TELESP), *Annual Report*, 1979.

this period, especially in view of the fact that increasingly larger proportions of total investment spending was directed to domestic suppliers. The realization of this procyclical role for public enterprise was one of the key elements that led to heightened central control over the state-owned companies in the early 1980s.

Sectoral perspectives

The performance of Brazil's state-owned companies in fostering rapid industrialization in Brazil has been examined from a number of different viewpoints and at various levels of aggregation. The state companies from 1965 through 1980 grew to assume an increasingly important role in the Brazilian economy. Through a mixture of strategies, the state established and expanded enterprises in high-linkage economic sectors and, by and large, the performance of these enterprises was characterized by rapid rates of output growth and increasingly large contributions to national capital formation. Considering the various state-owned industries as a single unit, the public enterprise sector in Brazil has become an important determinant of the pace of economic activity. While much more needs to be known about the efficiency of public enterprise resource use, the evidence assembled here suggests that the public enterprise sector has stimulated rather than repressed the growth of the Brazilian private sector. Public enterprise in Brazil was set up to provide a stream of cheap intermediate products for private industry, and most of the state companies examined have achieved the output to accomplish this objective.

Yet the Brazilian experience reveals contributions to the national development effort that go beyond investment and production by individual state enterprises. When, as in the case of Brazil, state-owned enterprises are located in the basic infrastructure areas of the economy, they exercise a lot of influence through their voluminous equipment orders. For example, by the mid-1970s, Brazil's forty largest state firms were responsible for 40%–50% of equipment orders from local capital goods producers and for a similar percentage of imported capital equipment.[10] For specially made (i.e., not mass produced) capital equipment, the Brazilian Association for the Development of Basic Industry (ABDIB) estimated that anywhere from two-thirds to three-fourths of the orders placed with local producers resulted from state-enterprise investment projects.[11] Thus, by the late 1970s the Brazilian government realized that it had gained, in the form of the procurement policies of its companies, a useful policy tool to achieve a number of important objectives.

One such policy objective, clearly, is to regulate cyclical economic activity, as discussed in the preceding section. Thus, when Brazilian authorities in late 1980 resolved to promote a slowdown in economic growth, one of the first and most important moves they made was immediately to cut state-enterprise investment budgets. The impact of this move was felt very rapidly throughout the Brazilian industrial structure.

But in addition to this cyclical use of public enterprise investment, the Brazilian government has also sought to use state-company procurement as a wedge to force backward linkage, that is, import substitution in the capital goods industry. For example, a 1975 presidential decree led to the creation in each major public enterprise of a commission charged with finding ways of diverting an increasing share of equipment orders to local producers and of relying to a greater extent on domestic engineering consultants.[12] While, as discussed below, these commissions have met with mixed success, the point is that the Brazilian state-enterprise sector had by the end of the 1970s achieved a size that allowed it to play a key role in filling out the national industrial structure and promoting the growth of domestic technology creation capacity. Importantly, the firms benefiting from this import substitution strategy were usually private companies, not other state companies, and, for the most part, locally owned rather than the subsidiaries of multinational companies. The case studies of public enterprise in the next sections will help illustrate the complex role these companies have played in recent Brazilian growth.

Public steel

The production of steel in Brazil more than tripled from the late 1960s through 1980, largely on the strength of the vigorous expansion of capacity in the "Big 3" of public steel: CSN, USIMINAS, and COSIPA (Companhia Siderúrgica Paulista). Together with a number of smaller subsidiaries of SIDERBRÁS, these firms expanded the share of public steel in total Brazilian ingot production from less than 49% in the early 1970s to almost 65% by 1980.[13] Overall, the Brazilian steel industry expanded by almost 13% per year between 1974 and 1980, at which point it was producing about 2% of total world output.

Privately owned companies in the steel industry play an important role, but by comparison to their state-owned counterparts, they use outmoded technologies and operate at smaller scales in producing nonflat steels for use in the construction sector. While public and private steel companies coexist in Brazil, for the most part the two ownership groups do not compete. The state firms specialize in hot and cold rolled steel sheets and coils (coated and uncoated), tinplate, and semifinished steel ingot ready for rolling. The output mix is well suited for large-scale production involving heavy investments in modern technology. In addition, CSN, the oldest of the state companies, produces a series of nonflat products, such as rails, structural shapes for construction, and seamless tubes in which it shares markets with private producers of nonflat products. Given their product emphasis on basic flat rolled steel, the public firms are linked as key suppliers to many of the most dynamic subsectors of Brazilian manufacturing including automobiles, electrical materials, and electronics.

With its feverish pace of investment and expansion during the 1970s, public steel captures well the strongly procyclical character of public enterprises during this period. "Lumpiness" of investment makes it difficult for the steel industry to grow in a "balanced" way with its major user industries. During much of the 1960s, public steel had been saddled with substantial idle capacity as the recently constructed USIMINAS and COSIPA facilities became available just prior to the industrial slowdown of 1963–7. Once the boom in industrial growth got underway after 1968, rates of capacity utilization in public steel rose rapidly. This led to fears of an impending shortage of domestic steel, fears apparently justified by the rapid and unprecedented growth of imports needed to supplement the domestic production of the Big 3 state companies.

Against this background, numerous national steel plans were formulated in the late 1960s and early 1970s, each aiming at substantial increases in state enterprise output. The plans went beyond the basic goal of complete import substitution to endorse the idea of Brazil as a major exporter of hot- and cold-rolled steel and semifinished steel. Export capacity was to be built into the Big 3 plants and entirely new steel companies, of which the Tubarão Steel Company was the most noteworthy example, were designed with the express purpose of servicing export markets. Many of Brazil's ambitious export hopes were undone by the emergence of a worldwide surplus of steelmaking capacity after 1973–4. The practical impact on public steel in Brazil was to reduce priorities on Tubarão and other export-oriented mills and to cut back on capacity expansion goals at all of the state firms.

The expansion programs at CSN, COSIPA, and USIMINAS were launched in the early 1970s and scheduled for completion by the late 1970s, although the completion date was later delayed until the early 1980s in most cases. Two important phases occurred in the construction of additional steel capacity. From 1971 to 1974, investment in public steel advanced at rates ranging from 70% to 100% annually as each of the steel companies essentially doubled steel-making capacity. Then from 1976 through 1979 (with the exception of 1977), the investment of public steel was again strongly procyclical, increasing in real terms at rates ranging from 11% to 40%. This extraordinary pace of investment permitted rapid rates of output growth after 1975. CSN, USIMINAS, and COSIPA doubled steel output from 4 million tons in 1975 to 8 million in 1979, with additional increments planned for the early 1980s.

As important as this growth in output was toward sustaining Brazil's rapid output growth in the 1970s, the Big 3 in steel greatly solidified their links with the domestic capital goods industry during the decade. During the first phase of the expansion of the steel industry in the early 1970s, only about 20% of all equipment used in the expansion was purchased from Brazilian manufacturers. By the second major investment stage in the late 1970s, more than 70% of needed equipment was being purchased domestically.[14]

Mining

The Companhia Vale do Rio Doce (CVRD) over the thirty years from 1950 to 1980 emerged as the world's leading company in the oceanborne iron trade, a position it is likely to maintain and consolidate in the future. CVRD's extraordinary growth performance in this period is captured in data relating to growth in production (from a few million tons per year in the early 1950s to 71 million tons in 1980), in total export earnings (an estimated $1 billion in 1980, or 5% of Brazil's total merchandise exports), and in Brazil's share in total world oceanborne iron ore trade (approximately 25% in 1978).[15]

The significance of CVRD's growth and investment performance lies in its implications for world trade in iron ore (the company's main line of business) and for the development of Brazil's natural-resource sectors. From the international standpoint, CVRD should be seen in the forefront of a worldwide trend toward an increasing role in the world iron ore industry for state-owned enterprises in developing countries. Vernon and Levy have observed that this represents a radical departure from an older pattern in which privately owned steel mills in the industrialized countries had ownership links with "captive" mines.[16] Historically, the advantage of the older relationship pattern for the mine had been to guarantee a customer for the mine's output, especially during cyclical downswings in world steel production and, hence, periods of surplus iron ore capacity. CVRD has survived and prospered in the iron ore industry for a number of fortuitous reasons including the high quality and ready accessibility of Brazilian ores, the decline of ore output in the United States and the Soviet Union, and the emergence of Japan and other natural resource-scarce countries as major steel producers. But another crucial factor in CVRD's long-term success has been its entrepreneurial acumen in arranging and maintaining long-term contracts with steel producers throughout the world, especially in Japan, Germany, and Eastern Europe.

Within Brazil, CVRD's growth and diversification efforts have had a broad impact that goes well beyond the company's substantial contribution to annual export earnings. The impact can be described in terms of the company's policies regarding investment, procurement, diversification, and provision of infrastructure. While CVRD's share of total state-company investment spending is relatively small, its investment performance was particularly dynamic during the Brazilian boom period of the early 1970s as the company expanded capacity for ore production and pelletizing operations. However, for most of the 1970s, CVRD's investment spending was strongly anticyclical, declining steadily in real terms after 1973. The prolonged slump in world steel production that followed the 1973–4 rise in oil prices caught CVRD with substantial excess ore capacity and dealt a heavy financial blow to its ambitious diversification plans. Total ore production stagnated during the late 1970s. Even though its total investment declined in real terms in the late 1970s, CVRD became one of the most aggressive state companies using procurement policy to forge links with domestic suppliers. For example, in 1976, a year of relatively heavy investment, CVRD placed 60% of its investment goods orders with domestic producers, compared with domestic procurement levels of less than 20% of total purchases in the early 1970s.[17]

CVRD's performance in two other important areas does not show up on its balance sheets or income statements. First, much of its investment has gone to develop a large infrastructure consisting of ports, roads, and railroads in the Minas Gerais–Espirito Santo region. In addition to the stimulus provided to regional development, this infrastructure is also at the service of numerous private companies that compete with CVRD in domestic markets for ore and in the iron ore export trade. During the 1980s, CVRD will be constructing a similar infrastructure complex in the Carajas region in the north of Brazil. Second, CVRD has been of help in redirecting attention in Brazil to the relatively underdeveloped minerals sector. While many of CVRD's diversification projects were postponed or restructured when its basic iron ore market weakened in the 1970s, the company's numerous joint ventures in pulp and paper, bauxite, manganese, titanium, iron ore pelletization, and a large number of potential mineral-related projects in the Carajas area still have provided a strong impetus to natural resource development. In addition, such projects have attracted increasing amounts of foreign investment and technology transfer under terms and conditions that assure substantial Brazilian control over future resource development projects.

Telecommunications

Even though they do not rank as a high priority area for public investment, the state-owned telecommunications companies have managed to maintain relatively high levels of investment during the process of transforming the structure of the Brazilian communications industry. Public investment in telecommunications was an important stimulus to aggregate demand during the early 1970s, but tended to fall in real terms after 1974 as the telecommunications sector was unable to maintain priority investment status in the face of fiscal belt-tightening moves by the government. The relative deemphasis on telecommunications should last well into the 1980s. But despite the cutbacks, the telecommunications firms did accomplish between 1965 and 1975 a structural transformation of communications in Brazil. By the end of this period, Brazil had largely overcome long years of neglect in building effective and well-maintained systems of intraurban, intercity, and international communications.

Public telecommunications can be subdivided into two distinct activities: long-distance operations and intraurban systems. The public long-lines enterprise Empresa Brasileira de Telecomunicacões (EMBRATEL), was particularly successful in installing a modern, technology-intensive communications system that effectively linked Brazil's far-flung regions for the first time and greatly increased communications with other countries. The expansion of intercity trunks, voice circuits, and satellite facilities permitted an increase in domestic long-distance telephone conversations from 16 million per year in 1970 to more than 400 million per year a decade later as well as a jump of similar proportions in completed international calls.[18] Additional investment by EMBRATEL led to greatly increased telex traffic, and to nationwide television broadcasting and data transmission.

The dramatic steps taken in improving long-distance communications contrast with much slower improvement in intraurban telephone systems where the technical difficulties of the physical expansion of facilities in congested urban areas combined with the economic problems of antiquated plant and equipment and high investment costs have slowed the pace of growth. However, a substantial pickup in investment in the urban systems began to mature by the late 1970s. For example, Telecomunicacões de São Paulo (TELESP), the phone company for the greater São Paulo area, was able to increase the number of phones in service in the city from about 800,000 in 1973 to almost 2.4 million in 1979. While still far from the U.S. standard of some 65 phones per 100 inhabitants, the number of phones in São Paulo per 100 inhabitants increased from 7.2 in 1973 to 12.6 by 1979.[19] Along with the expansion of physical facilities in urban areas came a marked improvement in the technical quality of the system, redeeming to some extent the once notorious reputation for poor service of the Brazilian phone system.

The public telecommunications sector, possibly due to the dominance of a security-conscious military in its key decision-making posts, has been among the most active in forging links with domestic supplier industries and in giving preference to domestic producers of technology. Most basic telecommunications equipment has long been produced in Brazil by local subsidiaries of the major international firms, such as ITT and Ericsson. Industrial policy in the TELEBRÁS system has also been designed to help domestic suppliers to provide increasingly sophisticated equipment, such as multiplexing equipment and computerized switching facilities, also using components produced domestically.

Electricity

State companies dominate in the production and distribution of hydroelectricity, Brazil's most abundant primary energy source. In the early 1980s, of Brazil's estimated hydro potential of 213,000,000 kw, only 48,000,000 kw or 22.6% was in use or under construction although definite plans had been formulated to tap an additional 85,000,000 kw or 40.3%.[20] Hydraulic energy supplied 16.7% of primary energy consumed in Brazil in 1969, 26.4% in 1979, and, on present trends, 36% by 1985.

Table 5.10. *Brazil: primary sources of energy consumption, in percentages*

Energy source	1969	1979	1985[a]
Petroleum	38.7	42.0	25.6
Hydraulic	16.7	26.4	35.8
Charcoal, other	40.6	26.2	23.0
Coal	4.0	4.3	10.8
Alcohol	—	1.1	4.8
TOTAL	100.0	100.0	100.0

[a]Official projection of Ministry of Mines and Energy.
Source: Ministry of Mines and Energy, *Balanço Energético Nacional,* various years.

In the 1969–70 period, the increased use of hydroelectricity made it possible to limit the increase in Brazil's relative dependence on fossil fuels. Petroleum provided 38.7% of total primary energy consumed in 1969, and this rose to 42% by 1979. National energy plans call for this trend to be reversed by 1985, however, with petroleum's share falling to just over 25%. Increased use of hydroelectricity and, secondarily, alcohol, should make possible this reduced dependence on oil (see Table 5.10). Brazil's installed capacity in hydroelectric facilities grew at an annual rate of 11% from 1962 to 1979 with emphasis on enormous new facilities in the Southeast. ELETROBRÁS anticipated a further 15% annual surge in capacity during 1980–4, including the boost to be provided by the 5,600mw facility at Itaipu.[21]

The strong output performance of the Brazilian power sector has been made possible by the financial strength of the ELETROBRÁS group and the consequently large volume of investments of the group in civil construction and in generation, transmission, and distribution equipment. Electricity has been, so far, the single most important public enterprise sector in terms of investment and impact on the economy. Through the 1960s, electric power investment provided the basis for the growing role of public enterprises in total gross fixed capital formation. During 1966–9, for example, the electrical sector alone accounted for 55% of total public enterprise investment, the equivalent of 1.5% of GDP. During the 1970s, annual electricity investment averaged almost 2.3% of GDP and was one of the strongest contributors to the rapid pace of economic growth in Brazil at the end of the decade.[22]

Like almost every public enterprise sector, the electrical industry has made a concerted effort to increase the amount of equipment purchased domestically. The Brazilian capital goods industry has acquired the capacity for the production of basic hydroelectric equipment, suitable especially for smaller-scale units. However, ELETROBRÁS in recent years has emphasized the development of a few large-scale projects (Itaipu, Tucuruí, Ilha Solteira) involving advanced technology and an important need for imported machinery. Nevertheless, ELETROBRÁS estimated the share of domestic industry in the supply of equipment at 80% in the late 1970s.[23] Apart from equipment purchases, the projects of state-owned electricity firms have clearly been major factors behind the growth of civil construction in Brazil during the 1960s and 1970s. Many of the large Brazilian construction companies that sprang up as a result of the electricity-building program have taken on large projects abroad in the 1970s and 1980s. The service earnings of these companies have come to figure importantly in the balance of payments.

Petrochemicals

PETROBRÁS and its vast system of subsidiary petrochemical companies stand close to the heart of Brazil's principal dilemma in the last quarter of the twentieth century: the dependence on imported oil. Brazil's impressive industrial structure had been built on the assumption of relatively inexpensive prices for crude oil and for refined petroleum and petrochemicals. While the use of fuel oil to produce electricity in Brazil has never been of consequence, the industrial and agricultural sectors are heavy users of petroleum and petrochemicals in production processes. In addition, the transportation system relies heavily on trucks and airplanes, rather than railroads or ships. To illustrate, more than 70% of the total volume of cargo transported in Brazil in the late 1970s was moved by trucks on highways.

Thus, the modern performance of PETROBRÁS, like that of the Brazilian economy itself, should be evaluated in two periods: before and after 1973. In the earlier period, PE-TROBRÁS, while not ignoring the need for investment in prospecting and exploration, concentrated on building up refinery capacity, distribution systems, and petrochemical complexes to meet the strong demand for these products. Needed supplies of crude oil were increasingly imported as policy-makers implicitly accepted a pessimistic assessment of hydro-carbon availability in Brazil. In this view, long disputed by nationalist sentiment, a country with Brazil's geophysical characteristics was likely to have only a large number of very small, predominantly noncommercial hydrocarbon deposits. Reflecting this assessment, PETROBRÁS's substantial investment budget during the 1960s and early 1970s gave relatively little emphasis to domestic exploration. Thus, the amount of crude oil pumped by PETROBRÁS between 1968 and 1973 remained constant while the volume processed in its vast refinery system doubled during the same time period.[24]

The emphasis on refining and distributing imported crude rather than risking capital in the search for domestic supplies was quite rational from the entrepreneurial viewpoint. The strategy allowed PETROBRÁS to increase its net profits by avoiding large charge-offs resulting from what were likely to be fruitless exploration activities. In any case, after 1973 the strategy seemed acutely short-sighted from the social standpoint, and PETROBRÁS hastened to shift gears to pursue a vigorous program of domestic and foreign exploration abroad, the latter particularly in joint-venture arrangements with Middle East countries. Domestic crude output began to increase again in 1980, but no major increments in domestic production could be anticipated before the mid-1980s at the earliest.

The output and investment performance of PETROBRÁS is best seen, then, in the context of the firm having had to change direction after 1973 away from concentration on refining, distribution, and the production of a large number of petrochemical products to an emphasis on exploration and

domestic production. In the boom period (1967–73), PE-
TROBRÁS faced rapid growth in demand for the major products refined from crude: automotive gasoline, diesel fuel, and
fuel oil (bunker) (see Table 5.11). With the growth rate of
domestic production of crude practically at zero throughout,
this strong demand was satisfied by an increasing dependence
on imported crude. Thus, PETROBRÁS emphasized its refinery capacity and, through its subsidiaries, related petrochemical capacity. Real investment increased substantially each
year as the PETROBRÁS system acted as one of the most
important sources of rising investment demand during the
boom period. In an environment of stable international oil
prices and strong annual growth in demand for fuel, PETRO-
BRÁS was also able to strengthen its ties to the domestic
capital goods industry, increasing the multiplier effect of its
large volume of investment.

The rise of OPEC disrupted this predictable environment
for PETROBRÁS just as it threatened to make obsolete the
whole pattern of postwar economic growth in Brazil. Through
the remainder of the 1970s, Brazil settled on a petroleum
policy that emphasized rationing through the price mechanism, reduced consumption via lower rates of GDP growth,
and increased domestic production of crude (see again Table
5.11). For PETROBRÁS, the new priorities spelled strong
annual increases in the real volume of investment, and total
petrochemical investment increased from 0.9% of GDP in
1977 to 1.5% of GDP in 1979.[25] Thus, as the Brazilian economy began to slow down, PETROBRÁS acted in a strongly
anticyclical manner. While investments continued to flow into
transport, major petrochemical complexes, refineries, and so
on, an increasingly large share of annual capital spending was
preempted by exploration and production. This component
increased steadily from about 33% of the annual investment
budget in the mid-1970s to 55% by 1979 and involved an
increasing demand by PETROBRÁS for imported equipment
(e.g., drilling rigs for offshore exploration, sophisticated seis-
mic devices). It also led, as was discussed in Chapter 4, to the
signing of risk contracts with multinational companies, thus
breaking the state monopoly on petroleum exploration that
had been in effect since 1953.

Table 5.11. *Fuel consumption, imports, and energy policy, 1967–79: key indicators, in percentages*

	1967–73	1974	1975	1976	1977	1978	1979
Growth of apparent consumption of fuels[a]	15.0	7.4	5.6	8.8	2.1	8.5	6.4
Growth of GDP	10.0	9.8	5.6	9.0	4.7	6.0	6.4
Growth elasticity of fuel use[b]	1.5	0.76	1.0	0.98	0.45	1.42	1.0
Change in real price of fuels[c]	0.0	8.9	31.5	17.5	8.4	-6.1	13.8
Growth rate of domestic crude production[d]	0.0	4.6	-2.6	-2.7	-3.5	-3.4	3.0
Growth rate of crude imports[e]		1.9	5.7	15.9	0.0	11.6	12.1
Dependence on imported crude[f]	70.0	79.0	82.0	79 b	87.0	86.0	86.0

[a]Includes gasoline, fuel oil, diesel fuel, and several less important fuels derived from petroleum. Source: 1967–73, IBGE, *Anuário Estatístico do Brasil*, p. 207; 1973–9, PETROBRÁS, annual reports.
[b]Defined as percentage change in apparent fuel consumption per unit percentage change in GDP.
[c]Difference between price indexes known as Col. 53 and Col. 2, which are published monthly in *Conjuntura Econômica*; price changes calculated on basis of yearly average price level.
[d]Sources: IBGE, *Anuário Estatístico do Brasil*, p. 207; PETROBRÁS, annual reports, 1974–79.
[e]Source: 1974–9, Central Bank of Brazil, Annual Report, 1979, p. 117.
[f]Defined as imported crude as percentage total crude produced and imported. Data on changes in crude inventories not available.
Source: Inter-American Development Bank, *Economic and Social Progress in Latin America*, annual report, various years.

In all, the reorientation of PETROBRÁS's substantial investment and the signing of the risk contracts resulted in a significant increase in drilling activity – more than 300 wells drilled in 1979 compared with less than 200 in 1976. Similarly large increases were reported in the total depth of drilling operations.

PETROBRÁS's recent performance record must be seen in the context of the weakness of Brazil's overall petroleum policy since 1973. The emphasis on price rationing and conservation did not succeed in lowering the growth elasticity of demand for fuels in Brazil; in consequence, as overall macroeconomic policy permitted rapid rates of growth from 1973 to 1980, these were matched by unit increases in the consumption of fuels (see again Table 5.11). Thus, despite the increasing relative price of petroleum fuels in Brazil after 1973, fuel use still grew by an average of more than 6% per year.

At most, Brazilian energy policy managed to slow somewhat the rising demand for fuels and to alter the relative composition of fuel use, that is, away from gasoline and toward increased use of diesel and bunker.[26] Indeed, the policy of price increases fell most heavily on gasoline; in fact, diesel use continued to be heavily subsidized throughout the 1970s. Thus, PETROBRÁS faces something of an impossible task in the future and, barring great good fortune in discoveries, is likely to be limited to importing, refining, and distributing foreign crude. Pressures on the firm will be eased only by a change in the pattern of Brazilian growth that might lead to lower energy requirements and reduced dependence on fossil fuels.

Railroads

Railroad transport in Brazil demonstrates the same "sick industry" symptoms characteristic of rail systems in many parts of the world. The rail network has been shrinking for years, plant and rolling stock are antiquated, and the major railroads Rede Ferroviária Federal (RFFSA) and Ferrovia Paulista (FEPASA) require large state subsidies to cover their costs of operation. The causes of the railroad problems are also familiar from the experience in other countries: government price controls, competition from trucks and airplanes, and an overlay of government-imposed social objectives that discourage efficiency and initiative.

Yet, for all the common ills, the plight of the railroad industry is made more serious in Brazil by the country's high degree of dependence on imported petroleum. The rail system was designed primarily to transport coffee, other agricultural products, and certain natural resources (e.g., iron ore) from productive centers in the interior to port cities such as Santos and Rio de Janeiro. In contrast to the experience in other countries (particularly the United States), the railroad system played only a very minor role in Brazil in promoting industrial growth by linking domestic regions through the large-scale transport of machinery and raw materials. This integrating role in Brazil fell largely to the highway system which, in its dynamic growth in the postwar period, both fed upon and contributed to the rapid rates of expansion of agricultural and industrial output. From 1967 to 1976, Brazil's network of paved roads more than doubled while the rail system actually decreased in length from 32,182 km to just over 30,000 kms, due to the elimination of some uneconomical lines. In 1977 only 17% of total cargo transported in Brazil was carried by rail.[27] Indeed, even the reported share of the railroads tends to overstate their importance. If the data are adjusted to exclude the transport of iron ore along a line administered by a railroad belonging to CVRD, RFFSA and FEPASA hauled only 8.5% of total cargo transported in 1977.[28]

Since the mid-1960s, RFFSA and FEPASA have made efforts to eliminate redundant personnel, to cut uneconomical routes, and to modernize equipment. Investment data suggest that railroad investment from the late 1960s through 1976 grew strongly in real terms. Yet by the end of the 1970s the railroads were rapidly approaching the limits of the indebtedness that had permitted the rapid expansion of investment through 1976. Furthermore, the accumulated financial drain of carrying out certain social objectives mandated by the government (e.g., passenger transport, especially commuters between Rio and São Paulo and their respective working-class suburbs; passenger traffic between sparsely inhabited rural regions; uneconomical freight lines) also combined to limit investment capabilities. Thus, the railroads have continued to play only a small role in Brazil's total transportation system.

Conclusions

The overall investment and output record of Brazil's state-owned enterprises is one of very strong growth. These firms have been generally successful in putting in place the essential infrastructure base upon which the economic expansion of the postwar period was built. Along the way, the large state-owned companies have become much more visible in the economy, as suggested by data portraying their steadily increasing shares of national investment and output. Behind these numbers lies a record of organizational accomplishment that also deserves recognition. The Brazilian public enterprises were somehow able to assemble the raw materials, train the workers and managers, and master the technology that resulted in the steady expansion of the economy's infrastructure core over the last thirty years.

What the data do not show also deserves attention: for the most part the physical growth of the public enterprises examined here has been complementary to, rather than competitive with, the growth of private sector entrepreneurship and investment in Brazil. One could argue plausibly on the record that the vigorous expansion of state enterprises – at least of those examined in this study – has permitted an equally vigorous growth of private enterprise in Brazil. All in all, looking at the record of Brazilian public enterprises in the postwar period and also at the performance of the overall economy, it is difficult to believe that Brazil could have done much better – within the confines of the growth model selected – had policymakers along the way *not* opted to use public companies to develop the basic sectors of the economy and instead waited for private enterprise to enter these areas.

The Brazilian experience is also important for what it says regarding the benefits of a large state-enterprise system in basic sectors apart from the obvious ones of producing more steel or generating more electricity. Because of the important input–output links that develop with the industrial sector, a large block of state companies gives policymakers additional control levers over cyclical movements in the economy. The rapid expansion of many state industries after 1968 was a key to the Brazilian boom that occurred in the early 1970s. By the same token, the large cutbacks in public enterprise investment budgets was one of the surest means policymakers could find to induce the sharp slowdown necessary for balance of payments adjustment in the early 1980s.

Finally, a large state-enterprise group in the basic industries of a large economy gives the government important leverage in filling out the industrial structure through the domestic production of sophisticated capital equipment and in raising the overall level of technological sophistication. Arguably, Brazil has the largest capital goods industry of any developing country. This industry is composed of many private companies who got their start because of large orders from CSN, ELETROBRÁS, PETROBRÁS, and the other large state-owned companies. Using state-enterprise procurement policies to force import substitution must have resulted in some inefficiencies, but the fact that many of these same privately owned capital goods supplying industries are now able to export from Brazil suggests that they have "grown up" and are competitive internationally.

It is important to note that the strategy by which a Brazilian state company producing a basic product has been used as a wedge to promote backward industrial linkages through the growth of private supplier networks is still very much in evidence. The same pattern appears in the development of the Brazilian nuclear, aerospace, defense, and computer industries, among other examples, which are being developed in the 1980s.

Thus, the macroeconomic overview of the relationships between the state companies and the process in economic growth in Brazil suggests that at least some important successes were achieved. More needs to be said about the economic costs of this success. This is the topic of Chapter 6.

6

Sources of growth and rates of return

Brazil's public enterprises turned in impressive growth performances over the last two decades by amassing and deploying large amounts of labor and capital and absorbing new technologies. This chapter looks in more detail at how these various factors were combined and examines the economic and financial rate of return achieved on Brazil's substantial investment in public enterprises. What can be said about productivity in the state-owned firms? How profitable have these firms been? How does this productivity and profitability record compare with available evidence on the private sector in Brazil? With the record of public enterprises in other developing countries? These are the types of questions addressed here.

Production and productivity: a framework

In general, the factors determining productive capacity in an enterprise are summarized in a production function in which the rate of output is expressed as a function of a flow of inputs. In addition to capital and labor, determinants of output include natural resources, management skills, the scale of production, and so on.

Statistical representations of the production function commonly make explicit consideration of just two inputs: capital and labor. Both of these are usually assumed to be homogeneous. Increases in output are attributed in part to change in the quantity of either input. The changes in output not explained statistically by changes in factor usage are usually attributed to a "catch-all" category known as "technical progress" or the "residual." Subsumed within such broad terms are many output determinants – economies of scale, innovation, and so on – which are more difficult to identify statistically, but nonetheless important in explaining increasing productivity.

It is well to recognize some of the many constraints that limit rates of technical progress in developing countries. Managers must learn by doing rather than from prior experience. Proper selection of equipment must be made; a management structure must be designed and staffed; a work force must be trained; and complicated machinery must be maintained properly. Other technical problems are even more intractable, especially the lack of reliable sources of supply for components, materials, and services. Economic obstacles to the introduction of new products and/or techniques by public enterprise may also be significant. These include a chronic lack of financial capital and foreign exchange, the smallness of the domestic market compared with minimum efficient scales of production, and the relatively high cost of capital. With these environmental constraints in mind, we can turn to the interplay of capital, labor, and a catch-all "residual" in determining output growth in selected, large Brazilian public enterprises.

Growth of inputs and outputs in public enterprises

Estimates were made of growth in value-added, the capital stock, and the labor force in the selected enterprises from 1965 through 1979. These estimates and the methods used to obtain them are set forth in more detail in Appendix B. Data on value-added and capital stocks are in constant 1970 prices. The capital stock estimates were obtained by adding or subtracting estimated net investment flows to a 1970 base-year estimate for each public enterprise industry. Industry-specific rates of depreciation of the capital stock are also reported in Appendix 3.

The most important insight to be gained from inspection of changing capital–labor ratios in Table 6.1 is the dramatic substitution of capital for labor that since 1966 has occurred in every public enterprise sector. On average, the typical public enterprise employee was endowed with three times as much

Table 6.1. *Capital–labor ratios in selected public enterprises,*
1966–79 (Cr$ 000 per man-year, constant 1970 values)

	1966–8	1970	1975	1979
Mining	64	123	191	320
Steel	122	100	227[a]	297
Petrochemicals	42	118	349	556
Communications	58	60	169	284
Electricity[b]	366	368	512	741
Railroads[c]	—	8	67	148
Average for public enterprise (excluding railroads)	104	163	328	515

Notes: The methods for estimating a capital stock for each public enterprise
sector are set forth in Appendix B. These involved adding or subtracting net
investment flows to 1970 base-year capital stock estimates. Investment
figures were deflated using the wholesale price index (FGV, column 12).
Assumed rates of physical depreciation are reported in Appendix B. A
three-year moving average was selected as the base period when alternative
procedures led to misleading results.
[a]Excluding ACESITA.
[b]Excluding data for Light, the large distribution company purchased by
ELETROBRÁS in 1979.
[c]Capital stock estimates for the railroads are believed less reliable than
those for other sectors.
Sources: Labor force estimates, see Table 6.2. Capital stock estimates, from
company balance sheets. See Appendix A.

physical capital in 1975 as in 1966 and at least five times as
much by 1980 (see Table 6.1).

Some of the trends behind this shift in factor proportions
are apparent. High levels of investment spending in most of
these firms during the last fifteen years have been noted, but
it is also important that employment in this set of large enterprises grew very slowly throughout the period (see Table
6.2). Under various military governments, Brazilian public
enterprises in basic industry and the utilities have not pursued
aggressively the social objective of employment creation nor
would they appear to fit comfortably within the common
stereotype of the public enterprise as being an overstaffed
bureaucracy top heavy in redundant clerical personnel.

Table 6.2. *Employment in selected large public enterprises, 1965–79*

	Mining	Steel	Petrochemicals	Telecommunications	Electricity	Railroads	Total	% manufacturing employment
1965	9,868	—	36,180	—	11,200	—	97,048	
1966	10,078	31,247	36,027	22,776	12,200	159,712	275,034	
1967	10,141	31,397	34,550	26,649	14,400	154,533	271,670	
1968	10,146	31,214	36,432	32,016	22,133	154,427	286,368	14.1
1969	9,924	31,065	35,266	36,627	25,877	152,229	291,515	
1970	11,115	31,881	36,114	40,253	39,889	148,492	307,744	
1971	11,671	32,156	35,877	42,546	41,310	149,000	312,560	
1972	12,000	31,838	33,175	44,362	43,087	144,442	308,989	
1973	13,244	34,052	34,001	48,090	44,699	139,567	313,653	
1974	17,375	37,743	37,379	45,126	50,159	136,192	320,418	9.4
1975	21,507	46,086	41,842	45,076	72,570	133,033	353,420	
1976	21,643	54,341	46,651	43,278	75,896	138,774	380,583	
1977	23,000	56,444	47,780	44,887	81,392	117,104	370,607	
1978	17,913	58,576	49,352	47,835	84,535	113,285	371,496	
1979	19,527	60,035	51,461	48,610	121,656	112,656	414,072	8.6[a]

[a]Estimate based on assumed 5.5% growth of labor force in late 1970s.

Sources: Annual reports of the companies listed in Appendix A. (Employment data may also be found in: *Visão, Quem é quem na economia brasileira,* annual editions, 1966–76.) Manufacturing employment 1968–74, FIBGE, *Séries Estatísticas Retrospectivas,* 1977, p. 156. Public enterprise employment in electricity adjusted to exclude Light.

The railroads have been the one sector in which redundancy and patronage have long been problems, but here the employment trends are both interesting and illustrative. Total employment in the various federal and state networks approached 200,000 workers in the late 1950s and early 1960s. While the advent of the military regime in 1964 meant very little in terms of allocating additional public investment to railroads, successive administrations in the rail systems were pressured by post-1964 federal and state governments to reduce operating deficits, since these had to be funded by deficit spending. Administrators responded by freezing new hiring and allowing normal attrition of the work force. Employment dropped steadily to just over 100,000 in 1980. While the railroads remain much more labor-intensive than other public sectors, capital-intensity in this sector increased rapidly during the 1970s and the trend should continue through the 1980s.

The aggregate employment data for the large public enterprises suggest that these firms have become less important in terms of national employment growth. Thus, the state companies represented more than 14% of total employment in Brazilian manufacturing in 1968, but probably less than 9% of the total by 1979 (see Table 6.2). To sum up, several factors are important in understanding the observed trends in factor proportions. Managers have clearly had the latitude to focus upon achieving industrial efficiency without concerning themselves with the social objective of increasing employment. Again, public enterprise managers in Brazil for most of the last two decades have not had to concern themselves with strong labor unions that could have lobbied to affect employment levels. This experience contrasts very sharply with that of public enterprise managers in Mexico who have had to negotiate cautiously with powerful labor unions in electricity, oil, rail, and other sectors.[1] Whether or not Brazil's public sector unions will gain increased bargaining power with movement toward democracy remains an interesting question for the 1980s.

Additional economic and political arguments could help explain the trend toward increased capital-intensity. First, the

Table 6.3. *Capital–output ratios in selected public enterprises, 1966–79*

	1966–8	1970	1975	1979
Mining	2.08	2.12	2.41	4.62
Steel	4.92	2.79	3.54	5.66
Petrochemicals	0.50	1.22	1.46	2.86
Communications	3.61	4.57	6.15	7.08
Electricity	8.90	9.56	10.63	13.86
Railroads	n.a.	2.63	13.58	16.16
Public enterprises	2.73	3.33	4.06	6.68
Public enterprises (excluding railroads)	n.a.	3.54	3.74	6.50

Notes: Output (value-added) is in constant 1970 Cr$; nominal values deflated by general price index (IGP, column 2). Value-added defined as gross sales minus expenditures, except for salaries, worker benefits, net interest, indirect taxes. Capital stock in constant 1970 Cr$. See note to Table 6.1. Derived by method described in Appendix B.
Source: Raw data obtained from annual reports of companies listed in Appendix A.

public enterprises did modernize significantly over the last two decades and probably replaced older technologies with more capital-intensive methods of production. Second, public sector managers may simply have found it cheaper to substitute capital for labor. Exemptions from import duties on capital equipment, the availability of investment finance from the government and official international agencies, and other policies may well have acted to encourage capital-intensiveness. Third, public enterprise managers, sensing that their stewardships would ultimately be judged by the amount of additional plant and equipment they put in place, may have acted to maximize installed capacity without regard either to relative input prices or the impact of the strategies on employment growth in a labor-surplus economy.

Granted that growth in the public enterprise sector has been highly capital-intensive, how productive have these increments to capital been? This question may be approached through an examination of capital–output ratios found in Table 6.3. The estimates presented require great care in interpretation: capital–output ratios (COR) are sensitive not only to measurement error, but to the level of capacity utilization in the industry and to systems of administered pricing that may cause observed output to be under- or overvalued. The data attest to a significant increase in "roundaboutness" in Brazilian public enterprises. The average COR for the selected public enterprises (excluding railroads) rises from about 2.7 units of capital to produce 1 unit of output in the 1960s to 3.7 units by 1975 and 6.5 in 1979.[2] Again, monopoly pricing or government price controls distort these figures somewhat by making "output" difficult to measure, but the trend toward increasing capital requirements is clear.

While output has been produced using more capital in all sectors, the average CORs disguise considerable variation in levels between public enterprise sectors. The electricity firms are considerably above this figure, as are those in communications and railroads, although capital stock estimates for this last sector are believed less reliable. Public enterprises in mining and petrochemicals show CORs significantly below the average figures.

The relatively greater use of capital throughout the public enterprise sector suggests that labor productivity must have been increasing rapidly as well. The data on labor productivity in Table 6.4 strongly support this supposition for the period through the mid-1970s. Average output per worker in Brazilian public enterprises more than doubled between 1966 and 1975, with strong gains in most industries, especially steel and petrochemicals. However, productivity growth slowed down sharply in the late 1970s. Productivity probably stagnated and may even have declined in the key sectors of mining, steel, and petrochemicals. The reasons behind this disturbing trend include tightened government price controls, some excess capacity, and a faster pace of employment growth; it is also possible that the overall efficiency of resource use began to deteriorate after the mid-1970s.

The significance of these findings on productivity and employment in Brazilian public enterprises are better appreciated in a comparative perspective. First, in terms of the absolute *level* of value-added per worker, how do the public enterprises stack up against the Brazilian manufacturing sector?

Table 6.4. *Output–labor ratios in selected public enterprises,*
1966–79 (Cr$ 000 per man-year, constant 1970 values)

	1966–8	1970	1975	1979
Mining	32.4	58.2	79.3	72.1
Steel	23.1	35.9	64.0	53.1
Petrochemicals	71.4	96.1	248.8	199.0
Communications	15.6	13.1	27.4	40.5
Electricity	45.8	38.5	48.1	53.4
Railroads	1.6	3.0	4.9	9.2
Public enterprises	16.3	25.3	56.5	58.4
Public enterprises (excluding railroads)	37.3	46.0	85.3	79.1

Sources: Output (value-added) is as defined in Table 6.3; employment data, Table 6.2: average work force during year.

Using 1970 as a base year for comparison, aggregate data suggest that the range of value-added per worker in Brazilian manufacturing was from about Cr$2,000 per worker in the least productive manufacturing pursuits to about Cr$64,000 per worker in the most capital-intensive establishments, with a median productivity of about Cr$20,000.[3]

Results reported in Table 6.4 suggest that in absolute terms productivity in public enterprises in 1970 exceeded slightly this median figure. However, if the railroads are excluded, average productivity in 1970 in the public enterprises was probably more than double the manufacturing average (i.e., Cr$46,000 vs. Cr$20,000). Again, productivity in public mining and petrochemicals was probably as high or higher than comparable figures in any branch of Brazilian manufacturing.

A more important comparative question concern changes over time in value-added per worker. Preliminary evidence on this point is presented in Table 6.5. From 1966 through at least 1975, the pace of productivity growth was much brisker than in manufacturing as a whole. Slower employment growth in the public enterprises is one important reason for this pattern. Employment in the manufacturing sector as a whole expanded 1.9 times between 1966 and 1975; employment in

Table 6.5. *Comparison of index numbers of labor productivity (real value-added per man-year) and employment in selected large public enterprises and Brazilian manufacturing (1966 = 100)*

	Labor productivity		Employment	
	Public enterprises	Manufacturing sector	Public enterprises	Manufacturing sector
1966	100	100	100	100
1970	140	131	138	111
1975	237	202	164	193
1978	220	217	186	202

Sources: Public enterprise output (value-added), Trebat, "An Evaluation," Appendix C, Table 52; employment, Table 6.3; output and employment for manufacturing sector (*indústria de transformação*), Instituto Brasileiro de Geografia e Estatística (IBGE), *Anuário Estatístico do Brasil,* various years, 1966–76; manufacturing, 1978, national accounts data used in calculation, results from industrial censuses not available. *Conjuntura Econômica* 33 (December 1979):70. Employment data: *Relatório Anual do Banco Central do Brasil, 1979* (June 1980), p. 29.

the large public enterprises – excluding railroads – advanced 1.6 times during the same period. Yet these trends appear not to have continued after 1975. Value-added per worker in the public enterprises (excluding railroads) stagnated in the latter 1970s and may have declined while productivity in manufacturing continued to expand.

Again, the trends in employment growth are the key: the public enterprises continued to expand their work force after 1975 while the pace of employment growth slackened in industry. On balance we can conclude for the period from the mid-1960s to the late 1970s that value-added per worker in the public enterprise sector tended to be higher in absolute terms and increasing at a faster pace than in Brazilian manufacturing. Nonetheless, the data suggest that a reversal of this trend may have set in during the late 1970s with possibly important implications for performance in the future.

A final point in this sector is to link up our findings on the

Table 6.6. *Ratio of increases in real wages to increases in labor productivity*

	1970	1975	1979
Mining	1.0	0.9	1.31
Petrochemicals	1.0	0.41	0.65
Railroads	1.0	0.95	1.35
Electricity	1.0	1.55	1.28
Steel	1.0	0.81	1.1
Telecommunications	1.0	0.84	0.70
Public enterprises	1.0	0.67	0.81
Public enterprises (excluding railroads)	1.0	0.80	0.98

Sources: Wages per worker derived from information in annual reports of companies listed in Appendix A, deflated by Rio de Janeiro cost of living index. Labor productivity: Table 6.4.

increasing average productivity of labor in public enterprises with trends in real wages. Have workers benefited directly from improved productivity? And how do wage levels and trends in public enterprise compare with those in Brazilian manufacturing?

Table 6.6 has been derived by dividing the index of real wages from 1970 to 1979 by the index of productivity growth. Thus, the resulting ratio is equal to 1.0 in 1970 (the base year) and then either increases or decreases according to whether the annual adjustment in real wages is greater or less than the corresponding increase in productivity. Were observed increases in labor productivity passed through to workers in the form of increased real wages? Apparently both productivity and real wages increased by an average 6% per annum in public enterprises (excluding railroads) during the 1970s, thus the ratio of 0.98 between the two indexes in 1979. However, cyclical changes in this ratio are striking. During the early 1970s, labor in public enterprises appears to have been "exploited" to the extent that less than 80% of its productivity gains were passed through to wages. Thus, labor's share in value-added declined somewhat in this period, leading to a

Table 6.7. *Annual percentage increases in productivity and real wages in public enterprises and manufacturing, 1970–9*

	1970–5		1976–9	
	Public enterprises	Manufacturing	Public enterprises	Manufacturing
Productivity	11.0	9.1	0	2.4
Real wages	8.2	7.4	3.2	7.7

Sources: Tables 6.4, 6.5, and 6.6. Real wages in manufacturing, IBGE, *Anuário Estatístico*, various years. Deflator: Rio de Janeiro cost of living index.

corresponding rise in the share of capital and other factors. From 1975 through 1979, wages tended to increase faster than productivity to the point of almost closing the gap.

These trends in real wages and productivity are summarized in Table 6.7. The data show that both productivity and real wages increased faster in the public enterprises than in the manufacturing sector as a whole, although real wages for both groups lag behind productivity increases. The late 1970s was a catch-up period for real wages and led to an increase in labor's share in value-added. Nevertheless, the main characteristic of the late 1970s was the sharp decline in productivity in the public enterprises.

Available data on the absolute levels of wage payments in public enterprises and in manufacturing are not comparable. The industrial censuses provide data on salaries while the wages data used in this study are much broader and encompass social security payments and other types of worker benefits. Thus, the public enterprise data are likely to overstate the case, but the differences between overall wage payments in manufacturing and in the public enterprises are large enough to suggest strongly that wages are, on average, higher in the state-owned firms.

If we take 1974 as an example (the last year for which census data are now available), the average wage in manufacturing industry was approximately Cr$1,130 per month, while the "total remuneration" figure in the public enterprises exceeded Cr$3,000 per month. Further data refinement is needed, but it is unlikely that the manufacturing figure could be in excess of approximately Cr$2,000 per month. The public enterprises do appear to pay higher wages. Obviously, the faster growth of productivity (through the mid-1970s) is one explanation. Another could be a possibly higher proportion of skilled workers and technicians in state firms.

To sum up, the important points raised in this discussion of the sources of growth and wage trends include the following. Brazilian public enterprise growth over the last two decades has been led by growth in capital. Capital requirements (i.e., units of capital needed to produce one unit of output) have increased steadily across sectors and over time. If we take the last two decades as a whole, the increasing use of capital has been accompanied by strong increases in value-added per worker. Furthermore, lagging, low-productivity public enterprise sectors have tended to improve their performance relative to the group mean. From another viewpoint, employment growth has been slow in the public enterprises but real wage increases have tended to keep pace with productivity gains. On balance, the public enterprise performance in raising productivity and real wages compares favorably with the Brazilian manufacturing sector. In absolute terms, the public enterprises appear to be "high wage" firms by comparison to Brazilian industry overall. But while "stylized facts" such as these do characterize Brazilian public enterprise performance, the empirical evidence did suggest a stagnation in productivity in the late 1970s.

Public enterprises compared with the private sector

The preceding examination of public enterprise performance in isolation provides a vantage point from which to examine the results of a large cross-sectional study of 731 major Brazilian firms in 1974.[4] Using financial and labor force data, Suzigan compared indicators of size, productivity, and profitability after classifying these firms into three ownership groups: public enterprises, multinational enterprises, and private do-

Table 6.8. *Indicators of productivity and factor intensity in 731 large Brazilian firms, 1974*

Ownership group	Fixed assets per worker	Sales per worker	Captial per unit output
Public enterprises	212	125	253
Multinationals	65	99	48
Private domestic firms	42	78	53
Average	100	100	100

Source: Wilson Suzigan, "As empresas do governo e o papel do estado," p. 102. The large public enterprises selected by Suzigan are not identical to those used in this study.

mestic enterprises. Selected results from this study, the most comprehensive of its type, are reproduced in Table 6.8. The data on comparative profitability will be examined later in this chapter. The reader is alerted to the fact that the Suzigan study encompasses a larger number of public enterprises in a greater variety of economic sectors than is the case in this study.

For each of the variables considered, Table 6.8 depicts the position of each of the three ownership groups – the state, multinationals, and the Brazilian private sector – relative to the overall group mean in 1974. The proxy variable for the capital–labor ratio (see column 1) underlines the role played by the Brazilian public sector in providing economic infrastructure and basic industrial inputs for the Brazilian private sector. The average state-owned firm uses more than three times as much capital than the average large multinational; more than four times as much as the average, large indigenous enterprise. Column (2) in Table 6.8 provides a rough proxy for labor productivity across the ownership spectrum, that is, net sales per worker. On this basis, labor productivity is considerably higher in the state enterprises than in either the multinational group or the Brazilian private firms. Yet the difference is not nearly as large as the difference in relative capital–labor endowments. Finally, column (3) confirms the massive capital requirement in state firms by comparison to their private sector counterparts. On average, the state firm requires five times as much capital to generate a unit of output as do private Brazilian firms.

Return on investment. Measuring the profitability of public enterprise investment presents a host of theoretical and practical problems treated at length in the literature.[5] What is the opportunity cost of public enterprise investment?[6] How should "surplus" be defined? How should externalities generated by such investment be taken into account, as, for example, public investment in electricity that makes possible the development of an entire region? What about government price controls? Different accounting standards that impede comparability?

The approach adopted here has been to work with two (hopefully correlated) measures of profitability. The first measure, which we refer to as the "real" rate of return, is broad and corresponds more closely to an economist's definition of the return to capital. The second measure of profitability is one more familiar to the accountant or stock analyst: net earnings in percent of stockholder equity or the financial rate of return. Use of this measure permits greater comparability with profits in private firms and with state-owned enterprises in other countries.

Real rates of profit define surplus as that part of value-added not distributed in the form of wages, salaries, and worker benefits. Thus, the total return to the capital factor picks up such items as net interest payments, rent, and indirect taxes, which the accountant would certainly not consider as surplus available for distribution to stockholders. The rationale for adopting this broad definition of surplus is that decisions on where the public enterprise may borrow and for how much, how heavily its output is taxed, and so forth, reflect the government's political decisions on how to distribute the surplus generated by economic activity and do not really alter the size of the surplus. The denominator in this first definition of profitability is the actual physical stock of capital, expressed (of course) in value terms and suitably adjusted for depreciation.

Brazilian public enterprises, with the exception of the railroads, have been generally profitable (see Table 6.9). Granted that the measure of surplus is a broad one, the average rate of return on capital in public enterprises (excluding railroads) hovered at or above 20% during most of the late 1960s and well into the 1970s. Even if the opportunity cost of capital had been as high as, say, 15% in Brazil, investment in public enterprises could still have been worthwhile from a strictly economic viewpoint.[7]

Two crucial refinements to this general finding are needed. First, the profitability performance is not uniformly strong across sectors. Mining and petrochemicals, the two natural resource sectors, clearly form a "high surplus" category and lift the average for all other public enterprises. The electricity and telecommunications firms comprise a "low surplus" category, with rates of return generally in the 5%–10% range. The profit performance in public steel lies between these extremes and is close to the overall state-enterprise average. Finally, rates of return in rail transport are consistently negative, a not surprising performance given the bleak record of most railroads in the world (see Table 6.9).

Second, public enterprise profitability has changed over time. The average rate of return dipped very sharply from about 21% in 1975 to 12% by 1979.[8] In a number of key public enterprise sectors (mining, steel, petrochemicals), the dip in profits after 1975 coincided with a trend toward declining profitability evident in these sectors since at least 1970. But in most sectors the rate of return on capital in 1979 was much lower than the levels recorded in the mid-1960s and significantly below profitability in 1975. PETROBRÁS and its subsidiaries in petrochemicals are the best example of this trend. The rate of return in this sector declined from 60% in the early 1970s to 30% by 1979.

While careful not to lose sight of the fact that profitability in Brazilian public enterprises has been generally good, we must seek to explain the post-1975 drop. Statistical errors may have played a role: the capital stock may not have been properly measured and a lag should have been allowed between investment (i.e., growth in the capital

Table 6.9. Net real rates of return in public enterprises, 1966–79, in percentages

	1966–8	1970	1975	1979
High surplus				
Mining	33.7	30.8	28.5	22.9
Petrochemicals	124.0	61.9	64.2	29.4
Average surplus				
Steel	11.3	21.4	19.0	11.2
Low surplus				
Communications	23.5	9.8	7.7	7.8
Electricity	n.a.	8.0	5.9	5.0
Railroads	n.a.	–3.1	–5.3	–3.2
Public enterprises (excluding railroads)		19.9	20.7	11.8

Notes: Net real rates of return are defined as: $\pi_t = (VA_t - W_t) / K_t$ where all variables are expressed in constant 1970 Cr\$. Value-added was deflated using the general price index (FGV, column 2). Wages were deflated by the cost of living index for Rio de Janeiro. Capital estimates were deflated by the wholesale price index (FGV, column 12). Value-added is net of accounting depreciation. The wage bill includes social security payments. See Appendix B for definition.

stock) and the appearance of output made possible by this investment.

Yet, apart from these possible measurement difficulties, two separate sets of circumstances may be alleged to explain declining profitability. On the one hand, profits may have been squeezed by a combination of factors, largely beyond the control of the public enterprises, especially:

1. Tighter government price controls as successive governments struggled with a worsening inflation problem;
2. Slower than expected market growth for the public firms as the pace of economic growth in Brazilian industry slackened in the late 1970s; and
3. Rising raw materials costs, especially for the petrochemical companies and for energy-intensive industries such as steel.

On the other hand, a less charitable but nonetheless possible explanation is that the public firms as a group have simply been overusing capital by an emphasis on growth, rather than profit maximization. In this view, public enterprise managers saw their main mission not as earning maximum profits, but building infrastructures that could generate pecuniary economies for downstream user industries. If so, was this growth-maximizing strategy truly in the public interest, or did it reflect privileged access to capital and the accumulated bureaucratic power of state-enterprise managers to set their own course? Again, assuming the less charitable alternative to be the case, the large state-owned enterprises that are the focus of this study may have begun imposing a heavy burden on a capital-short economy beset by the balance of payments and inflationary problems in the latter half of the 1970s.

Resource use: A summing-up

In the course of this study, a reasonably complete time series has been assembled on labor and capital absorption and also on the production of value-added in Brazil's largest state-owned enterprises. Drawing upon all of this information, a simple calculus can help answer the following question: "When all is said and done, did Brazilian public enterprises produce output at least equal to and, hopefully, greater in value than the cost of all the resources they used up?"[9] If so, a prima facie and purely economic case can be made on behalf of public enterprise performance. If not, we will have to consider the possibilities that the public enterprises have been wasteful or mismanaged, or that their performance can be justified only by taking price controls into account or by finding a way to value "hidden output" such as externalities bestowed on user industries or social services provided by the firm for which it does not receive an explicit subsidy.

This rate-of-return calculus considers the entire period from 1967 to 1979 as one single time period for purposes of calculating marginal product and marginal resource costs. The gross social benefits (GSB) resulting from the activities of the public enterprise j are defined as the difference in value-added (VA) when output in 1979 is compared with the figure corresponding to 1967, or:

$$GSB^j = VA^j_{1979} - VA^j_{1967}$$

where value-added is expressed in real terms. It is then necessary to arrive at an estimate of the cost of the two factors, labor and capital, used up in the production of this incremental output. For each public enterprise sector, an estimate of the marginal cost of labor (MCL) may be obtained by multiplying an appropriate annual wage by the change in employment occurring between 1967 and 1979, or, again for firm j:

$$MCL^j = \bar{W} (L^j_{1979} - L^j_{1967})$$

where $\bar{W}$ is the average wage prevailing in firm j's industry in 1970.

Analogously, the marginal costs of the capital (MCC) used up are found by multiplying an estimated "user cost" of capital by the change in the physical capital stock occurring between 1967 and 1979. Thus:

$$MCC^j = (\bar{r} + \bar{d}) (K^j_{1979} - K^j_{1967})$$

where $\bar{r}$ is the social opportunity cost of capital and $\bar{d}$ is a sector-specific rate of depreciation of the capital stock, K. In this exercise, $\bar{r}$ was set equal to 12%, an arbitrary but, hopefully, reasonable figure.

The sum of labor and capital costs defined in these ways yields an estimate of firm j's "marginal resource cost" or:

$$MRC^j = MCL^j + MCC^j$$

Finally, the "net social benefits" (NSB^j) arising from the activities of firm j are defined:

$$NSB^j = GSB^j - MRC^j$$

Thus, $NSB^j > 0$ will be prima facie evidence that, from a purely economic viewpoint, the performance of enterprise j (or group of enterprises in the same industry) has been satisfactory. And, $NSB^j < 0$ means either that economic performance was not satisfactory or we must certainly look beyond the analysis of income statements and balance sheets to evaluate performance.

At the risk of belaboring the point, the case of $NSB^j = 0$ is also of interest, but from a slightly different perspective. The question may be asked: What would the social opportunity cost of capital in Brazil have had to have been for GSB^j to be just equal to MRC^j? And how does this shadow rate of return compare to our (reasonable) estimate of a 12% social opportunity cost?

Finally, NSB^j has been calculated under two different assumptions regarding the lag between investment spending and the appearance of output. Method A assumes no lag whatsoever, while Method B assumes a four-year lag between investment and output. The assumed lag structure is defined in the notes to Table 6.10.

The results of this exercise to compare resource costs and output gains over the twelve-year period from 1967 to 1979 confirm earlier findings on the rate of return to capital. State enterprises in mining and petrochemicals (basically CVRD and PETROBRÁS) emerge as high "net social benefit" sectors. This is seen in Table 6.10 by the fact that net social benefits are positive and large. Indeed, the state's investment in these sectors would have been profitable even if the social opportunity cost of capital had been as high as 17% in the case of petrochemicals or 21.3% for mining. Furthermore, allowing for a lag between investment and output (Method B), the implicit rate of return was as high as 26% in both sectors.

The results for these two sectors once again underscore the economic motivations for public ownership of rent-generating

Table 6.10. *Estimated net social benefits of public enterprise resource use, 1967–79, (Cr$ 000 in constant 1970 values)*

		Marginal resource costs (MRC)	Gross social benefit (GSB)	Net social benefit (NSB)	Net rate of return at which $MRC = .MB$
Petrochemicals	(A)	6.358.934	7.717.776	1.358.842	17.0
	(B)	4.763.817		2.953.960	26.9
Mining	(A)	1.267.139	1.784.585	517.446	21.3
	(B)	930.779		663.647	25.8
Steel	(A)	3.257.460	2.819.163	-438.297	9.0
	(B)	2.320.723		498.440	17.1
Teleco munications	(A)	2.730.350	1.643.142	-1.087.208	3.5
	(B)	2.197.488		-544.346	6.6
Electricity	(A)	10.806.208	4.045.761	-6.760.447	0.6
	(B)	8.312.817		-4.267.05	2.5
Railroads	(A)	2.647.582	858.828	-1.788.754	0.5
	(B)	2.064.582		-1.205.654	2.1
Public enterprises (non-rail)	(A)	25.331.061	18.010.427	-7.320.634	5.9
	(B)	19.420.629		-1.410.202	10.4

Notes: (1) Marginal resource costs (MRC) are defined as follows: $MRC = \bar{w} \Delta L + (12 + \delta) \Delta K$, where: $\bar{w}$ = average wage in 1970 in each public enterprise industry; ΔL = change in employment between 1967 and 1979; δ = a sector-specific rate of depreciation (see Appendix B); ΔK = net change in the capital stock between 1967 and 1979. (2) Marginal benefits are defined as the change in value added between 1967 and 1979. (3) Method A assumes no lag between investment and output. (4) Method B assumes a four-year lag between investment and output. Weights were selected arbitrarily. The net change in the capital stock was calculated according to the following formula: $.5(I_{64}) + .75(I_{65}) + .9(I_{66}) + I_{67} + \ldots + I_{76} + .5(I_{77}) + 0.25(I_{78}) + 0.1(I_{79})$, where I is real net investment in a given year.

natural resource sectors. CVRD (in mining) and PETROBRÁS and its subsidiaries in petroleum and petrochemicals have allowed the state to appropriate a surplus that is the basis for the rapid expansion and diversification observed in these sectors.

The state-owned steel enterprises are a borderline case of overall profitability. If no investment–output lag is assumed, net social benefits are negative and would not be positive unless the opportunity cost of capital were as low as 9%, versus the 12% figure used to construct Table 6.10. However, the steel firms were engaged in large expansion programs in the late 1970s. Since the impact of these construction programs on capacity and output will not show up fully until the 1980s, it is reasonable to adjust the 1979 estimate of capital used up in steel production to reflect this lag. Thus, Method *B* procedures suggest large positive net social benefits generated by public steel. Further, the steel sector would yield nonnegative benefits even at an opportunity cost of capital of 17.1%. Finally, steel prices have been subject to more frequent and stringent price controls than has been the case in most public enterprises, a fact tending to reinforce the overall impression of good economic performance in public steel.

A purely economic case is much more difficult to make in behalf of the remaining public enterprise sectors, no matter the lag structure used to calculate capital costs. The railroads, of course, did not perform well economically, yielding large negative net social benefits. What is surprising is that the crucial electricity sector and public telecommunications do not perform much better than the railroads. Both sectors also used up economic resources worth far in excess of the additional output produced. In the case of electricity, these net social benefits would turn positive only under the assumption of a social opportunity cost of capital in a range of 0.6%–2.5%, far below any common-sense notion of a minimally acceptable rate of return. For telecommunications, the required range is not much higher: 3.5%–6.6%.

Putting all these sectors together (except railroads) permits a summary statement of the pure economic return to large

Table 6.11. *Rate-of-return performance of public enterprises, 1967–79*

	No investment–output lag	Four-year lag
Mining	Strong	Strong
Petrochemicals	Average	Strong
Steel	Weak	Average
Telecommunications	Weak	Weak
Electricity	Weak	Weak
Railroads	Weak	Weak
Public enterprises (excluding railroads)	Weak	Average

public enterprises (see Table 6.11). It is difficult to make a strong argument on behalf of overall economic performance unless the opportunity cost of capital used up was in the range of only 5.9%–10.4%. The results for all of these sectors are summed up in Table 6.11. The narrow economic performance (i.e., before adjusting input or output values to reflect externalities) of public enterprises are classified as "strong," "average," or "weak" on the basis of the difference between rate of return that would set *GSB* equal to *MRC*, assuming a 12% return on capital.

Care must be taken not to read too much into these results. Perhaps the need for longer lags than those assumed or poorly designed price policies explain weak performance. Surely, no adequate reckoning has been made of "social output," for example, money-losing rail service for low-income workers, expensive hydro development that will eventually make possible less political dependence on OPEC, and so on. And we are not really addressing the question: "Could private enterprise have done any better given the same circumstances?" However, with these qualifications in mind, the fact remains that public enterprises in electricity, communications, and railroads during 1967–79 absorbed resources worth considerably more than the output obtained from their economic activities. Did these firms overbuild? Were they wasteful? These remain as possible explanations to the patterns revealed by the data.

Table 6.12. *Comparison of profits in large Brazilian firms, classified by ownership group, 1974 and 1978 (net earnings in percent of net worth)*

	1974[a]	1978[b]
Public enterprise	11.4	7.9
Multinationals	20.6	14.9
Private domestic	22.8	10.6

[a]Private sector profit rates are reported net of income tax. Because public enterprises were exempt from profits taxation until 1975, the difference in rates of return for 1974 is larger than indicated in the table.
[b]1978, calculated on basis of largest 25 firms in each ownership group as reported in *Visão, Quem é quem na economia brasileira,* 1980.
Sources: 1974, Wilson Suzigan, "As empresas do governo e o papel do estado," p. 102. See also notes to Table 6.8.

Profitability in comparative perspective

The measures of profitability and overall rates of return have produced impressions about performance within the public enterprise, but broad comparability of results with the Brazilian private sector and with state-owned enterprises in other countries can be achieved only if we move to the accountant's definition of profitability, that is, net earnings in percent of total stockholder equity (i.e., capital plus reserves.) This measure was avoided earlier because it is distorted by differences in accounting standards, the inclusion of earnings (whether positive or negative) of real estate or money market transactions not directly related to the company's operating performance, and so on. Yet, while differences in magnitudes may exist, all measures of the firm's surplus should be highly correlated. Results of two separate examinations of profit rates for large Brazilian firms in two "normal" years – 1974 and 1978 – are presented in Table 6.12.

In both years, the return on financial investment in public enterprises (here including the railroads) is on the order of one-half the return earned by the private sector. The main lesson of Table 6.12 – that public enterprises are less profitable – does deserve one important qualification, however. Both multinational enterprises and private domestic firms in Brazil are probably "undercapitalized" in the sense that they rely heavily on debt, rather than equity financing. Multinational companies, especially during the 1970s, were able to arrange substantial loan financing from their parent companies abroad. Servicing these loans was a legitimate, though indirect means for potentially side-stepping Brazil's dividend remittance guidelines. Private Brazilian-owned firms are eligible for cheap investment financing from government agencies. Thus, private firms in Brazil probably have an incentive – which public firms lack – to minimize the equity component of their balance sheets. This makes them seem more profitable than they really are. If better measures of profitability were available, private companies would probably still be more profitable than their state-owned counterparts, but not by as much as Table 6.12 would suggest.

Finally, how does the profit performance of public enterprise in Brazil compare with the record of state firms in other countries? Comparative data, some of it summarized in Table 6.13, suggests that the profitability of Brazilian public enterprises is well above average by international standards and by a wide margin higher than that of state firms in other Latin American countries. Concluding a broad survey of financial performance in developing countries, a World Bank study reported that "The picture of state-owned enterprises is a rather dismal one involving large and mostly continuing financial losses."[10] Worldwide, public enterprises able to generate internal savings sufficient to cover wear and tear of their capital were found to be "the exception and not the rule."[11] However, as Sheahan points out, the profitability performance of state enterprises outside of Europe and Latin America has not been "uniformly bleak."[12]

Turkish and Indian public enterprise would appear to conform to the rule of low profitability. State firms in Turkey

Table 6.13. *Profitability performance of public enterprises in selected countries*

Country	Year	Profitability
Turkey	1968	2.6^a–4.8^b
	1972	6.2^b
India	1972–3	3.8^c
	1974–5	11.5^d
	1976	2.0^e
Korea	1972	High
Egypt	1972–7	$10–15^f$
Brazil	1974	11.4^e
	1978	7.9^e
Argentina	1972–8	Low
Mexico	1972–4	-3.8^e
Chile	1978	-3.12^e
	1978^g	-1.04^e
Peru	1973	1.4^e

[a]Profits as percent of capital stock.
[b]Pre-tax earnings + interest in percent of net worth.
[c]Overall rate of return.
[d]Gross profits in percent of capital employed.
[e]Net profits in percent of net worth.
[f]Current surplus, net of interest, depreciation, and rent, in percent of fixed assets plus inventories.
[g]Excluding CODELCO, the state-owned copper concern.
Sources: Turkey, India, Korea: IBRD: *State Intervention in the Industrialization of Developing Countries*, p. 16. Also for Turkey, Cihan Belen, "The Role of the State Economic Enterprises in the Development of Turkey," Ph.D. dissertation, University of Connecticut, 1975, p. 96.
Egypt: Heba Ahmad Handoussa, "The Impact of Economic Liberalization on the Performance of Egypt's Public Sector Industry," paper presented to the Second B.A.P.E.G. Conference on Public enterprise in Mixed Economy LDCs, Boston, April 3–5 1980, p. 13.
Argentina: Alberto Joaquin Ugalde, "El comportamiento financiero de empresas públicas en el período 1966–1978 y sus perspectivas," paper presented to the Second National Convention of Finance Executives, Buenos Aires, May 1979.
Mexico: IBRD, *Mexico Manufacturing Sector: Situation, Prospects, and Policies* (Washington: IBRD, 1979), p. 71.
Chile: *Chile Economic News*, September 1980.
Peru: E. V. K. Fitzgerald, *The Political Economy of Peru, 1956–78* Cambridge University Press, 1979), p. 196.

have been hampered by price controls and burdened with excess labor because of political patronage schemes. Average profitability has been in the 2%–6% range, certainly less than the opportunity cost of capital. Profitability in Indian public enterprise has been almost as low over an extended period of time.

Korea and Egypt appear to have achieved levels of state enterprise profitability equal to or greater than those in Brazil. Jones finds that a generally strong profit performance by Korean public enterprise reflects relatively high levels of engineering efficiency.[13] Handoussa considers that government measures to rationalize employment policies and the availability of foreign exchange are responsible for improving the once poor economic environment for public enterprise in Egypt.[14] Profits in Egyptian public enterprise have been in the 10%–15% range in recent years.

While additional study is needed, available evidence suggests that public enterprise in Italy and France, and throughout Latin America, has not performed nearly as well as state firms in Brazil. With regard to Italy and France, Sheahan reports that while certain companies have been well managed and done well, "more generally, most of the public firms in both countries manage at best to break even or earn very modest profits, certainly below any rate of return sufficient to cover the opportunity costs of their capital."[15]

Of all regions of the world, contrasts with the fairly strong performance of Brazilian public enterprise are sharpest in Latin America. Argentine public enterprise has suffered from cyclical swings in economic activity in that country, but has also been saddled with on-again, off-again price controls that have limited internal cash generation and made necessary large current transfers from the treasury. Price controls and weak managerial structures help explain the poor record of Mexican public enterprises. In the 1972–4 period, 33 public sector firms in manufacturing recorded losses equivalent to 3.8% of net worth.[16]

Furthermore, Mexican firms in electricity, railroads, and steel during 1972–8 either broke even or lost large amounts of money.[17] The Chilean state-owned copper concern, CODEL-

CO, has been well managed and, in times of favorable world prices, highly profitable. However, the financial performance of other large public enterprises in Chile has been weak, with aggregate losses exceeding 1% of net worth in 1978. Peruvian public enterprises, on balance, also barely break even. While not discounting poor management as a factor behind low profitability, Fitzgerald cites policies of price restraint and the "single-minded pursuit" of increased output as the most important reasons for low profits in Peru.[18]

Conclusions

What overall impressions remain concerning profits and overall rates of return in Brazilian public enterprise? Looking at the group of large public enterprises in isolation, they have been generally profitable, on balance earning a rate of return on capital close to its opportunity cost. As far as an overall rate of return is concerned, the additional output produced by the public enterprises has been somewhat below the marginal cost of inputs used up in production. Two qualifications are needed: First, performance varies widely by sectors. While only the railroads lose money, rates of return have been low in telecommunications and electricity, with this latter sector being, by far, the largest user of capital in the public enterprise group. Mining and petrochemicals anchor the opposite end of the profitability spectrum, while steel is something of an in-between case. Second, profitability began to decline in almost all sectors during the latter 1970s. While this trend reflected the generally slowing pace of growth in Brazil and stiffer price controls, it could also be a warning sign of a possible overuse of capital in major state-enterprise sectors.

In comparative perspective, Brazilian public enterprises appear to be less profitable than large private sector counterparts, with profit rates on average about one-half of private sector levels in recent years. The difference is not as big as it seems, however; it is distorted by undercapitalization of Brazilian private firms because of dividend remittance laws in the case of foreign enterprise and generous loan-subsidy programs available to domestic firms.

Though detailed comparative studies are needed to prove the point, Brazil's state firms probably rank among the more financially successful in the world. Certainly, average levels of profitability are much higher than in other major Latin American countries.

Factors internal to each country – size of market, level of education, rate of growth of income, and so on – undoubtedly have much to do with public enterprise performance. The overall regime for public enterprises is also crucial, particularly such elements as the degree of autonomy permitted to state-enterprise managers, government pricing policies, and the overall quality of state-enterprise management. Brazilian firms did, by and large, enjoy wide latitude during most of the late 1970s, even though their autonomy had become increasingly restricted by the early 1980s. Chapter 7 considers how government pricing policies may have affected Brazilian public enterprise performance over the last two decades, and Chapter 8 treats a consequence – investment finance.

7

Policies on pricing

Public policies on pricing of outputs and inputs and on the recruitment of managerial personnel are keys to overall state-enterprise performance in any setting. The examination of the record shows that, on the whole and with few exceptions, Brazilian public enterprises turned in strong growth records and were reasonably successful from the standpoint of profits. How much of this performance can be traced back to price policies?

An obvious problem is to resolve the tension between "microtechnical" considerations (e.g., prices that allocate resources "properly" or "fairly") and political considerations (e.g., prices that will provide the public firm with investment finance or that will contribute toward moderating increases in the cost of living). The theory of public enterprise pricing guidelines has been treated at great length in the literature, but the complexity of the topic does not admit much agreement on proper policies.[1] Most of the discussion assumes that public enterprises operate in sectors in which competition is weak or nonexistent, so control over pricing is needed to achieve a more efficient allocation of resources and to avoid welfare losses. Under such market structures, it is not sufficient to tell public enterprise managers to follow commercial guidelines in setting prices. In the search for a basis for pricing that avoids the extremes of complete price-setting freedom and arbitrary price controls, discussion usually centers upon the applicability of marginal cost pricing in public enterprises. This is because, under certain very restrictive assumptions, the most efficient allocation of resources is obtained when prices everywhere in the economy are set equal to (or equiproportionate to) marginal costs.[2] These assumptions are violated in a real world of market imperfections, taxes, public goods, and divergences of private from social costs. In such a world, it is inefficient to adhere to marginal cost pricing within the confines of the public enterprise sector alone, so suboptimal or "second-best" pricing strategies are more appropriate.[3] Other matters discussed at length in the literature include how to define social marginal costs (e.g., short-run versus long-run costs), how inputs, especially capital, should be priced, and so on.

One need not dwell at length on the finer points of marginal cost pricing to realize that, despite its predominance in the literature, the concept is seldom considered by policymakers in setting pricing guidelines. In the Brazilian case, the reasons for departure from allocative purity would be at least fourfold. First, a strong, legalistic tradition persists in which public utility prices are adjusted with the goal (not always attained) of providing the firm with a "fair" rate of return on its capital. The "fair" rate is usually about 12% of the book value of fixed assets. Second, Brazil over the last two decades has generally been more concerned to provide the public sector firms with enhanced self-financing rather than to allocate resources efficiently. The experience of the late 1950s and early 1960s, when price controls led to inadequate expansion of public utility infrastructure, prepared public opinion to accept regular utility price increases after 1964. Third, public enterprise prices have often been manipulated for the sake of political goals, in Brazil especially that of mitigating the visible effects of strong inflationary pressures. Policymakers have frequently yielded to the temptation to clamp down on public enterprise prices, especially those for steel, electricity, and other key intermediate inputs as a means of dealing with inflationary outbreaks. Fourth, public enterprise prices in Brazil, as elsewhere, have been held down occasionally as a means of subsidizing a particular social group, industry, or region of the country. For example, the railways are commonly pressured to maintain uneconomic lines in operation or to keep prices low in order to subsidize particular regions. Steel prices are carefully monitored in the light of their impact on downstream users, including the auto industry. Urban bus and rail lines are constrained to keep prices down for the sake of their low-income users.

Trends in price levels

The evidence on price-level changes provides an opportunity to gauge their impact over time on pricing strategies in the public enterprises. Table 7.1 presents estimates of indexes and rates of price increases for each of the public enterprise sectors. In order to take advantage of official statistics relating to public enterprise prices, an additional catchall category – utilities and urban transport – is included. This category covers such public enterprise goods and services as natural gas, suburban train service, electricity, water, and residential phone service. The sources for each of these public enterprise price indexes are explained in Appendix B. Finally, for comparative purposes, the general price index for Brazil is included in Table 7.1.

Table 7.2 reports "implicit" or representative price indexes for the subset of public enterprises considered in this study. Two alternative indexes for public enterprise prices were constructed. The implicit index in column (1) includes the petrochemical companies, while that of column (2) excludes these firms. Both indexes can then be compared to the price index for industrial products in Brazil in order to measure differences between public and private sector price movements over the last decade. It should be noted that the public enterprise prices in both Tables 7.1 and 7.2 are reported net of special earmarked investment taxes, which are a substantial part of the final selling price in several industries.

The information presented allows us to sketch a price history for the public enterprises. Two alternative hypotheses of trends in prices over time should be kept in mind: first, that government price controls have held down charges; and second, that public enterprises have used monopoly or oligopoly power to raise prices to customers.

A review of the price-level data for the public enterprises from 1960 to 1979 suggests two themes. First, authorities have squeezed hardest on public enterprise prices when infla-

Table 7.1. *Price indexes and percentage annual rates of change of prices for public enterprise output, 1960–80 (1965–67 = 100)*

Year	Steel	Rate of change	Petroleum	Rate of change	Iron ore	Rate of change	Electrical energy	Rate of change	Utilities and urban transport	Rate of change	Rail freight transport	Rate of change	Telecommunications	Rate of change	Brazil general price index	Rate of change
1960	7		6		12		4		4		9		2		7	
1961	9	29.0	10	29.0	15	25.0	6	50.0	6	33.0	14	55.0	4	100.0	9	29.0
1962	18	100.0	13	30.0	20	33.0	8	33.0	8	42.0	15	7.0	5	25.0	14	56.0
1963	31	72.0	24	77.0	28	40.0	15	100.0	15	91.0	22	47.0	8	60.0	24	71.0
1964	54	74.0	45	100.0	63	125.0	30	100.0	33	116.0	45	104.0	16	100.0	46	92.0
1965	84	55.0	80	78.0	91	44.0	68	126.0	66	100.0	70	56.0	28	75.0	72	57.0
1966	99	18.0	99	24.0	99	9.0	98	44.0	101	53.0	108	54.0	118	321.0	100	39.0
1967	117	18.0	120	21.0	111	12.0	134	37.0	133	32.0	123	14.0	154	31.0	128	28.0
1968	152	30.0	155	29.0	138	24.0	156	16.0	159	20.0	119	-3.0	169	10.0	159	24.0
1969	196	29.0	195	26.0	165	20.0	202	29.0	197	24.0	196	65.0	251	49.0	192	31.0
1970	253	29.0	225	15.0	199	21.0	257	27.0	254	29.0	260	33.0	351	40.0	230	20.0
1971	319	26.0	276	23.0	235	18.0	305	19.0	315	24.0	322	24.0	551	57.0	277	20.0
1972	360	13.0	350	27.0	266	13.0	366	20.0	392	24.0	322	0	766	39.0	324	17.0
1973	432	20.0	401	15.0	293	10.0	405	11.0	443	13.0	360	19.0	1,001	30.0	373	15.0
1974	653	51.0	641	60.0	391	33.0	512	26.0	526	19.0	477	33.0	1,171	17.0	480	29.0
1975	960	47.0	881	31.0	621	59.0	744	45.0	718	37.0	665	39.0	1,348	15.0	613	28.0
1976	1,197	25.0	1,398	59.0	978	57.0	894	20.0	966	35.0	829	25.0	1,618	20.0	852	39.0
1977	1,822	52.2	2,110	51.0	1,273	30.2	1,073	34.5	1,292	33.7	1,190	43.5	2,297	42.0	1,215	42.7
1978	2,419	32.8	2,799	32.6	1,630	28.1	1,402	30.7	1,851	43.3	1,616	35.8	2,642	15.0	1,686	38.7
1979	3,469	43.4	4,696	67.7	2,562	57.2	2,075	48.0	3,779	104.2			3,725	41.0	2,597	54.0
1980	6,362	83.4	7,485	159.4	5,412	112.6									5,199	100.2

Table 7.2. *Comparisons between implicit price indexes for public enterprise products and the industrial products price index, 1960–79 (1966 = 100)*

Year	Implicit price index for public enterprises	Implicit price index for public enterprise excl. petrochemicals	Price index for industrial products	Ratio of (1)/(3)	Ratio of (2)/(3)
1960	6.3		7	0.9	
1961	9.1		9	1.01	
1962	12.4		14	0.89	
1963	20.4		24	0.85	
1964	41		46	0.89	
1965	79	79	75	1.05	1.05
1966	100	100	100	1.0	1.0
1967	122	132	125	0.98	1.05
1968	152	149	163	0.93	0.91
1969	193	191	196	0.98	0.97
1970	236	245	229	1.03	1.07
1971	288	299	269	1.07	1.11
1972	349	348	312	1.12	1.11
1973	395	390	358	1.10	1.09
1974	473	513	463	1.02	1.11
1975	812	751	599	1.36	1.25
1976	1,200	1,020	818	1.47	1.25
1977	1,619	1,301	1,139	1.42	1.15
1978	2,155	1,711	1,585	1.36	1.08
1979	3,294	2,473	2,462	1.33	1.01

Note: The representative or "implicit" price indexes for the public enterprises considered were constructed in the following manner. The industry-specific price indexes reported in Table 7.1 were applied to corresponding series of value-added by public enterprise industry. The alternative time series of undeflated and deflated value-added were then each summed across the six industries considered. The implicit price index was derived as a ratio between a yearly aggregate value-added figure in nominal terms and the corresponding figure for value-added in real terms. That is, the value of the implicit index, P in year t was defined:

Table 7.2 (*cont.*)

$$P_t = \frac{\sum\limits_{i=1}^{6} V_{it}}{\sum\limits_{i=1}^{6} \dfrac{V_{it}}{P_{it}}}$$

i = one of six public enterprise industries; V_{it} = nominal value added by industry i at t; P_{it} = an own-price index number for industry i at t. 1977–9, excludes telecommunications ; 1979, excludes railroads.
Source: Price index for industrial products FGV, column 26, as published in *Conjuntura Econômica*.

tion has been a major problem for economic policy. This was the case during two time periods: 1961–3 and 1976–9. Second, when inflation has not been a major priority for public policy, the public enterprises have enjoyed a greater degree of freedom in setting prices. From 1964 through 1975, for example, relatively greater price-setting freedom resulted in public enterprise prices that either kept pace with or advanced more rapidly than prices elsewhere in the economy. Thus, Brazil has generally allowed public enterprises to capitalize themselves whenever this behavior was not in conflict with overall antiinflation strategy.

While these generalizations must be qualified on a sector-by-sector basis, their validity is supported by Table 7.1. During 1961–3, when inflation averaged 51% a year and led to rising social unrest, the relative prices of public enterprise output fell sharply. Brazil initiated an ultimately successful stabilization program in 1964 and, as inflation became progressively less of a priority for economic policy, the relative prices of public enterprise goods and services at first gained ground, then remained fairly constant through 1969. A succeeding period, from 1970 through 1975, is clearly marked by sharp rises in relative public enterprise prices and the lowest annual inflation rates in the entire two-decade period. Finally, from 1976–9, and probably well into the 1980s as well, inflation gradually reemerged as the fundamental macroeconomic policy concern. Public enterprise prices fell rapidly in relative terms as authorities once again sought to minimize the direct and indirect impact on the general level of price increases for key intermediate products.

Table 7.3. *Brazil's inflation and public enterprise prices*

Period	Inflation (%)[a]	Regime	Public enterprise prices
1960–3	51	Civilian	Decreasing
1964–6	61	Reformist military	Increasing
1967–9	24	Military	Stable
1970–5	21	Military	Increasing
1976–80	52	Military	Decreasing

[a]Average annual increase in general price index (FGV, column 2).

price increases for key intermediate products.

Some of the evidence on general trends in public enterprise prices is assembled below in Table 7.3. Again, care in interpretation is essential, since aggregate public enterprise pricing trends may not hold at the level of individual public enterprise sectors. An impression is that the overall rate of inflation in Brazil has probably been the most important single determinant of changes in relative prices. Populism, here interpreted as holding down public prices to redistribute income and gain votes, may have played a role during the 1960–3 civilian regime, but it was not an important factor under the various military governments thereafter. Even during the beleagured civilian regime, inflation was the principal worry and the main reason why prices for utilities, rails, petrochemical, and (sporadically) steel failed to keep pace with movements in the general price index.[4]

The period of 1964–6 in which public enterprise relative prices did increase despite an average annual inflation rate of 61% would appear to be an exception. This was the period of "corrective inflation" policies, in which policymakers sought to deal with some of the causes of inflation, even at the expense of a short-term rise in prices.[5] The policy of corrective inflation affected primarily the public enterprise utilities and was intended to serve the dual purpose of, first, reducing the need for federal subsidies that had contributed to the budget deficit and, second, laying the basis for the modernization and expansion of basic infrastructure.[6] During this period, the relative prices of output in telecommunications, railways, and electricity increased. On the other hand, steel prices, carefully controlled by government in order to ease pressures on the general price index, were substantially reduced in real terms.

For the succeeding period of 1967–9, prices of most public enterprise products kept pace with industrial prices as inflation slowed to 24% annually. Steel prices were a possible exception; these prices continued to lag behind the general index, but not by as much as in the earlier period.

Brazil's lowest rates of inflation during 1960–80 were recorded during 1970–5, a period also characterized by rapid advances in public enterprise prices. The initial rise in public sector prices in 1970 was caused by rapid increases in utility and steel prices. While petroleum prices, of course, began to rise quickly in 1974–5, relative prices increased through 1970–5 even if we exclude the oil sector (see Table 7.2). Most of the public sector enterprises (steel, railroads, and electricity are examples) were either in the midst of or planning large increases in capacity during the early 1970s. Profits were also generally high during these periods. Thus, the price increases should probably be interpreted as the means by which firms strengthened their financial base in order to carry out their investment projects.

A new era of declining relative prices set in after 1975. The cumulative impact of balance of payments deficits and rising inflationary pressures forced many expansion projects to be cut back and brought stabilization again to the forefront of policy concerns. Policymakers at first attempted to cope with the new "macro" environment by policies of predetermining maximum increases in public enterprise prices. Thus, steel and utility prices came under increasing pressure in 1976. As the crisis deepened and inflation continued to rise, the criticism of public sector prices continued and firms began to surrender some of the price-setting autonomy they had gained during the early 1970s. While prices generally increased by 40%–50% in the four years from 1975 to 1979, steel prices increased only about 38% annually, while electricity and telecommunications tariffs were adjusted only about 30% each year. Only petrochemical prices kept pace with the general

price index, but, obviously, these reflected the need to promote conservation of energy resources. The same pressures to
contain public enterprise prices applied into the early 1980s
as Brazil's underlying rate of inflation continued to rise.

How can these findings on public enterprise prices be related to the information available on their output during the
same period? When the relative prices do increase, are such
movements associated with relatively large increases in output indicating, for example, movement along an upward-sloping
supply curve? Or do such changes reflect the use of market
power so that the output is actually restricted in classical
monopoly fashion? Similarly, when relative prices decrease,
might this indicate increased output along downward-sloping
supply curves (increasing returns to scale)? Or have reduced
relative prices encouraged firms to restrict output in order to
maintain profitability? A simple test based in part on Figure
7.1 may provide some answers.

Assume a public enterprise with potential monopoly power
practices marginal cost pricing and is in short-run and (for
simplicity) long-run equilibrium at P_1 and Q_1 with market size
AR_1. What we observe with the passage of time is an increase
in prices from P_1 to P_2. As one extreme case, the increase in
price may have come about through a shift to monopoly
pricing; output is restricted in classical fashion from Q_1 to
Q_m. As another extreme, let the firm experience an unex-
pectedly large increase in demand, say, from AR_1 to AR_2. If the
firm adheres to a policy of short-run marginal cost pricing
pending an increase in capacity, exactly the same increase in
price as before may occur. However, output will tend to
increase as well. In the short run, the increase in output will
depend upon the slope of the supply curve, but over the long
run the firm will expand capacity to the extent necessary to
match the increase in demand.

A rough test for the presence of either of these extreme
cases is the following. Price increases that are in some sense
"above average" will imply increased use of monopoly power
if these increases are not accompanied by rapid output growth.
If they are, rising prices reflect rising costs or upward-sloping
supply curves, not the use of market power.

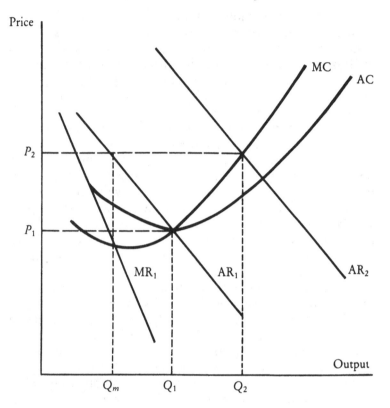

Figure 7.1. Alternative price and output positions.

Increases in output and prices from 1970 to 1975 and from 1976 to 1979 in each of five public enterprise industries were examined according to these criteria. (The mining sector was dismissed as a special case of a competitive industry.) Increases in industrial prices and industrial output in the economy were considered as the norms for the Brazilian case, and ratios were calculated between these norms and observed increases in the public enterprise industries. The results are reproduced in Table 7.4.

In the 1970–5 period, most public enterprises recorded above-average price increases by comparison to industry, but *also* above average output growth. In 1976–9, the pricing

Table 7.4. *Ratios of increases in public enterprise prices and output to industry norms, 1970–9*

	1970–5		1976–9	
	Prices	Output	Prices	Output
Petrochemicals	1.8	1.83	1.15	0.75
Railroads	0.96	1.89	1.04[a]	1.23
Electricity	1.17	1.39	0.79	1.12
Steel	1.72	1.34	0.99	1.15
Telecommunications	1.12	1.43	0.77	1.50

[a] 1976–8 only.
Sources: Public enterprise prices, Table 7.1; Public enterprise output, Tables 5.4 and 6.3. Industrial prices, Table 7.2 (FGV, column 26). Industrial output, *Anuário Estatístico do Brasil*, 1979, p. 828.

experience of the public enterprises much more closely approximated that of industry as a whole, while in the electricity sector, tariffs were readjusted at a slower rate. Nonetheless, each of the public sector enterprises still expanded output at faster rates than did industry as a whole. These findings suggest that the state-owned enterprises have not taken advantage of oligopolistic market structures to raise prices while constricting output. When public enterprises did enjoy price increases relative to industry, output also increased rapidly. This would suggest for 1970–5 rapid output expansion along steeply sloped short-run supply curves. Even when prices in real terms remain constant (or decline, as they did in electricity), output growth has remained strong in the public enterprise sector. This would suggest either constant or decreasing costs (increasing returns to scale) or a willingness by state-enterprise managers to accept a reduction in profitability in order to maintain output growth. In other words, managers have preferred to meet demand at the given price rather than to adjust supply to maintain profits.

How exactly have prices been set in Brazil's state-owned companies? This question is addressed in the following two brief case studies of price-setting procedures.

Cases in public enterprise pricing

Rate making in electricity

The purpose of this case study is to shed light on pricing in Brazilian public enterprise in general, rather than to treat the complex problems of electricity pricing per se. A brief review of the institutional landscape is helpful.[7] As set out in the legislation, government objectives for the electricity companies are the following:

1. To meet the demand for power and to prevent bottlenecks in the energy supply;
2. To earn revenues in excess of costs in order to (a) provide for an investable reserve; (b) reduce the need for capital contributions by government; and (c) attract foreign financing through demonstrated profitability;
3. To avoid excess capacity problems that would burden power rates for industrial users.

The basic legislation describing the procedures for electricity pricing in Brazil, the 1934 Code of Waters, established the right of a public electrical utility to recoup the costs of service, including a rate of return of 10%–12% on invested capital. The firm's accounting costs were defined to include the following:[8]

1. operating and administrative expenses;
2. the rate of return of 10%–12% applied to the indexed value of fixed and working capital;
3. straight-line depreciation ranging from 3% to 5% of year-end gross fixed assets;
4. an additional allowance of 3%–5% of fixed assets to form an amortization fund (the so-called Global Reversion Fund) which would be used to help finance utility expansion; and
5. recuperation of foreign exchange losses on external loans resulting from devaluations of the cruzeiro.

The five elements enumerated above comprise about 80% of the final price of electricity to the residential or industrial consumer, the so-called basic tariff. Two taxes augment the basic tariff: the Sole Tax on electrical energy, which amounts to an additional 15% of the basic tariff; and a mandatory loan assessed on all industrial customers, which amounted to about 11% of the basic tariff in 1979; in return the industrial customers who provide the loan receive ELETROBRÁS bonds bearing 6% per annum after monetary correction that are redeemable in twenty years.

Thus, from their inception the electricity companies in Brazil had a stable legislative basis for pricing and for generating financial resources to support their large-scale investment programs. Through the mid-1970s, the net operating income generated by the basic tariff plus the resources generated by the Sole Tax (on residential and commercial customers) and the compulsory loan (assessed on industrial users of electricity) were generating more than 50% of the electricity sector's very substantial investment requirements.

The dynamic aspects of pricing, especially as affected by investment policy, must also be examined. In electricity supply, pricing is affected by the following dynamic considerations:[9] (1) the required time stream of outputs six to eight years in the future; (2) expected future values of capital and operating costs; (3) the choice of a rate of discount to calculate the present value of fixed costs.

The sophistication of market studies at the large public enterprises to estimate future capacity requirements appears to have improved greatly. Such studies, which are monitored by ELETROBRÁS, attempt to predict future market size on the basis of past relationships between the demand for electricity and such variables as national income, population, industrial production, and projected growth in major industrial consumers of energy.

Nevertheless, market studies are difficult analytical exercises in any context, and especially in a developing country in which structural modifications in the economy affecting energy requirements may occur rapidly. In the face of uncertainty about the size of the market six years in the future, public enterprises in Brazil have a tendency to "play it safe" by deliberate overestimates of capacity requirements.[10]

Many plausible reasons for this built-in bias could be cited, including rivalry between firms for desirable hydro sites, competition for scarce government finance, "showcase" investment strategies, and so on.[11] Underlying these different explanations is the fact that there are few penalties for overbuilding capacity, whereas it is commonly believed in Brazil that electricity rationing – even if temporary – would be in the nature of a national catastrophe. As a result, Brazil, especially since the early 1960s, has enjoyed an abundance of generating power. Although the adequacy of current and planned increments to capacity is difficult for an outsider to evaluate, the country appears to have a relatively secure supply of hydroelectric power until well into the 1990s, even under optimistic assumptions regarding market growth.[12]

Together with the above-mentioned tendency to overestimate the level of future demand, there is a tendency to underestimate capital costs. This is based on the impression that the net cost of capital to the electrical firms is probably less than estimates of the opportunity cost of capital. The sources of capital for the electricity firms are (1) equity contributions and bona fide loans from the government, which are administered by ELETROBRÁS; (2) retained earnings; (3) loans from the BNDE and from international agencies like the World Bank; and (4) foreign private financing. While none of these types of capital is viewed as costless, the overall estimated cost of capital is probably somewhat less than opportunity costs for the following reasons: Retained earnings and equity contributions are discounted at 10%–12%, which is probably too low because the firms are not subject to the same profit tax rates as those applicable to private firms; in addition, no taxes are assessed on profits paid out as dividends to ELETROBRÁS. Loans from ELETROBRÁS, the BNDE, and the official international lending agencies carry interest rates of 3%–10%. Interest rates on foreign eurodollar financing range from 12% to 20%, but firms are able to pass on as legitimate costs any increases in debt due to depreciation of the cruzeiro, thus reducing the risk element.

Tendencies to overestimate market growth and to underestimate the social costs of capital can lead to an overbuilding of capacity. Under a "required revenue" structure such as the one actually used in electricity, the firm with excess capacity is faced with two strategies. First, the firm can maintain the full-cost-of-service principle and raise prices sufficiently to cover the increase in (private) costs resulting from operation of the new facility at less than optimal capacity. However, this solution requires an abrupt increase in rates, which firms are reluctant to adopt. Second, the firm may encourage greater use of existing facilities if it is prepared to accept a lower rate of return on capital. In fact, as Salles and Dutra note, public enterprises faced with excess capacity have frequently elected to follow this second alternative, thus earning rates of return considerably less than the legally permitted 10%–12%.[13]

As for the actual rate setting, the Code of Waters stipulates that electricity firms must apply for revisions in basic tariffs to a regulatory agency, the National Department of Waters and Electrical Energy (DNAEE), a division of the Ministry of Mines and Energy. From the time of the reorganization of the electricity sector in 1964 through 1974, the individual operating companies had considerable leeway in determining tariffs, which could differ by firms and regions. Annual price adjustments through 1974 were fairly automatic after the individual company reported to DNAEE its annual investment base (corrected for prior year price-level changes) and the forecast levels of cost of service and sales volume.[14] Interim surcharges could be added by the company for increases in such costs as interest on external debt because of devaluations of the cruzeiro.

The discretionary powers of DNAEE with regard to rate setting were increased after 1975 as the government sought ways in which to diminish the impact of increases in electricity rates on the overall rate of inflation in the economy. This was the beginning of a period of much more careful central scrutiny of electricity pricing that continued through the late 1970s and was tightened even further with the advent of SEST. This change in rate-setting procedures resulted in a steady decline in electricity prices in real terms after 1975 (see Chapter 8).

Trends in the electricity sector point to several important institutional characteristics of state-enterprise pricing in Brazil. The basic approach to pricing in monopoly or oligopoly markets is highly bureaucratic and formal. Rate making is performed on a "required revenue" or "fair rate of return" system that allows the firm to recoup a broad variety of operational and overhead costs, including a return on invested capital. Importantly, the basic legislation also incorporates additional taxes designed to raise resources for investment. Despite the safeguards built in by the extensive pricing legislation, the political environment does exercise an influence on rate setting. After 1974, in particular, the government did find ways in which to slow down increases in electricity prices in order to further its own antiinflation goals. However, these instances of government intervention in pricing are probably best seen as exceptions rather than the rule in electricity. The government generally views such price-control measures as being of limited usefulness and not worth pursuing to the point of seriously jeopardizing the financial stability of the public electricity sector.

International steel prices: A comparison

How do the prices of products produced by Brazilian state companies compare with prices for similar products in other countries? Steel would seem to be a good case for international comparison: The steel industry in Brazil is dominated by state companies, products are relatively standard across borders, and steel is a key ingredient in the cost structure of many industries. Have Brazilian industrial users of steel been forced to pay high prices for the output of protected, state-run steel companies?

The burden of the limited evidence we have on this point is that steel prices for a whole range of products are, from an international perspective, relatively low in Brazil. In his study of the Brazilian steel industry in the 1960s, Werner Baer already had suggested that Brazilian steel companies were highly competitive internationally.[15] Making proper allowance for exchange rate problems, he found that in 1967 the Volta Redonda plant of CSN could produce most of the major steel products at prices comparable to those then prevailing in U.S.

Table 7.5. *International comparison of prices for steel products (U.S.$/ton, December 1976 prices)*

Product	Brazil	United States	France	West Germany	United Kingdom
Heavy plates	264.30	374.72	325.89	347.13	342.72
Hot rolled sheets	239.44	330.10	287.29	323.19	303.26
Cold rolled sheets (commercial)	316.17	406.68	394.49	423.73	402.24
Cold rolled sheets (EEP)	409.56	419.98	445.95	490.77	456.96
Steel bars	273.37	255.72	258.13	320.79	265.53
Light shapes	311.81	306.44	321.17	343.78	360.00
Machine wire	263.78	338.41	313.61	317.52	349.44
Heavy shapes	290.25	342.82	307.66	314.09	403.02
Carbon steel	381.71	403.42	528.71	581.74	415.87
Chrome steel	392.36	482.79	596.66	629.62	512.64
Molybdenum steel	433.36	519.17	618.32	653.56	526.08
Steel for bearings	462.83	615.07	630.55	593.71	546.43

Source: Brazilian Steel Institute, as reported in L. A. Correo do Lago, et al., *A Indústria Brasileira de Bens de Capital*, p. 348.

mills and, in fact, enjoyed price advantages in the production of rails, heavy plate, and hot-rolled sheets. Additional comparative work led Baer to conclude that, as of the mid-1960s, Brazil's steel prices were probably the lowest among Latin American producers and comparable to the prices then being charged by Belgium, France, and other leading European steel producers.

These results for the 1960s are given extra weight by similar findings for the mid-1970s reported by the Brazilian Steel Institute.[16] Brazilian industrialists often complained about the high prices of locally produced steel, but an international comparison of prices for twelve major steel products in December 1976, revealed that Brazil was the least cost producer in ten of the twelve product lines, and highly competitive in one other (see Table 7.5). Again, exchange rate problems and steel price controls in Brazil may be distorting the picture somewhat, but the differences between prices charged in Brazil and those in the United States and Europe (Japan, unfortunately, was not included) are quite large for most products. Brazilian producers have reaped the benefits of low wage costs and, especially, modern steel-making technologies. In sum, it seems likely that the Brazilian state steel companies are capable of competing in international trade and that Brazilian industry has benefited from relatively low prices for steel.[17]

Conclusions

Setting prices in monopolistic or oligopolistic state-owned companies requires that a delicate balance be struck between many competing objectives. The companies should at least be given sufficient leeway on pricing to break even on current operations. Otherwise, the government will have to prop up its companies with budget subsidies. By the same token, the state companies should probably be allowed some surplus to help finance their investment programs. But raising public sector prices also puts pressure on the price index, a sensitive political issue, and can squeeze profits of downstream industrial users of state-company products.

Brazilian policymakers have had to juggle these types of conflicting objectives. As a general trend, public enterprise prices in Brazil have not been tightly controlled by the government or held down in order to subsidize users. Increases in public enterprise prices since 1964 have generally led or approximately kept pace with increases in prices elsewhere in the economy. At times, as in the late 1970s, the government has interfered with rate making, but not to the point of destabilizing state-enterprise finances. Throughout the period under examination, the government has been concerned to provide a stable planning environment for most state firms with emphasis on "realistic" or full-cost pricing in monopoly or oligopoly markets. Brazil has generally kept in mind the need for public enterprises to generate at least some savings from current operations. This was confirmed by previous findings (see Chapter 6) on the profitability of state enterprise in Brazil. This policy has generally paid off by encouraging steady expansions in public enterprise output while reducing the need for direct public subsidy of public enterprise operations.

The Brazilians have generally followed a technocratic, businesslike approach to management of its core public enterprises and this approach is reflected in the pricing of state-enterprise output. The approach can be contrasted with the apparently greater emphasis of the Mexican government on maintaining low prices for a wide range of intermediate goods (chemicals, steel, fertilizer) even if this approach results in large state-enterprise deficits.[18] In both Brazil and Mexico, it could be argued that the large public enterprises exist principally to benefit the large industrial users of their output and therefore, to promote faster industrial growth. But the Brazilian approach has resulted, over the last few decades, at least, in a faster pace of industrial growth at a lower social cost in terms of direct public subsidy to the state enterprises. Similarly, the Brazilian approach to public enterprise pricing should also be contrasted to the experience in Latin American countries in which populism has been a factor.[19] Argentina in 1973–5 and Peru in the early 1970s are just two examples of instances in which public enterprise prices were repressed as an active ingredient in the government's industrialization and income-distribution strategies.

On balance, then, Brazil's public enterprise pricing strategies have been just that – balanced. Occasional squeezes of public enterprise prices usually give way to readjustments in tariffs to allow firms to recover losses and to build investment reserves. The most recent example of a squeeze – the 1979–80 period – indeed did give way to large readjustments of public enterprise prices in the early 1980s. At the same time, and based on the results for the steel industry, at least, industrial users of state-company products have benefited from relatively low prices.

But for the state enterprises, the proof of the pudding in regard to the adequacy of price increases has always been their ability to finance ambitious investment plans, at least to some extent, out of internally generated funds. The issue of investment finance in state companies is the topic of Chapter 8.

8

The financing of public enterprise investment

From the mid-1960s through the early 1980s Brazil's state-owned enterprises carried out an enormous program of capital formation. In retrospect, the mobilization of savings that this entailed was a remarkable achievement in the context of a developing economy with thin domestic capital markets. Further, the financing of public enterprise investment in Brazil affected in important ways the behavior and relative autonomy of public enterprise managers and the overall performance of the Brazilian economy.

The sources of public enterprise finance in Brazil

The potential sources of finance for Brazilian public enterprise may be classified as either internal or external according to whether financing arises from cash flows under the direct control of state-enterprise managers or of agents outside the enterprise, including the government. Internal sources include retained earnings, depreciation funds, and proceeds from the sale of assets. *Receita vinculada* (earmarked tax revenues) resulting from a tax on the ordinary selling price may be considered "quasi-internal." The tax is imposed by the government and proceeds are, theoretically, at the disposition of government. But in most sectors where such earmarked taxes are important – telecommunications, petroleum, and electric power, among others – a large part of the proceeds may be considered as an increment to retained earnings since such funds support public enterprise investment and are exempt from ordinary budget review.

External sources of finance include state equity injections, equity raised directly from the public, and long-term borrowing from foreign and domestic credit institutions, both public and private. Several of these outside sources require brief comment. State equity injections are provided at irregular intervals depending upon the needs and self-finance potential of the firms. Such capital contributions have traditionally been provided directly by the treasury and have not carried any minimum dividend obligations. In recent years the growth of holding companies, such as ELETROBRÁS, has led to an increasing allocation of government equity investment through these new institutions.

Most Brazilian government enterprises are technically "mixed" rather than "public" enterprises. This means only that some degree of private equity ownership is permitted. Private risk capital frequently amounts to no more than 10%–15% of total subscribed (voting and nonvoting) capital. In recent years, the mixed-enterprise model has also been extended to include joint ventures between state enterprise and multinational foreign enterprise. In such cases, privately held equity accounts for a larger, albeit still noncontrolling, share of total capital.

Brazilian public enterprises have experienced success in raising funds through large loans and bond issues in eurocurrency markets. In fact, the state-owned enterprises have been among the most important borrowers in the world in these private foreign markets. It will be important to examine these sources of external capital, because they signify financing ordinarily not available to private Brazilian firms.

Other sources of long-term credit include public international lending institutions such as the World Bank and the Inter-American Development Bank, and the government-owned BNDE. Interest rate and repayment terms associated with such credits have varied from soft to ordinary commercial. The World Bank and allied institutions have been the main sources of such credits, which are usually provided in the form of project financing for public enterprises in sectors such as power, steel, and transportation. Brazil has been among the most important borrowers from the official multilateral lending institutions.

The significance of public enterprise financing in the Brazilian case can be determined by an empirical examination of three major issues: the degree to which public enterprises finance themselves in Brazil, the importance of direct public subsidies, and the role played by private capital markets in the provision of finance. Each of these issues is considered briefly in the next sections.

The degree of self-finance

The preference of state-enterprise managers for as high a degree of self-finance as possible is explained by the thinness of domestic capital markets, the financial costs involved in large-scale borrowing, and the desire to increase autonomy by reducing dependence on government budget allocations as a source of investment finance. Furthermore, and as was seen in the case of electricity in Brazil, governments may actively encourage increases in the proportion of investment financed internally by public enterprises. Increases in the level of national savings are more easily attained through monopoly pricing or investment taxation in the public enterprise sector than through an increase in general government revenues through tax reforms. Self-finance also removes a potentially heavy drain on government budgetary resources. Finally, a policy of a self-financing state-enterprise sector lessens the degree of head-on competition between public and private enterprises in domestic markets for loanable funds.

The costs involved in a strategy of public enterprise self-finance must also be recognized. These include ordinary allocative losses caused by departures from efficient pricing guidelines and also X-efficiency losses since, in effect, a self-finance policy means that the incomes of public firms will be raised regardless of efficiency levels in the state enterprise.[1] This point alludes to the danger that not all of the proceeds of the monopoly tax will be channeled back into productive capital spending. Another cost of a strategy of self-finance is that self-financing eliminates important control strings between the government and the public enterprise. Public enterprises are freer to determine their own diversification policies without direction from above and the government is deprived of the ability to redeploy the retained earnings of the public enterprise in other projects that may involve a higher social rate of return than those selected by the self-financing public firm.

Public provision of financing

Two additional issues surface in the event that the public enterprise cannot or should not be self-financed because of the economic or political costs of such a strategy. One of these is the role of public finance. Should any portion of the financing burden be assumed by the treasury? If so, what are the consequences for the distribution of public income? A general tax-based system of public enterprise financing implies that the community at large is being tapped in order to provide private goods for user industries, and such a system might be inequitable. The efficiency implications of the tax system in effect would also have to be considered a cost of the state's involvement in financing its enterprises.

Another cost of public provision of funds by equity transfer or by preferential tax treatment is that, since such funds are not specifically priced, the public enterprise may be given little guidance on what is an acceptable social use of the public's money. Gillis et al. note:

Even though equity investments normally should command an even higher required rate of return (than credit transfers), they are often treated by (public enterprises) as free resources with no explicit cost because the payment of dividends is typically not required to induce further government equity into the public enterprises. Hence, equity investment may often become a "back-door" subsidy that is seldom subjected to public scrutiny. Such hidden subsidies may lead to the use of public sector capital in undesired or inefficient activities.[2]

Thus, if not properly priced, the public provision of funds, in theory a means of controlling public enterprise behavior, can instead underwrite poor performance.

Borrowing from commercial banks

Some of the most important questions regarding public enterprise financing patterns concern the degree to which such firms should engage in commercial borrowing. Public enterprises unquestionably enjoy one major advantage over private firms with regard to access to ordinary commercial markets: Explicitly or implicitly such borrowing carries with it the full faith and credit of a sovereign government. The consequences of this identification with the government are important. First, state enterprises may take advantage of the fact that they command preferential access to commercial bank credit by "overborrowing," that is, by exceeding normally accepted debt–equity ratios. By the same token, lenders may be more lenient in reaching credit decisions involving a public enterprise borrower than when examining a credit for a private firm because of the belief that, somehow, the loan will be made good by the government should the public enterprise encounter difficulties.

Second, this preferential access to capital by the public firm can limit the supply of loanable funds available to the private sector. Third, borrowings by public enterprises in domestic capital markets are likely to be of such magnitude as to pressure interest rates upward and, thus, crowd out private borrowers even in the absence of lender discrimination in favor of the public firm. Fourth, dependence on commercial borrowing has important behavorial consequences for the public firm. It increases pressures on state-enterprise managers to service debt obligations in a timely fashion, that is, to adopt a more narrow commercial view of their responsibilities in order to safeguard corporate prestige and creditworthiness.

Finally, special consequences arise when public enterprises borrow from foreign commercial banks or in foreign currency markets. Borrowing in the eurocurrency markets has become the most important source of financing for many large Brazilian firms, again in part because such borrowing carries the full faith and credit of the Brazilian government. This type of borrowing has several identifiable costs. External borrowing may result in loss of control by the government if the large public enterprises are able to borrow on their own to finance investment without direct government supervision. At the same time, such borrowing can contribute to rapid growth in the country's external debt and growing strains on the foreign exchange reserves.

However, prohibitions on external borrowing by the public enterprises may not be feasible. External borrowing by public firms does mean that there is less pressure on domestic money markets, less impact on domestic rates of interest, and less crowding out of private borrowers. Further, foreign borrowing by public enterprises is often a convenient means of balance of payments financing, especially since foreign commercial banks look much less closely than do official institutions at the exact project to be supported. The borrowing results in an inflow of foreign exchange to the Central Bank, and some of this can be used to finance the balance of payments, since not all of the proceeds of the loan are needed for imports by the public enterprise that raised the money in the external market.

In the rest of this chapter, the pattern of public enterprise finance in Brazil will be examined from three angles: ability to self-finance, access to public provision of funds, and borrowing from commercial markets.

The extent of self-finance

The ability of Brazilian public enterprises to finance their own investment out of internally generated funds was strong through the mid-1970s (see Table 8.1). For example, from 1966 to 1975, the large public enterprises were able to finance from 40% to 60% of gross investment outlays using retained earnings and depreciation funds. A better picture of self-financing capability is gained by excluding the railroads, which have not generated any surplus in Brazil. In this case, the self-financing performance of the remaining public enterprise sectors through the mid-1970s appears even stronger, ranging from 81% in 1966 to 46% in 1975. Focusing on 1973–4, the average degree of self-finance in the public enterprises was approximately 45%, which compares with a figure of approximately 50%–60% for Brazilian private firms during the same period.[3] The self-financing level of the public

Table 8.1. *Investment and surplus (profits and depreciation allowances) for public enterprises, 1966–80 (current Cr$ 000)*

	Total investment (*I*)	Surplus (*S*)	Residual (*I-S*)	Self-finance ratio (*S/I*)	Self-finance ratio, excluding railroads, %
1966	1,026,395	616,083	410,312	60	81
1967	2,040,069	954,412	1,087,657	47	56
1968	3,044,573	1,382,662	1,661,911	45	51
1969	3,566,512	1,923,310	1,643,202	54	63
1970	6,317,567	3,489,137	2,828,430	55	63
1971	10,134,055	5,219,835	4,914,220	52	59
1972	14,065,013	6,395,576	7,666,437	45	53
1973	20,833,411	9,230,277	11,603,134	44	50
1974	31,953,318	14,712,189	17,241,129	46	54
1975	52,674,045	20,697,205	31,976,840	39	46
1976	92,811,000	27,512,900	65,298,100	30	35
1977	130,963,100	45,294,400	85,668,700	35	39
1978	178,911,400	59,974,100	118,937,300	34	37
1979	272,264,500	83,483,600	188,785,900	31	34
1980[a]	557,700,000	140,200,000	531,900,000	25	

[a]Not directly comparable to earlier years. Secretariat of Planning has provided this estimate of self-financing for large, federally owned companies in 1980. The definition of surplus did not include depreciation funds. Thus, the actual degree of self-financing reported is underestimated by comparison to the rest of the table. See: Secretaria de Planejamento-Secretaria de Contrôle de Empresas Estatais, *Empresas Estatais no Brasil e o Contrôle da SEST: Antecedentes e Experiência de 1980.* (Brasilia, 1981), p. 72.
Sources: Total investment and surplus (profits plus depreciation allowances) are from profit–loss statements and flow of funds statements of public firms in mining, steel, petrochemicals, electricity, telecommunications, and railroads. See Appendix B for explanation.

Table 8.2. *Internal financing as a percentage of gross investment (profits plus depreciation allowances as % of total direct investment)*

	1967–9	1970–1	1972–3	1974–5	1978–9
Steel	72	100	49	24	17
Petrochemicals	69	86	92	88	54
Mining	100	73	63	95	57
Electricity	49	37	28	29	30
Telecommunications	36	47	63	44	38

Note: Internal financing is defined as in Table 8.1. Railroad investment is assumed to be financed entirely with external funds.
Source: Income statements and flow-of-funds statements of firms as listed in Appendix A.

firms through the mid-1970s contrasts very sharply, however, with the results of a broad survey by Gantt and Dutto of public enterprise financing patterns during the 1960s.[4] This survey has suggested that few public enterprise sectors in the world earned enough surplus even to replace capital used up during production, much less to help finance new investment.

While the overall performance of Brazilian public enterprise may be satisfactory in comparative perspective, it began to weaken markedly after the early 1970s, leading to increased outside financing of public enterprise investment. For example, internal resources were sufficient to finance more than 60% of total investment in public enterprises other than railroads in 1970 (see the last column of Table 8.1). This figure declined steadily to just over 30% by 1979. Using a much larger sample of public firms than the one used in this study, the Secretariat of Planning estimated internal financing for Brazilian public companies at just 25% in 1980.[5] Two factors help to explain this declining self-finance performance: the significant increase in the level of real investment after 1970 and the more restrictive pricing environment for public firms after 1975.

Although significant variation occurs among public enterprise sectors in regard to their degree of self-financing, each of the public enterprise sectors considered here illustrates the trend toward a decreasing level of self-financing capability during the 1970s (see Table 8.2). The petrochemical firms (principally, PETROBRÁS) and the CVRD group were able at times to finance up to 100% of investment needs out of internal cash flow through the mid-1970s. During the late 1970s, however, both groups of firms were obliged to resort more heavily to outside financing.

Apart from the railroads, which are completely dependent on outside financing, the other public enterprise groups have financed some proportion of investment internally. Again, performance was better in the period through the mid-1970s. The degree of internal financing slipped in the steel sector from almost 50% in 1972–3 to 17% in 1978–9. This reflects the operation of both factors mentioned above: a large-scale expansion of steelmaking capacity after 1972 and a reduced ability by steel companies to adjust prices in line with inflation (see Chapter 7). Because energy investment takes the lion's share of total public enterprise capital spending, self-financing in public electricity firms deserves examination. This declined from almost 50% in the 1960s to 30% throughout most of the 1970s. Not surprisingly, ELETROBRÁS has been a principal absorber of public and foreign resources in order to close the widening gap between savings and investment.

Despite a generally favorable self-financing performance during most of the period under consideration, the public enterprises required large and increasing amounts of external resources to finance their investments. While hidden by a lack of official data on public enterprises until the early 1980s, this overall public enterprise deficit became a focal point of heightened inflationary pressures in Brazil during the late 1970s. The magnitude of the demand for external financing is seen best as a percentage of GDP. The current surplus (broadly defined) generated by public enterprises expanded from a little more than 1% to more than 2% of GDP by 1975 (see Table 8.3). This surplus then declined sharply to 1.4% of GDP by 1979. Over the same period, public enterprise investment surged from about 3% of GDP in the late 1960s to almost 6% by 1976 and 5% by the late 1970s.[6] Thus, the overall deficit generated by the public enterprise sector in Brazil has increased from about 1.5% of GDP in the late 1960s to 3%–4% of GDP by the late 1970s.

Table 8.3. *Overall public enterprise deficit: Brazil, 1966–80,
as a percentage of GDP*

	Current surplus	Investment	Deficit
1966	1.2	1.9	−0.7
1967	1.3	2.9	−1.6
1968	1.4	3.1	−1.7
1969	1.5	2.7	−1.2
1970	1.7	3.1	−1.4
1971	1.9	3.7	−1.8
1972	1.8	4.0	−2.2
1973	2.0	4.4	−2.4
1974	2.0	4.4	−2.4
1975	2.1	5.2	−3.1
1976	1.8	5.9	−4.1
1977	2.0	5.6	−3.6
1978	1.7	5.1	−3.4
1979	1.4	4.7	−3.3
1980	0.8[a]	3.8[a]	−3.0[a]

[a]Not directly comparable to rest of time series. *Source*: SEST, *Empresas Estatais no Brasil*, p. 72.
Source: Table 8.1.

While official data are lacking, the trend in the overall public enterprise sector suggested by the data in Table 8.3 is an extremely important explanation of the reasons why the Brazilian government after 1979 went to great lengths to exercise greater control over public enterprise investment budgets. After 1980, the government – through SEST – went a step further by liberalizing price controls "to allow the companies to utilize a greater share of their own resources in the carrying out of their activities...by means of a price and fee policy which is more adequate to the companies' cost structure."[7] Despite measures to reduce public enterprise investment in 1980, the surplus generated by the public enterprises also declined and the overall deficit remained at 3% of GDP (see, again, Table 8.3).

Data are not available on the size of the consolidated public sector deficit in Brazil, but this deficit was large, perhaps as large as 8%–10% of GDP in the late 1970s, and was the chief factor in the expansion of aggregate demand in the economy. Thus, the public enterprises probably accounted for about one-third to one-half of the total public sector deficit via large requirements for the financing of investment programs. The size of this deficit, and the consequent pressures both on internal prices and the balance of payments, caused the government to redouble its efforts to reduce the autonomy of public enterprises by controlling their budgets. These points are more clearly perceived after considering the ways in which Brazilian public enterprises arranged external financing.

External sources of public enterprise finance

The sources of investment finance for Brazilian public enterprise in 1976–9 are shown in Table 8.4. The results for 1978 are useful for purposes of illustration. On a weighted average basis, the public enterprises financed 33.5% of investment out of internal sources, approximately 20.3% out of resources provided directly or indirectly from the National Treasury, and 46.2% via increases in long-term indebtedness.

Public resources provided to the public enterprises are predominantly of two types: equity infusions by the National Treasury and the proceeds of special earmarked taxes. While some sectors, such as steel, receive most of their public subsidies in the form of straight capital contributions, the earmarked taxes are more important in sectors such as petrochemicals and electricity. But the main point holds: the largest and most important state companies in Brazil – those with the most ambitious programs of capital formation – depend relatively little on treasury subsidies to finance investment. Treasury subsidies are large, but those in Brazil go overwhelmingly to the smaller, less well-organized firms in the public enterprise sector.

Data recently made available for 1980 by SEST permit additional insight into this key point regarding public enterprise finance.[8] Official estimates of treasury resources provided to the large state-enterprise group show such resources to be

Table 8.4. *Sources of finance in public enterprises, 1976–9,*
as a percentage of total investment

	1976	1977	1978	1979
Operating Income				
Steel	10.6	36.6	17.0	17.0
Petrochemicals	63.2	57.3	55.9	50.9
CVRD	36.9	58.4	49.5	64.6
Telecommunications	32.1	32.1	48.2	27.1
Railroads	0.0	0.0	0.0	0.0
Electricity	27.0	27.4	28.6	30.3
Public Resources				
Steel	35.9	28.3	31.6	31.6
Petrochemicals	15.3	10.5	13.8	8.8
CVRD	5.0	1.9	1.9	1.2
Telecommunications	38.3	38.3	30.0	42.5
Railroads	10.0[a]	10.0[a]	5.0	13.0
Electricity	32.7	24.7	23.0	27.1
Long-Term Borrowing				
Steel	55.2	35.1	51.4	51.4
Petrochemicals	21.5	32.2	30.3	40.3
CVRD	58.1	39.7	48.6	34.2
Telecommunications	29.6	29.6	21.8	30.4
Railroads	90.0[a]	90.0[a]	95.0	87.0
Electricity	40.3	47.9	48.4	42.6

[a]Estimate.
Source: Annual reports of companies listed in Appendix A. See Appendix B
for explanation.

relatively small as a percentage of total investment spending
in these companies, despite the fact that the large firms accounted for 75% of total investment by state firms. For example, treasury resources provided to the consolidated
PETROBRÁS group in 1980 amounted to just 2% of the
group's investment. No treasury resources were provided to
the CVRD group, nor to the Itaipu Binational Entity, the
joint Brazilian–Paraguayan venture that is developing the Itaipu
hydroelectric project. The treasury funds channeled to the

other large groups range from 13% of investment for ELE-
TROBRÁS and SIDERBRÁS to 28% for TELEBRÁS.

The implication is that treasury subsidies in 1980 went
predominantly to the railroads and to hundreds of smaller
federal enterprises. These smaller companies (e.g., PORTO-
BRÁS, the DNER) accounted for Cr$165 billion in invest-
ment spending in 1980, about 25% of the federal company
total, but received almost Cr$300 billion in subsidies from
the treasury.

Public enterprises in Brazil have also accessed domestic
capital markets for equity capital, but since the proportion of
private ownership in most of the large public enterprises is
typically very small, this source of financing has not been
very important. For example, during the mid-1970s, equity
sold in domestic capital markets provided a mere 2% of outside financial requirements of the large public enterprises.

The bulk of the external financial resources supplied to the
public enterprises are provided by borrowing. Long-term debt,
including bona fide loans from the government-owned National Economic Development Bank (BNDE) have consistently
accounted for 40%–50% of investment requirements. Most
loans have been provided by external multilateral lenders
(especially the World Bank) and international commercial
banks. (The significance of this form of financing is examined
in greater detail later in this chapter.)

Long-term trends in financing

What are some of the longer-term trends in the financing of
Brazilian public enterprise? The earliest evidence available on
this issue was provided by Villela, who reported a degree of
self-financing in the large public enterprises of almost 82%
during the 1956–60 period.[9]

In view of later trends, the degree of self-finance in this
relatively early era of public enterprise in Brazil was high.
The same study estimated that direct government subsidy
accounted for an additional 10% of investment needs in
1956–60, with the remaining 8% supplied by foreign lenders
and the BNDE.[10] If public enterprises had not been expanding

in the 1956–60 period, high rates of internal financing would have been expected, but in fact, rapid growth occurred in petrochemicals, steel, and railroads.

Later experience shows that while this very high level of self-finance had declined by the late 1960s, it remained relatively high through Brazil's boom period of 1973–4. At the same time, and while the situation varied significantly from sector to sector, the large public enterprises rarely depended upon the National Treasury or the proceeds of earmarked taxes for investment subsidies that exceeded 20% of requirements. The gap left by a diminishing ability to finance their investment out of internal funds and a relatively constant level of direct public funding was filled by borrowing on straight commercial terms from domestic and foreign lenders. This trend accelerated in the late 1970s as the level of total public enterprise investment grew to an all-time high, and government price controls (and other industry-specific factors) limited the self-financing capabilities of many firms. The impact of this increasing resort to indebtedness showed up in increasing interest expenditures and generally high and increasing debt–equity ratios. The deterioration in balance sheets was most apparent in the electricity sector, which also accounted for the highest levels of investment spending in the 1970s. The ratio of long-term debt to equity in electricity firms more than doubled from 1976 through 1979. A consistently high degree of borrowing in the steel sector also resulted in relatively high levels of indebtedness. Before considering the sources and implications of this borrowing, the pattern of public enterprise finance should be compared with that of the Brazilian private sector.

A comparison with the private sector

The financing patterns of major industries controlled by private firms in Brazil are compared to the typical public enterprise pattern for the period of the mid-1970s in Table 8.5. Both public and private firms in Brazil could count on internally generated surplus to provide from 50% to 60% of investment requirements in the mid-1970s. Major financing

Table 8.5. *Comparative financing patterns in public and private enterprise, 1973–5, as a percentage of total investment financed through each source*

	Public enterprise	Machine goods	Electrical materials	Transport materials	Plastic products
Internal surplus	50.5	56.0	64.5	54.0	59.5
Subsidy[a]	22.5	—	—	—	—
Fiscal incentives	—	1.5	1.5	1.5	1.0
Private sector equity	1.8	5.0	14.5	7.5	5.5
Loans, domestic	8.3	21.5	13.5	13.5	30.0
Loans, foreign	16.9	13.5	6.0	23.0	4.0
Other	—	2.5	—	0.5	—
Total	100	100	100	100	100

[a]Includes public capital contributions and proceeds of earmarked taxes.

Sources: Public enterprise financing for 1974–5, Table 8.4. Financing in private industries for 1973–4, *Conjuntura Econômica* 29 (October 1975):70.

advantages of the public enterprise sector included access to government equity contributions and the proceeds of government-imposed earmarked taxes. Other advantages accrued from administered pricing and comparatively low levels of taxation on profits. Private enterprises were able to benefit from tax-reducing fiscal incentive schemes, but these funds provided a relatively small proportion of investment needs, at least in the years considered (see Table 8.5). Private firms benefited from privileged access to loans from the BNDE and this could have accounted for the relatively larger volume of domestic long-term lending contracted by the private firms in comparison to their public counterparts.

Another contrast is that, with the exception of the foreign-dominated automobile industry, the industries controlled by private enterprise did relatively little borrowing abroad in the mid-1970s, whereas public enterprise debt was contracted primarily in foreign capital markets. Finally, private industries relied relatively more on private sector equity subscriptions as a source of finance.

Apart from public enterprise access to subsidized finance, the comparison with the private sector reveals that a principal difference in financing patterns lies in the institutional sources of long-term lending. In particular, two such sources may be identified: the state-owned National Economic Development Bank (BNDE) and foreign financial institutions. Each of these is a potential arena for competition between public and private enterprises in the demand for finance.[11]

Sources of long-term lending

BNDE. The Brazilian government, through its ownership of the National Economic Development Bank, is the most important institutional source of long-term financing in the economy. It has deliberately chosen to use its power to discriminate among borrowers to favor private domestic enterprises and to prohibit or discourage large-scale borrowing by public firms.

This represents a significant shift in government economic policy. In the 1950s, the bank's charter restricted its lending activities to infrastructural areas of the economy; thus public enterprises absorbed annually an average of 80% of available credits.[12] In 1965, however, the charter was revised and by 1975 all public enterprises together (not just those selected for the present study) received only 22% of the loans granted by the BNDE; thus, fully 78% of the new lending was directed to private firms. In the ten years through 1975, the BNDE committed important amounts of financing to public enterprises in only two sectors: steel and railroads.[13] This policy of directing credits preferentially to the private sector continued through the early 1980s.

Foreign borrowing. External borrowing represented the most important source of public enterprise investment finance in the 1970s. This borrowing took two predominant forms: traditional project financing, via credits from the World Bank and other multilateral lenders and borrowing from international commercial banks. The latter came to be the most important.

This type of public enterprise finance should be seen in the overall context of Brazil's external debt management policies in the 1960s and 1970s. Brazil during this period became the most important of the developing countries as a borrower in private international capital markets. For example, at the end of 1979 international commercial banks reported a gross exposure to all non-OPEC LDCs of U.S. $157.1 billion. Of this amount, loans to Brazil represented almost U.S. $40 billion, that is, more than 25%.[14]

Commercial lending to developing countries expanded rapidly after the 1960s for several reasons. These are, first, the invention of the eurodollar rollover credit and, second, the increasing popularity of non-project-related financing.[15] The key feature of the eurodollar credit was the periodic adjustment of the rate of interest attached to the loan in line with fluctuations in short-term rates of interest. Being able to protect themselves against unforeseen fluctuations in interest rates made banks more willing to break out of the more traditional import and export financing and to lend longer-term funds to developing countries such as Brazil.

Prior to the late 1960s, most medium-term commercial bank lending (i.e., credits with an original maturity of more than one year) took the form of project lending whereby loan disbursement and repayment was "tied" to the development of a specific investment project. This type of lending, typical of most World Bank loans, proved cumbersome to commercial banks. Untied lending, often involving many banks in a single large "syndicated" credit, came to replace project lending in the late 1960s and 1970s. This allowed countries such as Brazil to raise large amounts of medium-term funds in relatively short periods of time with a minimum of paperwork. More importantly from the point of view of the borrower, these funds could be allocated flexibly according to specific foreign exchange requirements rather than used exclusively for imports for a particular project. Thus, developing countries worldwide came increasingly to use eurodollar financing for general balance of payments financing, even though many such credits ostensibly were arranged on behalf of a particular project.

The commercial banks engaged in this type of "balance of payments" finance (as opposed to strict project financing) accepted a sovereign risk, that is, they now had to look at the country's general international reserve position and future balance of payments prospect as sources of repayment. The feasibility and profitability of a particular development project ceased to be a major concern for the banks. The stage was then set for a rapid expansion of borrowing by Brazilian borrowers, including public enterprises, during the 1970s. "The floating rate" concept for determining interest charges, the popularity of "untied" credits, and after 1973, the availability of large OPEC deposits for recycling increased greatly the ability of banks to engage in general balance of payments financing precisely at a time at which Brazil would be developing large needs for external financing.

Developments affecting the public enterprises and their borrowing requirements mirror changes that were occurring in the Brazilian economy. The first round of OPEC oil-price hikes in 1973–4 gradually forced policymakers to alter the strategy that had led to the economic expansion in Brazil from 1968 through 1973. Brazil's adjustment was slow and incomplete, as policymakers in the Geisel government (which took office in early 1974) were reluctant to depart radically from an economic model which until that time had been considered highly successful. The main lines of economic policy involved the squeezing of non-oil imports, subsidizing exports, and financing large and growing balance of payments current account deficits by borrowing abroad, especially via untied eurodollar loans from commercial banks.

While considerable lip service was paid by the Geisel government to the need to restrain domestic economic growth as a consequence of the worsening in the terms of trade, no sustained efforts were made to restrain the spending of the public sector. In fact, almost every public enterprise sector still had major expansion programs well underway or in the advanced planning stage as late as 1976. Several of the public enterprise sectors (steel and petrochemicals, for example) were to play leading roles in the "second wave of import substitution" proclaimed in the Second National Development Plan unveiled by the Geisel administration in 1975. At the same time, the nation's energy needs strongly dictated a step-up in spending by such companies as ELETROBRÁS, NUCLEBRÁS, and PETROBRÁS.

Thus, from the angle of the public enterprises considered in this study, the period after 1973–4 was one of unprecedented expansion. Investment by these companies in terms of percent of GDP rose from 3% in 1970 and 4% in 1972 to almost 6% in 1976. While this surge was, of course, only one of the factors behind the rise in aggregate demand after 1973–4, it does help to explain some of the stimulus behind the strong 7% rates of growth recorded by the economy in 1974–80.

Yet the strong growth performance brought problems for Brazil (see also Chapter 5) and, by extension, for the public enterprises. In the absence of effective macroeconomic policy constraints on aggregate demand, inflationary pressures grew from about 30% per annum in the early 1970s to more than 100% by the early 1980s. Stronger growth brought with it increased dependence on imported oil. In spite of high gasoline prices, petroleum imports increased by more than 30%

between 1974 and 1980. Most critically, the lack of effective adjustment policies in Brazil led to a widening of the deficits in the current account of the balance of payments and, consequently, increased vulnerability to OPEC price increases and dependence on commercial bank financing. Current account deficits, which had averaged about U.S. $6 billion annually in 1973–7, increased steadily to almost U.S. $13 billion in 1980. Brazil's medium-term external debt increased from about U.S. $12 billion in 1973 to almost U.S. $54 billion in 1980, with almost all of the increment provided by borrowing from international commercial banks (see Table 8.6).

The need to finance the current account deficit and to make repayment on maturing external debt drained Brazil's international reserves and boosted the economy's gross borrowing requirements sharply. Through the late 1970s and early 1980s, total borrowing needs grew from about U.S. $6–$8 billion annually to almost U.S. $20 billion (see Table 8.6).

With an increased need for investment financing, many of the state firms became active and well-known borrowers in the euromarkets in the 1970s. The government made increasing attempts to control such borrowing but was caught in a dilemma, because although, on the one hand, these types of state-enterprise foreign borrowings did permit the firms to carry on large investment programs, on the other, the unrestricted nature of the medium-term euromarket credits permitted the government to use the resulting foreign exchange for general balance of payments purposes. Thus, control over public enterprise borrowing by the Central Bank and, later, by SEST, was primarily a means of organizing Brazil's external borrowing program – for example, by preventing the presence of more than one Brazilian borrower in the market at any one time and ensuring that all borrowings were arranged on the best possible terms with regard to interest rates and lengths of maturity.

While an important share of net public enterprise external financing continued to be provided by the World Bank and other multilateral lenders, the international commercial banks provided the bulk of external financial requirements. For those public enterprises considered in this study, total medium-term

Table 8.6. *Brazil: Major balance of payments trends, 1974–80 (U.S.$ million)*

	Exports	Imports	Balance of trade	Balance on current account	Net capital inflows[a]	Balance of payments	Gross borrowing requirement[b]
1974	7,951	12,641	−4,690	−7,122	6,254	−936	7,757
1975	8,670	12,210	−3,540	−6,700	6,189	−950	7,508
1976	10,128	12,283	−2,225	−6,017	6,594	1,192	6,947
1977	12,120	12,023	97	−4,037	5,278	630	8,138
1978	12,659	13,683	−1,024	−6,990	11,891	4,262	11,161
1979	15,244	18,084	−2,840	−10,742	7,657	−3,215	17,797
1980[c]	20,132	22,961	−2,829	−12,180	9,380	−2,800	19,480

[a]Includes net errors and omissions.
[b]Gross borrowing requirements are defined as the sum of the current account deficit and principal repayments on medium-term external debt.
[c]Preliminary figures for 1980.
Source: Boletim do Banco Central do Brasil, various issues.

Table 8.7. *Brazil: public and private external debt:*
1974–80 (U.S.$ million)

	Total external debt	Public sector debt[a]	Of which public companies[b]	Private sector debt	Debt service ratio (%)[c]
1974	17,166	9,250	n.a.	7,916	n.a.
1975	21,171	11,461	n.a.	9,710	n.a.
1976	25,985	14,852	5,962	11,133	n.a.
1977	32,037	14,309	6,416	12,728	48.5
1978	43,511	27,556	9,071	15,955	60.5
1979	49,904	34,035	11,376	15,869	66.5
1980	53,847	37,270	n.a.	16,577	61.3

[a]Direct plus indirect, includes debt of state companies without federal guarantee.
[b]Medium-term debt of the large public enterprises considered in this study.
[c]Interest and principal on external debt as percentage of exports of goods and services.
Source: Banco Central do Brasil and Table 8.6.

external debt increased from about U.S. $6 billion in 1976 to U.S. $11.4 billion by the end of 1979 (see Table 8.7). In 1979, this level of indebtedness represented almost 23% of Brazil's total medium-term external debt and one-third of the total debt of the public sector. Short-term indebtedness of the public enterprises, for the most part short-term oil-financing facilities of PETROBRÁS, amounted to an additional U.S. $2.6 billion in 1979 and U.S. $5.3 billion in 1980.

The heaviest borrowers among the public enterprises were ELETROBRÁS and its subsidiaries, with almost U.S. $5 billion in medium-term debt at the end of 1979. The steel and railroad companies have also borrowed large amounts of external resources. For the most part, these borrowings are guaranteed by the Federative Republic of Brazil; thus, they represent for the lenders sovereign risk rather than project risk.

Through the end of the 1970s, the most creditworthy public companies – CVRD and PETROBRÁS – had been among the least active international borrowers since their strong in-

Table 8.8. *Medium-term foreign currency debt of major public enterprise sectors, 1976–9 (U.S.$ million)*

	1976	1977	1978	1979
Steel	850.1	1,170.4	2,035.4	2,034.9
Petrochemicals	855.9	617.7	698.7	861.2
CVRD	595.1	410.5	585.4	440.6
Telecommunications	755.4	903.1	1,086.4	1,206.4
Railroads	1,633.0	1,639.6	1,896.3	1,998.2
Electricity	1,272.6	1,674.6	2,768.6	4,878.5
Total	5,962.7	6,415.9	9,079.9	11,375.7
Total as % of public sector external debt	40.1	33.2	32.9	33.4
Total as % of total Brazil external debt	22.9	20.2	20.8	22.8

Source: Balance sheets of the companies listed in Appendix A. See explanation in Appendix B.

ternal cash flow positions resulted in a reduced need for all types of outside financing (Table 8.8). Both these firms should, however, become larger borrowers during the 1980s. CVRD will be attempting to develop the Carajas iron ore deposits in the north of Brazil, a U.S. $3 billion project (in constant 1980 dollars) scheduled for completion by 1985. PETROBRÁS, for its part, will continue to invest U.S. $1–$2 billion annually in the search for oil.

By being able to access international financial markets with relative ease in the 1970s, the Brazilian public enterprises had available an additional means of carrying out their investment programs, especially after they experienced a decreased ability to finance investment out of their own internal cash flow. Being identified in the eyes of lenders with the Brazilian government (whether or not the borrowing bore an explicit guarantee of the Republic) no doubt gave the public enterprises a financing advantage over all but the largest and best-known private companies in Brazil. Nevertheless, the Brazilian private sector also stepped up significantly its level of borrowing in the international capital markets during the 1970s. Most of the private borrowing was channeled through the Brazilian banking system (so-called Resolution 63 lending), although a substantial part of private borrowing was arranged via direct loans, for example, from parent companies to subsidiaries of multinational corporations doing business in Brazil.

By 1979, Brazil's external debt problems became too pressing to ignore, especially after a second round of OPEC price hikes in 1979–80. The percentage of Brazil's total exports of goods and services preempted by remittances for debt service purposes (interest plus principal) rose steadily during the 1970s to reach two-thirds of total exports by 1979 (see again Table 8.7). This ratio seemed likely to remain high through the early 1980s, at least, as Brazil would be forced to continue borrowing large amounts to finance oil payments and to continue essential infrastructure investments. For example, by 1980, Brazil was spending more than 100% of its export earnings on oil imports and debt service payments. In order to meet such large financial requirements, Brazil was forced to draw down international reserves as well as to borrow additional funds abroad. This situation seemed likely to continue through at least the early 1980s or until Brazil's relative dependence on imported oil was substantially reduced.

The resort by Brazilian state-owned enterprises to large-scale borrowing abroad had a number of important implications. From the point of view of the companies, large-scale external borrowing was a means to sustain ambitious capital formation programs even in the face of a deterioration in self-financing capability. From the point of view of the economy as a whole, state-enterprise borrowing had both advantages and disadvantages. On the one hand, it did result in a substantial inflow of foreign resources that otherwise might not have been available. On the other, public enterprise borrowing was part of a broader Brazilian pattern of excess dependence on external debt during the 1970s. The need to service the sharply increased level of debt produced a severe foreign exchange constraint, which resulted in lower rates of economic growth during the early 1980s.

The external debt issue was ultimately important in altering control relations between the government and the public enterprises. An important reason for its growth had been the imposition of price controls on selected sectors (notably, electricity) in advance of carefully designed central controls over state-enterprise budgets and expansion programs. Efforts by policymakers to control the amount of state-enterprise borrowing were then complicated by the fact that such foreign resources provided a useful means of balance of payments finance. Finally, and as exemplified by the creation of SEST, public enterprise borrowing was controlled by the dual approach of, first, reducing investment programs and, second, permitting price increases that would strengthen self-financing capability.

Case studies of financing public enterprise

Financing patterns in Brazilian public enterprise vary according to the industries concerned. The petrochemical firms and the CVRD group, for example, dealt with less complicated investment financing environments because they were in a relatively strong position to generate cash internally. The railroads, at the other extreme, were forced to rely entirely on long-term borrowing and, on occasion, large government equity infusions. The other public enterprise sectors considered here used some combination of self-finance, government-provided resources, and long-term borrowing. One of these sectors – electricity – managed to assemble a stable and successful scheme of investment finance. Another – the public steel industry – was unable to do so. The similarities and differences in the two cases merit closer consideration.

The case of electricity

The keys to the successful financing scheme mounted in public power involved (1) rate-of-return regulation, which led to a relatively high degree of self-financing; (2) a substantial flow of off-budget public resources via a series of special taxes; and (3) strong support from multilateral lending institutions and international commercial banks.

Table 8.9. *Average price of electricity, 1974–9 (in Cr$ per megawatt hour)*

	1974	1975	1976	1977	1978	1979
Nominal	273.78	374.30	488.53	644.63	844.46	1,220.60
In 1974 prices	273.78	292.8	272.9	256.1	241.6	225.29

Note: Deflator: Wholesale price index (average variation during year).
Source: ELETROBRÁS.

Through the mid-1970s, the net operating income generated by the basic tariff plus the resources generated by the Sole Tax (on residential and commercial customers) and the compulsory loan (assessed on industrial users of electricity) produced more than 50% of the electricity sector's very substantial investment requirements. While it is stretching the concept somewhat, this degree of "self-financing" in the mid-1970s contrasted with an average rate of self-financing of 38% for investor-owned utilities in the United States.[16] U.S. utilities looked to long-term bond markets for the balance of their investment requirements. The practical equivalent of a long-term capital market in the case of the Brazilian electrical sector has been the public multilateral lender, for example, the World Bank, supplemented by medium-term (i.e., 8–12 years) financings from international commercial banks. From 1972 through 1975, institutions such as the World Bank and even bilateral lenders such as the U.S. Export–Import Bank agreed to provide ELETROBRÁS and its subsidiaries with more than U.S.$1 billion in low-cost, long-term loans.[17] Support from such institutions continued to be arranged thereafter.

The system of financing of electricity in Brazil was sound enough to withstand important changes in the firm's financial environment after 1974. The most important of these changes related to rate setting; another to the allocation of Sole Tax revenues. In real terms, the price of electricity in Brazil declined by almost 4% per year from 1974 through 1979 (see Table 8.9).

Table 8.10. *Sources of investment funds for electric power, 1968–79, in percentage of total financed through each source*

	1968	1970–1	1974–5	1978–9
Net operating income[a]	30.1	21.2	32.7	30.7
ELETROBRA	(7.9)	(8.1)	(29.7)	—
Companies	(22.2)	(13.1)	(3.0)	—
Sole Tax and compulsory loan	24.3	27.9	22.2	14.6
Federal and state subsidies[b]	21.8	22.1	19.7	9.2
Long-term debt	23.8	28.8	25.4	45.5
BNDE-held	(3.0)	(4.8)	(2.3)	(10.0)
Foreign-held	(20.8)	(24.0)	(23.0)	(35.5)
Total	100.0	100.0	100.0	100.0

[a]Defined as retained earnings, depreciation, and amortization.
[b]Annually budgeted funds plus state government shares in revenues of Sole Tax on Electrical Energy (IUEE).
Source: Annual ELETROBRÁS estimates of sources of finance, ELETROBRÁS, *Annual Reports*, 1968, 1970, 1975, 1979.

In addition to the more stringent rate-setting environment, the government moved to restrict severely ELETROBRÁS's ability to utilize the revenues produced by the Sole Tax on electrical energy. Prior to 1974, ELETROBRÁS retained 90% of the total revenues accruing to the federal government. In 1975, the government created a general "National Development Fund" outside ELETROBRÁS's control, which began siphoning off progressively larger shares of the Sole Tax revenues. By 1979, 50% of these revenues were directed to the fund with only 45% to ELETROBRÁS – the balance going to the Ministry of Mines and Energy. Finally, sharp decreases also occurred in budgetary allocations to public power companies.

The net impact of these changes in the basic financing scheme in electric power was to force a step-up in external borrowing. Thus, by 1978–9, the percentage of investment financed internally declined somewhat and significant declines occurred in the shares of investment financed by the Sole Tax and various government budget subsidies (see Table 8.10). The proportion of investment financed by long-term borrowing rose from 25% in 1974–5 to 45% in 1978–9. During this period, ELETROBRÁS continued to draw on its traditional multilateral creditors, but it also became one of the most active Brazilian borrowers in the eurocurrency markets. The longer-term implications of this change in financing structures were clearly to diminish ELETROBRÁS's ability to sustain a high level of investment in electricity. While investment in the energy sector, including hydroelectricity, does remain among the government's highest priorities, some cutback in ELETROBRÁS's plans to double installed hydro capacity during the 1980s could be anticipated. But the basic elements of what has been a successful financing scheme remain in place: (1) the ability of firms to generate significant internal financial resources, even in a period in which price controls caused the real price of power to decline; (2) important off-budget sources of public subsidy; (3) ready access to international capital markets; (4) good centralized financial administration of the electric power sector, as illustrated by the fact that ELETROBRÁS itself has been consistently profitable. ELETROBRÁS has had the political and economic strength to make efficient use of the funds available for electricity investment by acting, in essence, like an internal capital market. The holding company has derived substantial operating income of its own from dividends on its equity holdings in power companies, and interest and administration fees on loans.

The case of steel

Unlike the case of electric power, the public steel industry has been unable to mount a stable and durable system of investment financing. Planning in the steel sector has been more vulnerable than electricity to cyclical crises in the economy, which result in increased economic and financing restrictions on the public enterprise sector. Price controls have generally been tighter on steel products, even before the resurgence of inflationary pressures in the economy after 1974. Government-imposed price controls in 1964–7 severely restricted internal cashflow and left the three major public steel companies (CSN,

COSIPA, USIMINAS) in a weakened financial position when a major expansion of public steel-making capacity became necessary in the 1970s. With more liberal price adjustments in the 1970s, the financial position of the various steel companies stabilized; but after 1975, the real price of steel declined steadily and profitability plummeted in the late 1970s (see Chapter 7). The more restrictive pricing environment hit the steel sector harder than the electricity companies for a number of reasons, among these the lack of a special earmarked tax mechanism to generate tax revenues for deployment in steel.

For example, the second of a three-phase steel expansion program ("Phase II") was scheduled to take place in 1972–5. Three sources of financing for Phase II investments had been identified: current account savings (profits and depreciation), the public international lending agencies, and the government, the latter in the form of BNDE loans or equity subscriptions. Private capital markets were disregarded as a source of financing both because of the poor financial record of public steel and a concern not to burden the companies with additional high-cost financing. Actual costs during Phase II exceeded projections, however, and the relative shares of each source of financing had to be modified on an ad hoc basis (see Table 8.11). The share of the World Bank and the Inter-American Development Bank was considerably less than planned. Despite a more aggressive pricing strategy, the share of current account savings also declined from its planned level. The combined shares of these two sources of finance, planned for 75% of investment needs, amounted to 50%.

By the end of 1975, the balance sheets of the Big 3 public steel companies revealed a high debt/equity ratio of 1.5 and thereafter the financial positions worsened still further despite large infusions of capital by the government and loans from the BNDE. The difficulties with Phase II financing foretold even greater problems with Phase III, originally scheduled for the late 1970s. This phase of the expansion program ran into even tighter price controls limiting or even wiping out internal savings generation at most SIDERBRÁS subsidiaries. Attempts by the companies to push ahead with Phase

Table 8.11. *Phase II, steel expansion: projected and revised amounts of financing, 1972–5, (U.S.$ million)*

	Projected	%	Revised	%
IBRD/IBD and supplier credits	607	(47)	605	(30)
Current account savings	345	(27)	452	(22)
BNDE loans and treasury equity subscriptions	334	(26)	980	(48)
Total	1,286	(100)	2,037	(100)

Note: The development of severe financial constraints during Phase II forced the government to play a larger than anticipated role in financing the expansion of public steel. In particular, the BNDE expanded considerably its volume of lending. Predictably, increased indebtedness severely strained the liquidity of the largest steel firms, especially the Companhia Siderúrgica Nacional (CSN).
Source: CONSIDER, *Relatório*, 1975.

III resulted in further financial disequilibria. By the early 1980s, SIDERBRÁS subsidiaries (especially CSN and COSIPA) had accumulated enormous debts with domestic construction companies as timely payment became impossible. Total medium-term external debt (mostly to foreign commercial banks) of the SIDERBRÁS group jumped from U.S. $2 billion in 1979 to U.S. $4.4 billion by early 1981.[18]

Why did the steel sector experience greater difficulties than the electric power industry in arranging for investment financing? Generally, poorer management is one of the reasons. A number of the steel companies (USIMINAS is a notable exception) have had difficulties even in the absence of price controls on steel products. Several of the expansion programs were poorly conceived and implemented. The government has been reluctant to compensate for poor decision-making in the steel companies by granting price increases or increasing public investment subsidies.

Other factors behind steel's relative weakness include:

1. A better-organized industrial lobby against increased steel prices by the automobile companies, major industrial consumers. Dutra and Salles argue that these companies (and other major industrial consumers

of steel) have been able to bring pressures on the government to moderate price increases in steel.[19] By comparison, electricity companies service a much larger and diversified customer base and do not face such concentrated lobbying power.

2. The lower priority assigned to the steel industry by the government, which resulted in fewer resources, including loans from the World Bank and other multilateral lenders.

3. The fact that the holding company in steel, SIDERBRÁS, was unable to achieve on its own a position of financial strength or political influence. It was not successful in lobbying for tax mechanisms to generate investment resources for steel or in developing a budget of its own out of which it could loan to the companies.

Comparative financing patterns

How does the recent investment-financing performance of the large Brazilian public enterprises compare with experience elsewhere in Latin America? Some evidence on this point is assembled in Table 8.12. By comparison to public enterprises in Mexico, Chile, and Argentina, the level of self-financing in Brazil is relatively high. During the late 1970s, the large Brazilian public enterprises financed 34% of total investment out of internal sources, versus 14% in Argentina and only 8% in Mexico. The self-financing ratio of the Chilean state-owned firms was much higher, that is, 90% during the late 1970s. This extraordinarily high ratio is explained by the relatively low level of state-enterprise investment in Chile during the period – one of severe economic recession – and by the simultaneous efforts of the Chilean government to reduce drastically the level of public expenditure.

Because of Mexico's greater similarity to Brazil in terms of economic size, a comparison with it is more interesting and relevant.[20] The overall financial performance of Mexican firms studied is characterized by a current surplus that is relatively small in the light of investment finance requirements. The current surplus (sales minus operating expense) in percent of GDP ranged from 0.2% to 0.9% during 1972–8; public enterprise investment in percent of GDP ranged from 2.3% to 6%. In consequence, the overall deficit of the core Mexican public enterprises tended to be much larger than that of the large Brazilian public firms, about 4%–6% of GDP versus

Table 8.12. *Comparative state-enterprise financing patterns in Latin America as a percentage of GDP, annual averages*

	Current account surplus	Investment	Deficit	Self-finance ratio[a]
Argentina, 1977–8	0.6	4.1	−3.5	14.0
Brazil, 1975–9	1.8	5.3	−3.5	34.0
Chile, 1976–9	2.7	3.0	−0.3	90.0
Mexico, 1974–8	0.4	4.8	−4.4	8.0

[a]Current account surplus divided by investment.
Sources: Brazil, Table 8.3. Chile, Central Bank of Chile, unpublished data. (All public enterprises.) Current account surplus is defined as operating surplus after taxes and transfers. Investment expenditure is net of capital revenue. Mexico, data for 19 large federally owned public enterprises subject to budgetary control. *Source:* Secretariá de Programación y Presupuesto, *Boletín Mensual de información económica* 3, no. 4 (April 1979). Argentina, Alberto Joaquin Ugalde, "El Comportamiento Financiero de Empresas Públicas en el Período 1966–1978 y Sus Perspectivas," pp. 15–16 and Annex I. GDP numbers from IMF, *International Financial Statistics.*

3%–4% in the case of Brazil. Expressed in another way, the ability of Mexican public enterprises to finance investment out of internally generated resources is less than that of their Brazilian counterparts. In the period considered here, Mexican public enterprises typically financed only about 8% of investment requirements with internal resources, versus 30%–40% in Brazil.

A sector-by-sector view of the financing performance of Mexican public enterprises in 1972–8 shows PEMEX and the non-rail transport sector to be the only public enterprise sectors able to generate any portion of investment finance internally. PEMEX, by far the most important sector in the entire group, generated on the order of 40–50% of investment requirements internally during 1972–8. The non-rail transport firms actually showed a surplus after investment in a number of years.

The remaining four sectors – railroads, electricity, steel, and manufacturing – were unable to contribute any internal savings toward the financing of investment requirements. In

Brazil, among the large state enterprises only the railroads were unable to generate internally any part at all of investment needs. Brazil's weakest non-rail public enterprises, the steel companies, were able to generate nearly 20% of investment requirements during the late 1970s, versus 0% for their state-enterprise counterparts in Mexico.

The evidence presented is consistent with the hypothesis that Brazil has placed much greater emphasis on a policy of self-financing by public enterprise than other large Latin American countries, even though the degree of self-financing in Brazil did decline during the 1970s. Many public enterprises in Mexico, in particular, tend to be run as adjuncts of public finance.

Conclusions

Brazilian public enterprises demonstrate both the complexity and the diversity of financing patterns and also the relationships that can arise between macroeconomic variables and the patterns of finance of a large public enterprise sector. In general, Brazilian public enterprise has been successful in financing internally a substantial proportion of investment requirements. Obviously, this capacity to finance internally varies from sector to sector, and across the business cycle in Brazil, but, with few exceptions, the large public enterprises financed enormous programs of capital formation with little dependence on direct government subsidy. To be sure, indirect subsidies were important (earmarked tax revenues, for example, and BNDE loans), but the fact that self-financing capacity was good and that access to "safe" public funds was assured in key sectors (e.g., electricity) were important factors in explaining both the growth in investment and in autonomy of the state-enterprise sector through the mid-1970s. The Brazilian case offers at least the following lessons in the financing of public enterprise.

First, public enterprises in a developing country need not be adjuncts of public finance. The observation contrasts with a view frequently encountered in the development literature, for example, this quote from a broad empirical survey of

LDC government enterprises: "Government-owned enterprises, rather than serving as a focal point for collecting financial resources for their own investment or for other purposes, have generally placed a financial burden on parent governments."[21] The Brazilian experience contrasts very sharply with that of Mexico.

Second, a substantial degree of self-financing can bring with it other problems. In Brazil, public enterprises did achieve a substantial degree of autonomy by the mid-1970s, leading to a large volume of investments exceeding their internal financial capacity. The overall state-enterprise deficit grew steadily to more than 5% of GDP at a time when Brazil was experiencing mounting inflationary and balance of payments pressures.

Third, public enterprise financing in Brazil illustrates the possibilities and problems offered by relatively easy access to international capital markets. The possibilities include an ability to carry out investment plans that far exceed resources available internally. State-enterprise borrowing is a convenient means for a government to arrange balance of payments financing without borrowing in its own name. There are also problems: public enterprises may overborrow in the pursuit of their own goals and aggravate debt service difficulties for the country.

9

Conclusions

The Brazilian experience with public enterprise has been reviewed from a number of different viewpoints. The task has required the gathering and interpretation of many facts and figures. This leaves us with the question: "What does it all mean?" I have approached this in three ways. First, the major conclusions on the Brazilian performance itself are assembled and reviewed. Second, the relevance of the Brazilian experience for other developing countries is discussed. Third, in the light of past performance, I consider the future role of public enterprise in Brazil.

The Brazilian experience reviewed

A steadily increasing role for the state in the economy has been a generally "stylized fact" of the post-1930 Brazilian industrialization experience. This growing role can be measured in terms of the two categories of the "state as regulator" (e.g., controls over foreign trade, traditional fiscal functions) and the "state as entrepreneur." Through the combined impact of its spending, taxing, regulating, banking, and directly productive activities, the Brazilian state exercises an enormous direct and indirect effect on decision making and resource allocation throughout the economy. This role has grown in the absence of any specific socialist ideology and, indeed, has bloomed vigorously under governments, such as those of the post-1964 period, that expressed deep philosophical and practical commitments to retaining this central role of the marketplace as the guide to economic decision making.

To understand why Brazil has embraced the apparent contradictory principles of an activist state and a basically decentralized economic system one must understand its underlying concept of the proper role of the state. Stepan dubbed this Latin American conception as the "organic-statist" role of the state, an approach lying somewhere in between the extremes of classical Marxism and classical liberalism (see Chapter 1). In the organic-statist view, the state is imbued with a "moral obligation" to interfere in the resource allocation process in the event of social dissatisfaction with the decisions that result automatically from the free play of market forces. At the same time, this Latin American conception imposes certain limits on the permissible actions of the state. Private enterprise, in particular, has a legitimate and important role to play and it is commonly recognized that private risk taking is the best way of achieving the goal of efficient economic growth.

Thus, the Brazilian conception has been to emphasize a broad field of action to "correct" market decisions or to substitute for private enterprise in order to speed up economic development, while at the same time adhering to constraints on the permissible sphere of state intervention. Whether or not this basically *political* approach to the role of the state is consistent with economic resource constraints is another matter. The intent of this study was to examine as carefully as possible the *economic* consequences by focusing on the public enterprise sector.

The Brazilian state has concentrated its entrepreneurial activities in a fairly predictable pattern in heavy industry, transportation, and the utilities. The overall pattern of sectoral location is not that different from patterns observed in many other countries that have also used public enterprise. This suggests the operation of certain common economic causal factors (e.g., economies of scale) operating across national borders and leading to the formation of public enterprises. However, the growth of public enterprise in Brazil also involves political explanations, among these the national security concerns of the armed forces, relations with foreign capital, and governmental reforms leading to the creation of new public enterprises out of former government bureaucracies. The growth of public enterprise in Brazil has been associated with the rise of an economic role for the military, limitations on foreign ownership in what are deemed "strategic sectors" of the economy, and the creation of a new group of "state executives" out of former civil servants.

In sum, the *original* entrepreneurial role of the public sector is well explained by the desire of policymakers to speed up industrialization in Brazil by substituting the state for domestic private entrepreneurship that was not available or foreign ownership that was not politically acceptable. While the state's role in the industries it entered was presumed to be permanent, the whole idea of its involvement in the first place was to encourage the growth of downstream private enterprises, which would be the major beneficiaries of the output of the public enterprises. And, by and large, the growth of the Brazilian public enterprise sector from the 1940s through the 1980s has remained true to this original conception. The government has not created public enterprises randomly across sectors of the economy. Indeed, it is almost as if public enterprise in Brazil could be defined in terms of its capital intensity. With the state's role basically limited to infrastructure and heavy industry, it has been up to private enterprise (including many foreign-owned companies) to define and to fill out the productive structure in Brazil.

This is not to say that the consequences of the development of the public enterprise sector in Brazil were unforeseen. One such consequence must have been the enormous growth in the scale of public enterprise operations and in the size and importance of such firms in the economy. The capital expenditure plans of the state enterprises, to cite one example, have come to exercise an important impact on cyclical movements in the Brazilian economy. The overall operations of public enterprises influence domestic interest rates, the level of capacity utilization in industry, the balance of payments, and the level of external debt. Paralleling the growth in the size and importance of the state-owned enterprises has been the emergence of a politically powerful and generally able group of state-enterprise managers to direct their increasingly complex industrial operations. These state-sector executives have developed over time a vested interest both in protecting their firms and industries from outside interference and in gathering the financial resources needed for expansion of productive capacity. This combination has presented the Brazilian government with problems of control that were not foreseen in earlier decades. Traditionally, public enterprise in Brazil was not tied closely to central government administration. Indeed, in legal structure and operating style, the state-owned enterprises were often specifically charged to imitate private enterprise behavior. Central to the Brazilian conception of public enterprise was the idea that these units would not be an administrative or financial burden on the rest of the public sector, which chronically was stretched thin in terms of financial resources and managerial talent.

For the most part, the central government has not meddled excessively in public enterprise operations to the point of demoralizing management and debilitating the firm's financial structure. The public enterprise sector has responded by remaining relatively independent of government subsidy, and the individual firms certainly have not been characterized by waste and corruption. For a lengthy period from the mid-1960s, the large state-owned enterprises developed a fairly high degree of managerial autonomy while maintaining good operational performance.

More serious control problems in Brazil have instead been related to the fact that a good part of the public sector with an important impact on the economy was not effectively subject either to ordinary market discipline or fiscal controls. In historical retrospect, the period of deepening economic crisis from the late 1970s through the early 1980s will be seen as one in which Brazil's political and economic leadership came to recognize the need for greater administrative and financial control over the state-enterprise sector. This imperfect process of gathering central control, symbolized by the creation of a budgetary authority, put limits on the autonomy of the state as entrepreneur while consolidating and strengthening for the future its own regulatory role.

Most of this study dealt with the actual empirical results of the largest forty or fifty state-owned enterprises in Brazil, a selection that included six separate industries – railroads, steel, electricity, telecommunications, petrochemicals, and mining. The study also attempted to examine performance over a lengthy time period. Thus, it is difficult to resist the temptation to qualify endlessly any general statements about economic performance. Depending on the particular economic criterion adopted, some firms have done consistently well, other consistently poorly. Some state-owned companies can be seen to be strong performers in one time period, then weak performers in another. Bearing this in mind, an overview of public enterprise performance is now attempted.

The relationships of public enterprises to economic growth was one important angle of analysis in this study, with empirical emphasis on the investment and output performance of state companies in the six economic sectors. In my view, it is difficult to argue that Brazilian public enterprises have acted as bottlenecks to economic growth. From an international perspective, the growth rate of the Brazilian economy has been extraordinarily high, with total production of goods and services doubling every ten years; and all of this has occurred precisely at a time in which the public enterprises have increased their relative size in the economy. When one looks at sectoral trends in investment and output growth, the record is generally an impressive one.

One can argue that the state-owned enterprises, by their generally strong performance, have served to implement a generally inadequate economic model in Brazil, that is, one that is too capital-intensive, too highly protected from world trade, too narrowly focused on certain regions of the country, and so on. Yet it is not really proper to lay these problems of economic policy at the door of the public enterprise sector. Within the given economic model, the public enterprises had a specific investment and production role to play, and they have generally played it well. A broad range of privately owned firms and industries in Brazil have grown up over the years precisely because they have had close input or output links with the state enterprises. In my view, it is not plausible to argue that Brazil's rate of economic growth over the last three or four decades could have been significantly higher had the government elected not to use public enterprise in many basic industries and instead waited for the appearance on the scene of private entrepreneurs.

In retrospect, the major accomplishment of public enterprise in Brazil may have been to promote a drastic transformation of the economic structure after 1950 by speeding up the industrialization process. It is easy to underestimate the organizational, technical, and managerial difficulties involved in putting in place the basic infrastructure of a modern economy. Yet in almost every sector examined – steel, electricity, telecommunications, mining, and petrochemicals – state-enterprise managers did demonstrate true entrepreneurship in Brazil in the relatively successful completion of large capital formation programs. In the process, they contributed to raising the level of technical sophistication in the economy and created many opportunities for private enterprise. The modern Brazilian capital goods industry, largely created over the last twenty to thirty years and predominantly controlled by private capital, owes much of its growth to its customer or supplier state firms. And in a number of important industries – computers, aerospace, defense, to name the most obvious – we are seeing today the same process repeated of a Brazilian state company being used as a wedge to open up new possibilities, that is, to expand the productive capabilities and technological sophistication of Brazilian industry.

The nature and *costs* of the state sector's contribution to economic development in Brazil have also been considered. The growth of the state companies has been overwhelmingly capital-intensive, with little direct (albeit substantial indirect) employment creation. Some evidence exists that the public enterprises, notably in the electricity sector, may have over-built capacity, causing a misallocation of scarce capital. But, with allowance for the vagaries of central government interference with the pricing of output, the public enterprises have generally been profitable. They were not set up to be and, in fact, have not been, profit maximizers, but (and aside from the railroads) the major public enterprises in Brazil have generally earned enough in revenues to cover costs and to generate some surplus for investment. This study did not address the issue of the technical, engineering efficiency of the public enterprises; a larger rate of profit probably could have been attained had these industries been run privately. Indeed, the rate of return to state-enterprise investment is consistently lower, often significantly lower, than that obtained by private investors in other industries. Yet public enterprises have been subject to on-again, off-again price controls as well as saddled with the most heavily capital-intensive sectors in the economy. It stands to reason that, under any form of ownership, rates of return in the steel industry, for example, would tend to be lower than in other economic sectors. In defense of the profit performance of Brazilian public enterprise, most of the companies have made an effort to rationalize the overall size of their work forces (though they may be overstaffed at the management level) and their profit record over the years is generally much better than that of public enterprises in other developing countries.

An important reason why Brazilian public enterprise has been at least somewhat profitable has been the importance attached by Brazil to using the state enterprises as a means of generating a financial surplus for reinvestment. Aided by a legal framework for pricing that allowed firms to keep abreast of inflation, many state enterprise sectors in the late 1960s and early 1970s were quite successful in financing a large part of their capital expenditures out of internally generated resources. Later in the 1970s, the self-financing record declined sharply across the board, in part because profitability declined in many public enterprise sectors, but also because the overall investment effort of the public enterprises was increasing sharply.

The growing gap between savings and investment of the public firms complicated the management of aggregate demand, put strong pressures on interest rates, and required the increasing use of external commercial bank credits. These developments triggered a series of institutional reforms designed to bring the budgets of the state enterprises under closer control, with the aim of both improving profitability and cutting investment expenditures. These measures should stabilize the financial structure of the public enterprises in the future.

But in general, it remains true that Brazilian public enterprises over the last several decades were generally successful in arranging the financing of their ambitious capital formation programs without large dependence on public subsidy. Again, their record on this score stands in sharp contrast to that of public enterprises in many countries.

A broader interpretation

The Brazilian public enterprise experience, in sum, has demonstrated that state ownership of basic industries can be an effective substitute for private enterprise in stimulating rapid and sustained economic growth. This statement is not meant as a blanket endorsement of public enterprise as somehow "better than" private enterprise, only that within the confines imposed by Brazilian politics and economic policy, the state-owned enterprises have performed reasonably well and have permitted the Brazilian economy to grow much more rapidly than would have been the case in their absence.

Before recommending that any developing nation seek to emulate Brazil's path, it is well to recall some of the possibly unique characteristics and some obvious limitations of the Brazilian experience. It is important to realize that the creation and use of public enterprise in Brazil has not been indiscriminate. The great bulk of the state's investment is concentrated in a handful of infrastructural sectors. The government has not been reluctant to own and operate important industries, but it has not considered public ownership of the means of production to be an end in itself. Indeed, the prime purpose of Brazilian public enterprise has been to stimulate the growth of private ownership by opening up the industrial structure. Put in another way, direct employment creation has not been an important objective of Brazilian public enterprises.

Another relevant characteristic of the Brazilian experience is the long-standing concern to put state-owned companies on a commercial footing. For the most part, the state companies have been located in sectors where it has been theoretically possible to earn some profits and, by and large, managers have managed to accomplish this goal. The companies developed an early relative independence from the open-ended operating subsidy. By the same token, Brazilian firms, unlike those in many developing countries, have not been asked also to pursue social objectives that might have served to depress profits and to justify government subsidies.

The Brazilian experience also demonstrates well the need for a distinction between public ownership and public control. In particular, the development of large public firms implies the creation of vested interests in the form of enterprise management and the customers and suppliers of the public firm. Over the years, this has meant in Brazil a tendency for state companies to assume a fairly high degree of autonomy from the central government, at times complicating the task of overall economic management. In particular, it is not true to say that because the state-enterprise sector is large, therefore the Planning Ministry in Brasilia possesses important levers of control over the economy. Indeed, one could argue that a number of public enterprises – CVRD is only one example – have been effective because they are *not* closely controlled by Brasilia.

Thus, it is important from an international perspective to understand the limited role of public enterprises in the Brazilian economy, despite their size, and their high degree of ordinary commercial orientation. The findings of fairly favorable economic performance by the state enterprises should also be seen in the light of the very large size and rapid growth of the Brazilian economy, which allowed capital-intensive public enterprises to realize scale economies unattainable in many smaller developing countries.

A final point worth underlining relates to the skills of state-enterprise managers. Much more in the way of hard research needs to be done on this point, but it is clear that Brazil did have a relatively large supply of well-trained technocrats and professionals from which to recruit the managers of the state companies. Furthermore, these managers were well paid, and relatively free from the threat of removal for political reasons or because of a simple changeover at the top levels of government. This has allowed for a continuity in management, especially at the middle levels, which has been important in assuring a relatively stable planning environment.

The future of public enterprise in Brazil

At this writing, the Brazilian economy is in the midst of a serious crisis originally brought on by the permanent change in relative energy prices after 1973. Symptoms of the crisis include slowing rates of economic growth, high rates of inflation, mounting pressures on foreign exchange, and growing external debt. At the same time, the economy is coming under increasing social pressures to raise standards of living for the large majority of the population. Brazil retains enormous potential for long-term development, but it is at an historical crossroads. Fundamental development strategy must be revamped to achieve this potential. The new strategy must lead to reduced dependence on imported oil and external borrowing and to a generally less capital-intensive mode of development. It will necessarily involve the relative redirection of public and private investment out of import-substituting industry and into agriculture, alternative energy sources, and export pursuits in general. The Brazilian economy will also have to become more open to international trade. An integral part of the new strategy will also involve more explicit public measures to deal with Brazil's inequitable distribution of income. Necessarily, the implementation of this strategy will take more than a few years; rather, it will be Brazil's economic agenda in the 1980s.

In one important sense, the future role of public enterprises in the restructuring of the Brazilian economy is clear. As agents of sectoral economic policy, the state-owned companies have amply demonstrated their usefulness in the past. Many of the sectors in which public enterprises are or could be active will be important priorities for future government investment. Some obvious examples of state-enterprise involvement include oil exploration, new hydroelectric projects, and alternative fuels projects. But in addition, state-owned companies will be crucial to Brazil's hopes of developing important mineral deposits in the Carajas area and other regions of the country. A greatly expanded role may also be foreseen for state trading companies and state-owned commercial banks as the foreign trade sector continues to expand rapidly. Expanded agricultural research efforts and railroad rehabilitation are two more obvious avenues for the expansion of state enterprise in the future.

Brazil's economic difficulties in the 1980s are by no means insurmountable, but they will, in all likelihood, produce an economic environment fundamentally different from that prevailing in the thirty years from 1950 through 1980. Economic growth will almost certainly be lower, inflation higher, foreign exchange reserves under continual pressure. Brazil's ability to realize its development potential will depend on the managerial skills of policymakers and the productivity of public and private investment.

These same imperatives will hold for the public enterprise sector. Policymakers over the last thirty years or so have found ways to assure adequate, but not excessive controls of the state companies, to recruit able managers, to generate some financial surplus from the companies for reinvestment, and so on. They will be under pressure in the 1980s to refine these techniques and to prevent any serious regression in the performance of the government companies.

Brazil's ability to resume relatively high rates of economic growth by the latter 1980s are, in my view, closely linked to the success of the state companies in continuing to avoid the need for huge subsidies and in channeling investment funds into projects that will result in increased exports, improved energy efficiency, an expanding agricultural sector – in short, a new model of economic growth. The performance of the state companies in meeting the challenges posed by Brazil's industrialization drive of the last few decades gives some grounds for optimism that the public firms will adapt to the challenges of the 1980s. But the margin for error is a thin one: policymakers and state-enterprise managers will have to redouble efforts to prevent serious misallocations of capital through the public enterprise sector.

In sum, however, Brazil's experience with public enterprises serves to illustrate some of the limitations as well as the advantages of these instruments of public policy. In an era in which radical reassessments of the proper role of the state in economic development are taking place throughout Latin America, it is well not to lose sight of either.

APPENDIX A

Enterprises included and years covered

Mining	
Companhia Vale do Rio Doce	1965–79
Steel	
Companhia Siderúrgica Nacional (CSN)	1965–79
Companhia Siderúrgica Paulista (COSIPA)	1966–79
Usinas Siderúrgicas de Minas Gerais (USIMINAS)	1965–75
Companhia Ferro e Aço de Vitória (COFAVI)	1968–72
Siderúrgica Brasileíra (SIDERBRÁS)	1975–79
Petrochemicals	
Petróleo Brasileiro (PETROBRÁS)	1965–79
PETROBRÁS Química (PETROQUISA)	1968–79
Railways	
Rede Ferroviária Federal	1966–79
Ferrovia Paulista (FEPASA)[a]	1965–79
Other Transport[b]	
Cia. de Navegação Lloyd Brasileiro	1970–74
Cia. de Navegação do S. Francisco	1970–73
Serviço de Transportes da Bahia de Guanabara	1970–73
Empresa de Navegação da Amazonia, S.A.	1970–73
Serviço de Navegação da Bahia da Prata	1970–73
Cia. Brasileira de Dragagem	1970–73
Cia. Docas da Guanabara	1970–73
Cia. Docas do Pará	1970–73
Empresa de Reparos Navais "Costeira," S.A.	1970–73
Telecommunications	
Companhia Telefonica Brasileira (CTB)[c]	1966–72
Telecomuniçacões do Rio de Janeiro (TELERJ)	1973–79
Telecomuniçacões de São Paulo (TELESP)	1973–79
Empresa Brasileira de Telecomuniçacões (EMBRATEL)	1967–79
Telecomuniçacões do Paraná (TELEPAR)	1965–73
Telecomuniçacões de Minas Gerais (TELEMIG)	1968–75

Telecomuniçacões do Espirito Santo (TELEST)	1968–75
Telecomuniçacões de Brasilia (TELEBRASILIA)	1968–74
Companhia Estadual de Telefones (CETEL)	1965–73
Telecomuniçacões de Bahia	1965–70
Cia. Riograndense de Telecomuniçacões (CRT)	1965–72
Telecomuniçacões Brasileiras, S.A. (TELEBRÁS)	1974–79

Electricity

Cia. Brasileira de Energia Elétrica (CBEE)	1970–75
Cia. de Eletricidade de Manaus (CEM)	1970–75
Cia. Hidroelétrica do S. Francisco (CHESF)	1965–75
Empresa S. Catarinense de Eletricidade (ESCELSA)	1968–75
FURNAS Centrais Elétricas	1965–75
Cia. Paulista de Força e Luz (CPFL)	1965–75
Cia. de Energia Elétrica do Brasil (CEEB)	1970–73
Cia. Força e Luz de Minas Gerais (CFLMG)	1970–73
Cia. Força e Luz de Paraná (CFLP)	1970–73
Cia. Hidroelétrica de Boa Esperança (COHEBE)	1970–72
CONEFOR	1970–72
Centrais Elétricas do Sul do Brasil (ELETROSUL)	1971–75
Centrais Elétricas de São Paulo (CESP)	1966–75
Centrais Elétricas de Minas Gerais (CEMIG)	1965–75
Centrais Elétricas Brasileiras (ELETROBRÁS)	1970–80

[a]FEPASA was created in 1971 after the consolidation of a number of pre-existing rail systems operating in the state of São Paulo. Data on these pre-existing systems were combined to derive observations for 1965–70. These systems were: Estrada de Ferro Araraquara, Estrada de Ferro São Paulo-Minas, Estrada de Ferro Sorocabana, Cia. Paulista de Estradas de Ferro, and Cia. Mogiana de Estradas de Ferro.

[b]This sector was not included in the computations used in the book. However, reliable data are available for the years indicated.

[c]Before 1973, the urban telephone systems of Rio and São Paulo were operated under the aegis of a single company, the Companhia Telefonica Brasileira. After this date, separate entities – known as TELERJ and TELESP, respectively – superceded the CTB.

Sources and interpretation of data on public enterprises, 1965–1979

Introduction

A major impediment to the study of public enterprise performance in Latin America has been the lack of central data files. The creation of SEST – the federal budgetary authority – in 1979, was the beginning of a major step forward in resolving this problem in the case of Brazil, but no comparable data collection point existed during the time period covered by this study. Consequently, one of the most important tasks for the researcher is to marshal comparable data on numerous public enterprises in different economic sectors. The purpose of this appendix is to describe briefly the attempts made to surmount this difficulty in the case of Brazilian public enterprises from 1965 to 1979.

First, the most important sources of data on public enterprise performance are described. Second, the methods for classifying the bulk of raw financial data underlying this study are set forth. Third, the methods used to derive a number of the more important variables used in this study are described.

Sources of data on public enterprise performance, 1965–79

The principal sources of data used in this study included: (1) annual reports of public firms, holding companies, ministries, and ministerial bodies; (2) data files of the Centro de Estudos Fiscais, Fundação Getulio Vargas; (3) miscellaneous publications and internal documents of individual enterprises or similar works relating to particular industries in which public enterprises are dominant; (4) annual surveys of the financial condition of enterprises; (5) interviews with government officials and directors of public firms; (6) newspaper files, primarily those of O *Estado de São Paulo*; and (7) reports of the Secretary for the Control of State Enterprises (SEST).

Annual reports

As open capital firms, most Brazilian public enterprises are required to publish annual reports (*relatórios*). Containing a wide variety of data on production, sales, investment plans, as well as complete statements of the company's financial condition, these reports are the basis for any examination of public enterprise performance. In addition, a number of the principal ministries, for example, the Ministry of Mines and Energy, as well as interministerial agencies, such as CONSIDER, and holding companies, such as TELEBRÁS, also provide much relevant information in annual reports. The reports and miscellaneous documents published by ELETRO-BRÁS, in particular, now provide comprehensive physical and financial data on all the electricity firms.

Data files of the Centro de Estudos Fiscais

As part of its long-term examination of public enterprise performance, the Centro de Estudos Fiscais maintains extensive financial information on Brazilian public enterprises.[1] These files are reasonably complete up to 1970 for most of the firms listed in Appendix A. In some cases, data are now available to 1975. As of this writing, the Centro, under its director Margareth Hanson Costa, has plans to publish its extensive data in the near future.

While extensive use was made of these files in the present study, especially for the pre-1970 period, it bears repeating that the responsibility for the use and interpretation of the data is strictly that of the author and not of the Centro de Estudos Fiscais. Furthermore, the data obtained are unofficial and subject to revision.

Annual surveys of enterprises

Important supplementary sources of information are annually published surveys of financial characteristics of large Brazilian firms. The annual *Quem é quem na economia brasileira* of *Visão* is the most complete and authoritative survey.[2] The 1976 edition, for example, contains information on a total of 5,353 firms, including 443 public enterprises. The data in the *Visão* survey are derived from the major financial statements of each firm.

SEST publications

The establishment of SEST may lead to improved central control of the state-enterprise sector; it will certainly facilitate the task of basic research on the economic and financial performance of Brazilian public enterprise. In 1981, SEST was acting as the central budgeting authority for some 382 (out of a total of 560) federally owned state enterprises, including all of the more important firms. As explained in the text, SEST's financial controls over state enterprises extend to pricing, current expenditures, capital expenditures, budgetary transfers, and external and domestic credit facilities. The authority of SEST also extends to the formation of new state companies, capital increases, import ceilings, dividends of the federal government, managerial salaries, and employee benefit programs. As SEST was in a starting-up phase as this research was being concluded, official data on these different aspects of state-enterprise activity were of less value than interviews with various SEST directors. However, the control agency's annual reports should provide the raw material for future research efforts.[3]

In short, a canvass of the materials in this section led to the accumulation of information on both the physical and financial aspects of public enterprise operations. An attempt was made to sort out the financial data for comparative purposes.

Classification of financial data

Since accounting methods are not uniform from enterprise to enterprise, it was necessary to establish certain rules for the classification of financial data. For the most part, the procedures followed by the Centro de Estudos Fiscais were adapted to fit the needs of this study. Accordingly, the many different variables describing financial activity of the firm were classified in three main categories: (1) receipts and expenditures; (2) assets and liabilities; and (3) sources and uses of funds.

Receipts and expenditures

Receipts on current account include: (1) all sales revenues; (2) profits from the sale of assets; (3) all other general revenues (such as income from financial investments); (4) receipts of subsidies from the federal government. They exclude receipts of the proceeds of excise taxes on the sales of the corporation, which are made available by the federal government for investment finance.

Expenditures on current account include: (1) salaries, wages, and worker benefits; (2) purchase of materials, services, and so on; (3) payment of interest and other financial expenditures; (4) direct and indirect taxes; (5) depreciation; (6) all other general expenditures.

Salaries, wages, worker benefits. This variable includes the gross wage bill, social security contributions paid by employees, directors' fees (*honorários da diretoria*), fees paid to members of the fiscal council of the firm, profits distributed annually to directors and employees, and all worker benefits paid by employers such as INPS, FGTS, and PIS/PASEP.[4]

Accounting methods in Brazil usually do not require the public disclosure of some of the major components of this variable, particularly the gross amount of salaries to production workers or managerial compensation. Fortunately, special data collected by the Centro de Estudos Fiscais did include the total figure for all types of salaries, wages, and workers' benefits. For those firms or years in which such information was not available from the CEF, it was often possible to obtain the global figure from information contained in the body of the company's annual report. When no outside information of any type was available, an estimate was made by using the percentage share in total costs of "salaries, wages, and workers' benefits" of other public firms in the same industry. While the data on this variable used in this study are believed reliable, the reader is alerted to the possible need for data revision in the future.

Interest and other financial expenditures. The financial items that compose this variable include interest payments, bank fees and commissions, and charges for monetary correction.

Direct and indirect taxes. The most important taxes reported include the profit tax, the tax on industrial products (IPI), and the turnover tax (ICM).[5]

Assets and liabilities

The asset categories for which data were obtained include the following: (1) cash on hand (*disponível*); (2) short-term receivables; (3) inventories; (4) property, plant, and equipment at historical cost; (5) monetary restatement of property, plant, and equipment; (6) works in progress; and (7) financial investments.

Liabilities are classified as (1) authorized, subscribed, and fully paid shares (*capital social*); (2) retained earnings and legal reserves (*reservas*); (3) current liabilities; and (4) long-term debt.

Two comments are necessary in regard to this list of liabilities. First, the sum of categories (1) and (2) (*capital social + reservas*) are by definition equal to net worth (*patrimonio liquido*). Second, information on long-term debt for selected enterprises was further broken down into foreign- or domestic-held debt. This was possible because accounting practices require disclosure of debt contracted abroad.

Sources and uses of funds

Information on sources and uses of funds was collected in a less systematic fashion and was used primarily as a check on calculations derived using receipt-expenditure and asset-liability data. The major sources of funds for which data were collected include: (1) net profit for the year; (2) depreciation and amortization; (3) increases in long-term loans; (4) capital stock subscriptions received; and (5) other sources.

The uses of funds were classified as (1) additions to property, plant, and equipment; (2) increases (or decreases) in working capital; and (3) other uses.

The derivation of particular variables

The data described above were used in various combinations to arrive at estimates of (1) value-added; (2) investment; and (3) the capital stock. For some industries, the data were also used to develop price indexes. The computation of each of these variables is briefly reviewed below. The interested reader is referred to the author's doctoral dissertation for the relevant time series of these and other variables.[6]

Value-added. Net value-added is defined as the value of gross sales minus all expenditure categories, except net interest, indirect taxes, and expenditures on salaries, wages, and worker benefits. It should be noted that value-added in this study is net of accounting depreciation charges.

Investment. Whenever possible, the amount of investment spending was derived directly from the flow-of-funds table. Often, investment figures are also reported in the body of the report. In numerous other cases, however, especially for earlier years in the 1965–75 series, it was necessary to estimate this figure on the basis of balance-sheet information. In such cases, the investment figure was defined as the gross addition to property, plant, and equipment during the year plus the net change in works in progress. The data collection methods made it possible to separate additions to property, plant, and equipment from mere monetary restatement of such assets.

The following qualifications of the investment data used in this study are important.

Steel. Investment data (as well as data on value-added) refer to CSN, COSIPA, and USIMINAS only.

Petrochemicals. Investment data for PETROQUISA include not only the gross fixed capital spending of the company, but also its investments in subsidiaries and joint ventures.

Telecommunications. Investment and output series refer only to EMBRATEL, TELERJ, and TELESP.

Railroads. For 1965–8, data were obtained from Joyce Howland, "The Economics of Brazilian Transportation Policy, 1945–1970" (Ph.D. thesis, Vanderbilt University, 1972), p. 136. Investment figures for other years were obtained directly from company reports.

Capital stock. All estimates used in the text are expressed in constant 1970 prices and were derived in the following manner. First, the end-of-year 1970 book value of physical capital (property, plant, and equipment + monetary restatements + works in progress) was selected as the base-year estimate for each firm in each industry. Second, resulting values for each firm were added up to arrive at an industry figure. Third, the investment series for each industry was also expressed in 1970 prices, using the wholesale price index (FGV, column 12) as a deflator. Fourth, the gross investment figures were adjusted by subtracting an estimated depreciation allowance; the resulting net investment figures were then added or subtracted to the base-year capital estimates for each industry.

The assumed rates of depreciation of the capital stock are reported in Table A.1.

Price indexes

Steel. The index for 1965–75 is based upon average revenues per equivalent ingot ton of steel at the three largest public enterprises: CSN, COSIPA, and USIMINAS. Sales and production figures were derived from annual reports of these firms. Unfortunately, reports were not available for the period 1960–4; the wholesale price index (FGV, column 21) for metals and metal products was used, although this substitution is not completely satisfactory. Reports were also not available for 1976. Steel prices in this period were assumed to increase in accord with the increase in the wholesale price index for iron and steel (FGV, column 56).

Petrochemicals. The price index used is that for wholesale prices of fuels and lubricants (FGV, column 20).

Iron ore. The index in Table 7.1 was constructed on the basis of the average dollar price per metric ton of exported ore. The dollar price index was converted into cruzeiros using the average annual rate of exchange. The average dollar price of ore is reported in annual reports of the Companhia Vale do Rio Doce. For exchange rate data, see *Conjuntura Econômica* 30 (March 1976):93.

Electricity. The price index reported is spliced together from several sources. The average price per kilowatt hour for 1965–72 is reported in Ministério de Minas e Energia, *Relatório Anual*, 1973. For the period from 1960 to 1964, increases in power rates were assumed to change in accord with the utilities subitem of the consumer price index for Rio de Janeiro. Again, this is an unsatisfactory approximation. For 1973–6, the delivered price per kwh in Rio de Janeiro was used in order to bring the index forward. For this information, see *Conjuntura Econômica* 28 (February 1974):24; 29 (February 1975):20; and 31 (February 1977):14.

Utilities and Urban Transport. This is a catch-all category covering a basket of publicly produced goods and services such as natural gas, suburban train transport, electricity, water, and residential phone service, as well as some privately produced services such as bus transportation. The index is one of the components of the cost of living index for Rio de Janeiro.

Railroad Freight. The index is the cost of shipping one ton of rice over a distance of 600 kilometers, which was arbitrarily selected as a representative price of services. For 1960–72, see Howland, "The Economics of Transportation Policy, 1945–1970," p. 175. This index was updated by the author, using information culled from IBGE, *Anuário Estatístico do Brasil*, various years, 1972–6.

Telecommunications. The index is constructed on the basis of revenues per local phone call in the cities of Rio de Janeiro and São Paulo. For the period from 1960 to 1974, the relevant data may be found in Companhia Telefônica Brasileira (CTB), *Anuário Estatístico da CTB*, various issues, 1960–74. For 1975–6, the average charge per call was assumed to have increased in accord with the telephone price item used in the calculation of the Rio consumer price index. (See note on construction of electricity price index for appropriate references to *Conjuntura Econômica.*)

Table A.1. *Normal depreciation allowances: Ratio of replacement investment to net fixed assets*

Industry	Rate of depreciation
Railways	.056
Petroleum	.100
Electricity	.051
Communications	.080
Other industries	.073
Overall mean	.073

Note: Estimates on basis of average length-of-life figures for capital.
Source: Andrew H. Gantt and Guiseppe Dutto, "Financial Performance of Government-Owned Corporations," *IMF Staff Papers*, (March 1968): 110.

Notes

Preface

1. The debate over "statization" (*estatização* in Portuguese) arose in the mid-1970s out of the reaction of leading private sector business figures to the growing web of state regulation of economic activity in Brazil despite the frequent allegations of the government that their objective was to create an economic system based upon free enterprise. The flavor of the early debate is well captured in a polemical article by Luciano Martins, "Estatização da Economia ou 'Privatização' do Estado?" *Ensaios de Opinião*, no. 9(1978):30–7. See also Werner Baer, Richard Newfarmer, and Thomas Trebat, "On State Capitalism in Brazil: Some New Issues and Questions," *Inter-American Economic Affairs* 30 (Winter 1977):69–91; Douglas H. Graham and José Roberto Mendonça de Barros, "The Brazilian Economic Miracle Revisited: Private and Public Sector Initiative in a Market Economy," *Latin American Research Review* 13 (1978):5–38.

1. Introduction

1. Alfred Stepan has investigated the origins of this Latin American view of the state in the course of his work on Peru. Alfred Stepan, *The State and Society: Peru in Comparative Perspective* (Princeton, N.J.: Princeton University Press, 1978). A classic work on the relations between state and economic development in Latin America is by William P. Glade, *The Latin American Economies: A Study of Their Institutional Development* (New York: American Book, 1969).
2. Glade, *The Latin American Economies*, p. 409.
3. Stepan, *The State and Society*, esp. Chapter 1, pp. 3–45.
4. Ibid., p. 30.
5. Ibid., p. 41.
6. Ibid., pp. 44. My emphasis.
7. An influential early article was by Werner Baer, Isaac Kerstenetzsky, and Annibal Villela, "The Changing Role of the State in the Brazilian Economy," *World Development* 1 (November 1973):23–4.
8. A basic reference is Sergio Abranches, "The Divided Leviathan: State and Economic Policy Formation in Authoritarian Brazil," Ph.D. dissertation, Cornell University, August 1978.

9. Sergio Abranches and Sulamis Dain, "A Empresa Estatal no Brasil: Padrões Estruturais e Estratégias de Ação," Rio de Janeiro, FINEP, 1978, Xerox.

10. Luciano Martins, "A expansão recente do Estado no Brasil," Rio de Janeiro, IUPERJ, 1976, Xerox. The earlier reference is to Martins's "Politique et developement economique: structures de pouvoir et système de decisions au brésil," Ph.D. dissertation, University of Paris, 1973.

11. Renato Boschi, "National Industrial Elites and the State in Post-1964 Brazil: Institutional Mediations and Political Change," Ph.D. dissertation, University of Michigan, 1978. Published in Portuguese as *Elites Industriais e Democracia* (Rio de Janeiro: Edições Graal, Ltda., 1979).

12. Carlos Estevam Martins, *Capitalismo do Estado e Modêlo Político no Brasil* (Rio de Janeiro: Edições Graal, 1977), and also an important volume edited by Martins, *Estado e Capitalismo no Brasil* (São Paulo: Editora HUCITEC, 1977). Some of the valuable works included in this volume are Luciano Coutinho and Henri-Philippe Reichstul, "O sector produtivo estatal e o ciclo," 55; Fernando Henrique Cardoso, "Desenvolvimento Capitalista e Estado; Bases e Alternatives," pp. 205–20; and Eli Diniz Cerqueira and Renato R. Boschi, "Elite Industrial e Estado," pp. 167–204.

13. Peter Evans, *Dependent Development: The Alliance of Multinational State, and Local Capital in Brazil* (Princeton, N.J.: Princeton University Press, 1979).

14. Richard S. Newfarmer, *Transnational Conglomerates and the Economics of Dependent Development: A Case Study of the International Electrical Oligopoly and Brazil's Electrical Industry* (Greenwich, Ct.: JAI Press, 1980). Another important study by the same author is "State Elites in Power: State Control of the Electric Power Industry in Latin America" (Xerox), Department of Economics, University of Notre Dame, 1980.

15. At this writing, Margareth Hanson Costa and her team at the Center for Fiscal Studies, Fundação Getulio Vargas, Rio de Janeiro, are preparing for such data publication.

16. Albert H. Hanson, *Public Enterprise and Economic Development*, 2nd ed. (London: Routledge & Kegan Paul, 1965), p. 204.

17. Space does not permit mention of the relevant works on the economic analysis of public enterprise in practice. The interested reader is referred to the bibliography for a more complete listing. The important studies of public enterprise in developed countries have been contributed by observers of the British experience and include: W. A. Robson, *Nationalized Industry and Public Ownership* (London: Allen & Unwin Ltd., 1960); W. G. Shepherd, *Economic Performance Under Public Ownership: British Fuel and Power* (New Haven, Ct.: Yale University Press, 1965); Richard Pryke, *Public Enterprise in Practice* (London: Macmillan, 1971); Ralph Turvey, *Economic Analysis and Public Enterprise* (London: Allen & Unwin, 1972). The best available study of the U.S. experience is found in Clair Wilcox and W. G. Shepherd, *Public Policies Toward Business*, 5th ed. (Homewood, Ill.: Irwin, 1975). The most important recent study on

performance evaluation in a cross-national setting is by W. G. Shepherd, ed., *Public Enterprise: Economic Analysis of Theory and Practice* (Lexington, Mass.: Heath, 1976.) Basic references for the study of public enterprises in developing countries would include Hanson, *Public Enterprise and Economic Development*; V. V. Ramanadham, *The Structure of Public Enterprise in India* (New York: Asia Publishing, 1961); Gustav Ranis, ed., *Government and Economic Development* (New Haven, Ct.: Yale University Press, 1971), and Leroy Jones, *Public Enterprise and Economic Development: The Korean Case* (Seoul: Korea Development Institute, 1975). An important early work on Brazilian public enterprise was by Judith Tendler, *Electric Power in Brazil: Entrepreneurship in the Public Sector* (Cambridge, Mass.: Harvard University Press, 1968).

18. William P. Glade, "The Study of State Enterprise in Economic Development," paper presented at the Conference of Economic Relations between Mexico and the United States, Austin, Tex. (April 1973), p. 16.

2. The economic role of the state

1. This distinction was also used in an earlier, co-authored article, which provided an outline for this chapter. See Baer, Newfarmer, and Trebat, "On State Capitalism in Brazil: Some New Issues and Questions."

2. Glade, *The Latin American Economies*, pp. 156–7.

3. Ibid., p. 299.

4. Nicia Vilela Luz, *A luta pela industrialização do Brasil, 1808 a 1930* (São Paulo: Difusão Europeia do Livro, 1961).

5. Steven Topik, "The Evolution of the Economic Role of the Brazilian State, 1889–1930," *Journal of Latin American Studies* 11 (1979): 326.

6. For details, see Thomas H. Holloway, *The Brazilian Coffee Valorization of 1906: Regional Politics and Economic Dependence*, State Historical Society of Wisconsin for the Department of History, University of Wisconsin, 1975.

7. Agriculture's declining share is discussed in Paulo Rabello de Castro, "Repartição setorial da renda: ciclos e tendencias," *Conjuntura Econômica* 33 (December 1979):85–6.

8. Two standard sources on industrialization are Werner Baer, *Industrialization and Economic Development in Brazil* (Homewood, Ill.: Irwin, 1965); and Joel Bergsman, *Brazil: Industrialization and Trade Policies* (London: Oxford University Press, 1970). See also Wilson Suzigan, ed., *Indústria: política, instituições, e desenvolvimento* (Rio de Janeiro: IPEA, Série Monográfica no. 28).

9. Some references on the role of the state in Brazil are A. Villela and W. Suzigan, *Política do governo e crescimento da economia brasileira, 1889–1945* (Rio de Janeiro: IPEA/INPES, 1975); W. Baer, I. Kerstenetzsky, and A. Villela, "The Changing Role of the State in the Brazilian Economy," *World Development* 1 (November 1973):23–4; Fernando A. Rezende, *Avaliação do setor público na economia brasileira* (Rio de Janeiro: IPEA/INPES, 1973).

10. See Richard Musgrave, *Fiscal Systems* (New Haven and London: Yale University Press, 1969), pp. 69–90; Fernando A. Rezende, "A evolução das funçoes do governo e a expansão do setor público brasileiro," *Pesquisa e Planejamento Econômico* 1 (December 1971):235–82.

11. In national accounts data in Brazil, the "public sector" is comprised of the following: (1) organs of central administration of the three levels of government, excluding public enterprises; (2) *autarquias* and foundations; (3) nonprofit private entities set up with social welfare, educational, or research objectives and whose resources come predominantly from the government (examples: SESC, SENAI, SENAC); and (4) special regional development programs and retirement funds, such as P.I.N., PROTERRA, PRODOESTE, PROVALE, PIS, and PASEP. In accordance with international practice, public enterprises are excluded from the public sector for national accounts purposes.

12. As Baer points out, this figure, while high for developing countries, is not unusual by international standards. See W. Baer, I. Kerstenetzsky, and A. Villela, "The Changing Role of the State in the Brazilian Economy," p. 28, n. 28.

13. The Brazilian system of revenue sharing is discussed in Donald Syvrud, *Foundations of Brazilian Economic Growth* (Washington, D.C.: American Enterprise Institute, 1975), pp. 123–4.

14. See John F. Due and Ann F. Friedlaender, *Government Finance: Economics of the Public Sector* (Homewood, Ill.: Irwin, 1973), p. 672.

15. Luciano Martins has called attention to the growing importance of these and other types of funds to the overall expansion of the state of Brazil. See Luciano Martins, "A expansão recente do Estado no Brasil," unpublished research paper, 1976, pp. 8–10. The FGTS, or Job-Tenure Guarantee Fund, was established in 1966 to provide increased financial security for workers, because at the time employers were permitted greater flexibility to dismiss unneeded workers. The resources generated by the FGTS have been used to finance the operations of the National Housing Bank. PIS – the Social Integration Fund – and PASEP, a similar fund for public sector employees, are profit-sharing programs. The resources of these funds have been used to finance housing and general development projects and have provided funding for the National Economic Development Bank (BNDE).

16. The best explanation for the growth of these funds may be found in Werner Baer and Paul Beckerman, "The Trouble with Index-Linking: Reflections on the Brazilian Experience," *World Development* 8 (1980):677–703.

17. This point is also discussed in Baer, Newfarmer, and Trebat, "On State Capitalism in Brazil," pp. 87–8.

18. Martins, "A expansão recente do Estado," pp. 3–4.

19. Margareth Hanson Costa, "A discutida ampliação da intervenção estatal," *Conjuntura Econômica* 33 (December 1979):90–2.

20. Martins, "A expansão recente do Estado," p. 14.

21. Fernando Rezende and Flavio P. Castelo Branco, "O emprego público como instrumento de política economica," in Rezende da Silva et al.,

Aspectos da participação do governo na economia, IPEA Série Monográfica, no. 26 (Rio de Janeiro: IPEA/INPES, 1976), esp. Tables 2, 3, 4.

22. Ibid.

23. Costa, "A discutida ampliação", p. 92.

24. Ibid.

25. Baer, Newfarmer, and Trebat, "On State Capitalism," pp. 74–5.

26. A thorough description is provided in Cesar Guimarães, "Perfil da Expansão do Estado Brasileiro na Esfera Economica," unpublished paper, IUPERJ, Rio de Janeiro, 1977, pp. 19–101.

27. Annibal Villela and Werner Baer, *O setor privado nacional: problemas e políticas para seu fortalecimento* (Rio de Janeiro: IPEA, Coleção Relatórios de Pesquisa, no. 46, 1980).

28. Ibid., p. 113.

29. Ibid., p. 130.

30. Abranches has performed a very thorough analysis of the decision-making process of the CDI. See Sergio Abranches, "The Divided Leviathan: State and Economic Policy Formation in Authoritarian Brazil," Ph.D. dissertation, Cornell University, August 1978.

31. For a description of the expansion of the state in the financial sector after 1964, see Douglas H. Graham and José Roberto Mendonça de Barros, "The Brazilian Economic Miracle Revisited: Private and Public Sector Initiative in a Market Economy," *Latin American Research Review* 13 (1978):16–32.

32. Villela and Baer, *O setor privado nacional*, pp. 194–7.

33. Brazil's twenty largest commercial banks ranked by deposits, 1980 (Cr$ million)

33. *Brazil's twenty largest commercial*
banks ranked by deposits, 1980
(Cr$ million)

1. Banco do Brasil[a]	264,455.8
2. Bradesco	88,253.8
3. Banespa[a]	57,350.7
4. Itau	51,839.1
5. Nacional	33,511.7
6. Unibanco	33,206.2
7. Real	31,734.9
8. Bamerindus	24,936.4
9. Banerj[a]	24,662.6
10. Mercantil de São Paulo	20,169.2
11. Auxiliar	17,090.5
12. Citibank	17,079.7
13. Economico	16,328.0
14. Sul Brasileiro	16,176.1
15. Safra	15,942.0
16. Frances e Brasileiro	15,401.3
17. Comind	14,353.2
18. Banrisul[a]	14,323.8
19. Lar Brasileiro	13,988.2
20. Bemge[a]	13,557.2

[a]State-owned.
Source: Visão "Quem é quem na economia brasileira," August 29, 1980, p. 406.

3. Origins of public enterprise in Brazil

1. Suzigan, "As empresas do governo e o papel do estado na economia brasileira," in Fernando Rezende da Silva et al., *Aspectos da participaçao do governo na economia* (Rio de Janeiro: IPEA/INPES, 1976), p. 126.

2. These and other hypotheses are investigated from a comparative international perspective in Frederick Pryor, "Public Ownership: Some Quantitative Dimensions," in W. G. Shepherd, ed., *Public Enterprise: Economic Analysis of Theory and Practice*, pp. 3–22.

3. Sheahan, "Public Enterprises in Economic Development," pp. 205–6.

4. See Ronald I. McKinnon, *Money and Capital in Economic Development* (Washington, D.C.: Brookings Institution, 1973), p. 9.

5. It should be noted that the private sector may be weak precisely because of past government intervention in the market mechanism, an argument advanced by many authors, including McKinnon (see Ibid). If this argument is essentially correct, the obstacle of a weak private sector is

not overcome by further public intervention. The "weak private sector" hypothesis does not deal with the merits of this argument.

6. Charles Kindleberger and Bruce Herrick, *Economic Development*, rev. ed. (New York: McGraw-Hill, 1977).

7. Baer, Newfarmer, and Trebat, "On State Capitalism," pp. 87–8.

8. One major exception to this general lack of a pattern would occur when independence of a colonial/imperialist power is a primary motivation. Public intervention would be expected in tradeables that might previously have been dominated by the foreign power. I owe this point to William Steel.

9. The official census of federally owned enterprises yielded a total of 251 mixed economy and public enterprises. (See text for juridical distinction between these two major types of state companies.) See Secretaria de Contrôle de Empresas Estatais (SEST), *Empresas estatais no Brasil e o controle da SEST: antecedentes e experiência de 1980* (Brasília, 1981), Annex 20, pp. 94–120. The best source of information on state companies at all levels of government continues to be the annual survey of corporations published by *Visão* magazine and entitled *Quem é quem na economia brasileira*.

10. The most important piece of legislation affecting the creation and operation of state enterprises in Brazil is Decree-Law 200 of 1967, later supplemented by Decree-Law 900 in 1969. Both types of public enterprises are authorized to operate within the bounds of private law in Brazil. For additional discussions of legal aspects, see Manoel de Oliveira Franco Sobrinho, *Empresas Públicas no Brasil* (São Paulo: Editora Resenha Universitária, 1975).

11. This was originally pointed out by Luciano Martins.

12. For a review of the history of public enterprise in Brazil, see Baer, Kerstenetzky, and Villela, "The Changing Role of the State," pp. 23–8. See also Wilson Suzigan, "As empresas do governo e o papel do estado na economia brasileira," pp. 77–134; "Atividade Empresarial dos Governos Federal e Estadual," *Conjuntura Econômica* 27 (June 1973):76–82; Alberto Venancio Filho, *A intervenção do estado no domínio econômico* (Rio de Janeiro: Fundação Getulio Vargas 1967).

13. Werner Baer, *A industrialização e o desenvolvimento econômico do Brasil*, 2nd ed. (Rio de Janeiro: Fundação Getulio Vargas, 1975), p. 299.

14. Ibid.

15. Steven Topik, "The Role of the State and Economic Nationalism in an Underdeveloped Country: Brazil, 1889–1930," Ph.D. thesis, Department of History, University of Texas at Austin, 1978.

16. See Villela and Suzigan, *Política do governo e crescimento da economia brasileira, 1889–1945*, p. 139.

17. A. Villela and W. Suzigan, *Government Policy and the Economic Growth of Brazil, 1889–1945* (Rio de Janeiro: IPEA, 1977), p. 47.

18. Ibid., pp. 309–16.

19. Villela and Suzigan interpret this trend as follows: "The increase in government ownership was due not to expropriation and confiscation, but

to the unprofitability of Brazilian railroads. Unfortunately, increased government administration rendered the railroads even less efficient... The decline of administration by private firms aggravated the tendency of railroads to run a deficit. Frequent changes in management, administrative featherbedding, political pressures, and a reluctance to press for fare increases despite widespread inflation lowered the efficiency of the railroads run by the government. Even worse, the revenues of the federal lines were used as general government accruals, rather than retained by the railroads that generated them. As a consequence, there was no incentive for individual lines to increase their revenues," ibid., pp. 330–2.

20. Ibid., pp. 317–22.

21. Steven Topik, "The Evolution of the Economic Role of the Brazilian State, 1889–1930," *Journal of Latin American Studies* 11 (1979):327.

22. Fernando Rezende and Dennis Mahar, "The Growth and Pattern of Public Expenditure in Brazil," *Public Finance Quarterly* 3 (October 1975):31.

23. A description of the *autarquias* may be found in Alberto Venancio Filho, *A intervenção do Estado no domínio econômico* (Rio de Janeiro: Fundação Getulio Vargas, 1967), pp. 358–65.

24. Suzigan, "Empresas do governo e o papel do estado," p. 85.

25. The founding of the steel industry is recounted in John Wirth, *The Politics of Brazilian Development, 1930–1954*, pp. 77–132; Werner Baer, *The Development of the Brazilian Steel Industry* (Nashville, Tenn.: Vanderbilt University Press, 1969). Abranches, "The Divided Leviathan."

26. Wirth: *The Politics of Brazilian Development*, p. 127.

27. Ibid., p. 126.

28. Venancio Filho, *A intervenção do Estado no domínio econômico*, pp. 376–8.

29. See Sergio Abranches, "Empresa estatal e capitalismo: uma análise comparada," in Carlos E. Martins, ed., *Estado e Capitalismo no Brasil* (São Paulo: HUCITEC, 1978), pp. 13–14.

30. Sergio Abranches and Sulamis Dain, "A Empresa Estatal no Brasil: Padrões Estruturais e Estratégias de Ação," unpublished preliminary report, FINEP, 1978, pp. 33–43.

31. This enterprise, never consistently profitable, was sold to the private sector in 1968. To my knowledge, this was the only significant case of denationalization of a public enterprise in the postwar period until a flurry of sales of mostly small or money-losing public enterprises during 1982.

32. Wirth describes the formation of PETROBRÁS in *The Politics of Brazilian Development 1930–1954*, pp. 133–216.

33. Alexander Gerschenkron, *Economic Backwardness in Historical Perspective* (Cambridge, Mass.: Harvard University Press, 1962), p. 14. My thanks to Werner Baer for pointing this out.

34. Baer, *The Development of the Brazilian Steel Industry*. COFAVI was one of several small steel plants put up for sale to the private sector in 1982.

35. See Judith Tendler, *Electric Power in Brazil: Entrepreneurship in the Public Sector* (Cambridge, Mass.: Harvard University Press, 1968).

36. Graham and Mendonca, "The Brazilian Economic Miracle Revisited," p. 14.

37. Werner Baer, "The Brazilian Growth and Development Experience, 1964–1975," in Riordan Roett, ed., *Brazil in the Seventies* (Washington, D.C.: American Enterprise Institute, 1976), pp. 45–6.

38. For a review of the period of expansion, see ibid.

39. For a description of the intent of the reforms, see Helio Beltrão, "A revolução silenciosa," *Visão* (August 31, 1976), pp. 29–30.

40. However, the foreign companies were, after the arrival of PETROBRÁS Distribuidora, strictly limited in their ability to open new gas stations or distribution centers.

41. For details, see Evans, *Dependent Development*; also, Jose Tavares de Araujo Junior and Vera Dick, "Governo, Empresas Multinacionais, e Empresas Nacionais: O Caso da Indústria Petroquímica," *Pesquisa e Planejamento* 4 (December 1974):629–54.

42. Getulio Carvalho, "PETROBRÁS: A Case Study of Nationalism and Institution Building in Brazil," Ph.D. dissertation, University of Connecticut, 1975, pp. 26–7.

43. Evans observes: "In two years of negotiations (with private firms), PETROQUISA has managed to put together a set of companies which when they all go on-stream will double Brazil's petrochemical industry and be the biggest single impetus to industrialization that has been attempted in the Northeast region." Peter Evans, "Multinationals, State-Owned Corporations, and the Transformation of Imperialism: A Brazilian Case Study," *Economic Development and Cultural Change* 26 (October 1977):54.

44. Ibid.

45. Even though CVRD's financial problems became manageable after some paring down, management was blasted in editorials of the time for its "undeniable megalomania" (*Jornal do Brasil*, May 28, 1978) and its "irresponsible diversification" (*Estado de São Paulo*, September 17, 1978).

46. COBRA was set up essentially for political reasons, since a number of the largest multinational computer equipment manufacturers, eyeing an enormous potential market, were anxious to set up facilities in Brazil for the production of small computers. A state company was thought to be the best means of heading off what otherwise would have been a complete takeover of the incipient industry by foreign-owned companies. For details on this interesting case of state-enterprise creation, the reader is referred to Ivan da Costa Marques, "Computadores: parte de um caso amplo da sobrevivência e da sobernia nacional," *Revista de Administração Pública* 14 (Oct.–Dec. 1980):110–47.

47. Graham and Mendonça, "The Brazilian Economic Miracle Revisited," pp. 14–16.

48. *Visão, Quem é quem na economia brasileira,* 1967, 1971, 1975.

49. Source for Mexican estimate is Rene and Rocio Villarreal, "Las empresas públicas como instrumento de política económica en Mexico," *Trimestre Económico* 45 (April–June 1978):217; for Argentina, Alberto Joaquin Ugalde, "El comportamiento financiero de empresas públicas en el

periodo 1966–1978 y sus perspectivas," paper presented to the Second National Convention of Finance Executives, Buenos Aires, May 1979.

50. International Bank for Reconstruction and Development, *Chile: An Economy in Transition* (Washington, D.C.: IBRD, 1980), p. 88.

51. Villarreal and Villarreal, "Las empresas públicas," pp. 221–2.

52. International Bank for Reconstruction and Development, *Mexico: Manufacturing Sector: Situation, Prospects and Policies.* (Washington, D.C.: IBRD, 1979), p. 29.

53. *Chile Economic News*, September 1980, p. 4.

54. Glade, *The Latin American Economies*, pp. 432–45.

55. "Plan del Peru" (1971), as quoted in Fitzgerald, *The State and Economic Development*, p. 39.

56. However, many of the problems of foreign private enterprise in these sectors were caused by politically inspired rate controls.

57. On this, see Beny Palatnik and Luiz Orenstein, "Perspectivas do Proceso de Privatização no Brasil," *Encontros com a civilização brasileira* 15 (September 1979):43–62.

58. The "privatization" program by late 1982 had resulted in the sale of nine mostly small public enterprises. A long list of other companies was still up for bidding at the same time. These included three small steel companies: Cia. Ferro e Aço de Vitória (COPAVI), Cia. Siderúrgica Mogi das Cruzes (COSIM), and Cia. Siderúrgica da Amazônia (SIDERAMA).

4. The control of public enterprise in Brazil

1. For analytical and empirical discussions of the problem, the reader is referred to: Mario Einauldo, Maurice Bye, and Ernesto Rossi, *Nationalization in France and Italy* (Ithaca, N.Y.: Cornell University Press, 1955); C. D. Foster, *Politics, Finance, and the Role of Economics: An Essay on the Control of Public Ownership* (London: Allen & Unwin, 1971); Albert H. Hanson, *Public Enterprise and Economic Development*, 2nd ed. (London: Routledge & Kegan Paul, 1965); M. V. Posner and S. J. Woolf, *Italian Public Enterprise* (Cambridge, Mass.: Harvard University Press, 1967); Richard Pryke, *Public Enterprises in Practice* (New York: St. Martin's Press, 1971); William A. Robson, *Nationalized Industry and Public Ownership* (University of Toronto Press, 1960); Henry Tulkens, "The Publicness of Public Enterprise," in W. G. Shepherd, ed., *Public Enterprise: Economic Analysis of Theory and Practice* (Lexington, Mass.: Heath, 1976), pp. 23–32; John B. Sheahan, "Public Enterprise in Developing Countries," in Shepherd, ed., "Public Enterprise, pp. 205–34; W. G. Shepherd, "Objectives, Types, Accountability," in Shepherd, ed., *Public Enterprise*, pp. 33–48; W. G. Shepherd, "Entry as a Substitute for Regulation," *American Economic Review* 63 (May 1973):98–105. For an excellent recent discussion, with examples drawn from the Latin American experience, see Horacio Boneo, *Saber Ver Las Empresas Públicas* (San José, Costa Rica: EDUCA, 1979.

2. See discussion in Shepherd, "Objectives, Types, Accountability," pp. 38–40.

3. Richard S. Newfarmer has contributed an important case study of the interaction between public enterprise management and interest groups, such as governments and supplier firms. See *State Elites in Power: State Control of the Electric Power Industry in Latin America* (Department of Economics, University of Notre Dame, April 1980).

4. Hanson, *Public Enterprise and Economic Development*, p. 366.

5. Ibid., pp. 49–51.

6. Ibid.

7. Charles R. Frank, Jr., "Public and Private Enterprise in Africa," in Gustav Ranis, ed., *Government and Economic Development*, (New Haven and London: Yale University Press, 1973), p. 91.

8. A discussion may be found in Beatriz Wahrlich, "Controle politico das empresas estatais federais no Brasil – uma contribuição ao seu estudo," *Revista de Administração Pública* 14 (April–June 1980):5–38.

9. A discussion of these institutions is provided in Alberto Venancio Filho, *A intervenção do Estado no dominio econômico* (Rio de Janeiro: Fundação Getulio Vargas, 1968), pp. 438–58. See also J. G. Piquet Carneiro, "Para controlar a empresa estatal," *Revista de Finanças Publicas* 37 (Oct.–Dec. 1977):45–8.

10. For example, in late 1977 the tribunal had a staff of only 15 "tecnicos" with which to examine the books of more than 200 enterprises.

11. This role has been carefully described in Robson, *Nationalized Industry and Public Ownership*; and Foster, *Politics, Finance, and the Role of Economics*.

12. Posner and Woolf, *Italian Public Enterprise*, p. 125.

13. Boneo, *Saber Ver Las Empresas Publicas*, p. 60.

14. Ibid.

15. Judith Tendler, *Electric Power in Brazil: Entrepreneurship in the Public Sector* (Cambridge, Mass.: Harvard University Press, 1968).

16. Ibid.

17. Cited in Sergio Abranches and Sulamis Dain, "A empresa estatal no Brasil: Padrões estruturais e estratégias de ação," p. 52.

18. Otavio Marcondez Ferraz, "Discurso de Posse," *Revista Brasileira de Energia Elétrica* 1 (1964):34.

19. Martins, "A expansão recente do Estado no Brasil," pp. 42–3.

20. Decree-Law 200, Article 27.

21. Thomas E. Skidmore, *Politics in Brazil, 1930–1964: An Experiment in Democracy* (New York: Oxford University Press, 1967), p. 290.

22. Reported by Donald E. Syvrud, *Foundations of Brazilian Economic Growth* (Stanford, Calif.: Hoover Institution Press, 1974), p. 120.

23. One of the most important intellectual influences on stabilization policy after 1964 was former Finance Minister Eugenio Gudin. Gudin was quoted as follows regarding the weakened financial condition of public enterprises in 1963–4: "[Goulart] never took an interest in these problems, except in regard to the promotion of his Trade Union Republic. If the trade

unions requested it, he would double the salaries in PETROBRÁS; if they demanded the nationalization of [privately owned] refineries, he would do it; if they recommended a superintendent for [one of the railroads], he would name him. The succession of mistakes was the main cause of the Federal Government deficits and, thus, inflation" (Gudin, quoted in *Estado de São Paulo*, March 29, 1978).

24. Coutinho and Reichstul, "O setor produtivo estatal," pp. 58–9.

25. Martins, "A expansão recente do Estado no Brasil."

26. The dominance of engineering and other technical backgrounds among high-level public enterprise managers is apparent from a comparison with the training of comparably high-level civil servants. Martins found that 80% of the public enterprise group had either formal degrees in engineering or had completed their university education at one of Brazil's military academies where emphasis is placed on the applied sciences. Only about 8% had pursued courses of study that emphasized business administration. By contrast, the sample group of high-level civil servants had proportionately many more individuals with general business and legal educations. More than one-half of the group of 44 civil servants had studied business and law, whereas only 40% had engineering backgrounds (see Table 4.2).

27. Martins, "A expansão recente do Estado," p. 193.

28. Ibid., p. 185.

29. Ibid., p. 194.

30. Ibid., p. 196.

31. Abranches and Dain provide a case study of the federal railway system in "A empresa estatal no Brasil: padrões estruturais e estratégias de ação."

32. Abranches has contributed a valuable series of articles on CONSIDER, SIDERBRAS, and the workings of the decision-making structure for steel described here. See Abranches, "Governo, Empresa Estatal, e Política Siderúrgica no Brasil" (Rio de Janeiro, 1977), working paper. A complete discussion of the origins of the various decision-making structures for steel is also provided by William A. Wernecke, Jr., "The Mixed Corporation Model in Brazil: A Case Analysis of Three State Steel Firms, 1964/76," undergraduate thesis, Stanford University, June 1977.

33. The control of the Ministry of Communications over TELEBRAS and its subsidiaries is greater than that exercised by other ministries over public enterprises, because the ministry's range of responsibility is narrow relative to those of the Ministries of Mines and Energy and of Industry and Commerce. Besides being able to devote a large proportion of its staff and resources to overseeing public enterprises, the success of the ministry (and the political career of the minister) is much more closely identified with the success of public enterprises than is the case in other sectors.

34. Relatively little has been written about CVRD, an example of a highly successful state enterprise. In addition to the study by Abranches and Dain, several articles dealing with the company are available. See Janet Kelly Escobar, "Comparing State Enterprises Across International Boundaries: The Corporación Venezolana de Guyana and the Companhía Vale

do Rio Doce," in Leroy P. Jones, ed., *Public Enterprise in Less-Developed Countries* (New York: Cambridge University Press, 1982), and Raymond Vernon, "State-owned Enterprises in Latin American Exports," in Werner Baer and Malcom Gillis, eds., *Export Diversification and the New Protectionism: The Experiences of Latin America* (Champaign-Urbana: University of Illinois, 1981), pp. 98–114.

35. For a fuller explanation, see Raymond Vernon and Brian Levy, "State-owned Enterprises in the World Economy: The Case of Iron Ore," in Leroy P. Jones, ed., *Public Enterprise in Less-Developed Countries.*

36. Abranches and Dain, "A empresa estatal no Brasil," p. 65.

37. Several studies of decision making in PETROBRÁS are available. These include Getulio Carvalho, "PETROBRÁS: A Case Study of Nationalism"; Peter Seaborn Smith, *Oil and Politics in Modern Brazil* (Toronto: Macmillan of Canada, 1976); and Lawrence W. Bates, "The Petroleum Industry in Brazil," Ph.D. dissertation, University of Texas at Austin, 1975.

38. Smith, *Oil and Politics in Modern Brazil*, p. 164.

39. Ibid., p. 166.

40. Ibid.

41. *Estado de São Paulo*, October 5, 1976.

42. Decree 84.128, October 29, 1979.

43. Author's interviews with Brazilian policymakers, Brasília, February 1981.

44. For example, ELETROBRÁS encountered severe budget pressures in late 1970, partly as a result of SEST price controls. While, eventually, some rate relief was granted to the firm, this was not before the proud company was forced to skip loan repayments to equipment suppliers and the president of the company resigned in protest over the controls placed on ELETROBRÁS. Late payments to domestic suppliers were to become an even more serious problem for ELETROBRÁS and other large state firms as Brazil's financial crisis worsened through 1982.

5. Relationships with economic growth

1. Hollis B. Chenery and Moses Syrquin, *Patterns of Development, 1950–70* (London: Oxford University Press, 1975), p. 20.

2. Unfortunately, national accounts investment data for Brazil do not detail the amount of inventory change; thus, the aggregate figures include some amount of involuntary investment.

3. Early postwar industrialization policies are well described in Werner Baer, *Industrialization and the Economic Development of Brazil* (Homewood, Ill.: Irwin, 1965); Joel Bergsman, *Brazil: Industrialization and Trade Policies* (New York and London: Oxford University Press, 1971); and Wilson Suzigan, ed., *Indústria: política, instituições, e desenvolvimento* (Rio de Janeiro: IPEA, Série Monográfica, no. 28, 1978).

4. The aerospace and computer industry initiatives both involved the pioneering production under foreign licensing arrangements by government enterprises of the finished products, i.e., light commercial aircraft by

EMBRAER, small office computers by COBRA. Government policy then concentrated on building backward supply linkages to nationalize increasingly not only the manufacture of parts but also the essential technology involved. For a case study of the computer industry, see Ivan da Costa Marques, "Computadores: parte de um caso amplo da sobrevivência," *Revista de Administração Pública* 14 (Oct.–Dec. 1980):110–47.

5. Suzigan, *Indústria*, pp. 67–72. Incentive policies of the government are also discussed in Baer and Villela, *O setor privado national*, e.g., pp. 70–6. In the 1970s, the emphasis in many of these government programs broadened from promoting simple import substitution to encouraging as well the development of a Brazilian research and development infrastructure. The idea was to begin reducing Brazil's traditionally heavy dependence on imported foreign technology. For a description of changing government policies toward science and technology, see Fabio Stefano Erber, "Desenvolvimento tecnológico e intervenção do estado," *Revista de Administração Pública* 14 (Oct.–Dec. 1980):10–72. A useful additional reference is by Bela Balassa, "Incentive Policies in Brazil," *World Development* 7 (Nov.–Dec. 1979):1023–42.

6. I am grateful to Margareth Hanson Costa of the Fundação Getulio Vargas for making these data available.

7. A more detailed treatment of the cyclical role of public enterprise investment is provided in Henri Philippe Reichstul and Luciano Coutinho, "Tendências recentes do investimento empresarial do Estado," (FUNDAP/ CLACSO, São Paulo, December 1979).

8. Ibid., p. 67.

9. Ibid., p. 68.

10. Luiz A. Correa do Lago et al., *A Indústria Brasileira de Bens de Capital* (Rio de Janeiro, IBRE, Fundação Getulio Vargas, 1979), p. 241.

11. Ibid.

12. Decree 76404 (10/9/1975) mandated the creation in each state company of a "nucleo de articulação com a indústria," a unit to seek ways to promote closer supply links with domestic producers and to reduce imports. It was left to each company to figure out how exactly to shape its investment requirements to match existing *or potential* domestic supply capacity. A first step on the part of many companies was simply to announce purchases along with technical equipment specifications well in advance in order to give potential suppliers a chance to prepare to meet the anticipated orders.

13. SIDERBRÁS, Annual Report, 1979.

14. Annual Reports of CSN, COSIPA, USIMINAS. The steel industry traditionally had difficulties increasing domestic purchases because many of its projects were financed with World Bank loans that required competitive international bidding, precluding favoritism toward domestic producers. But in 1979, SIDERBRÁS, under growing government pressure to reduce equipment imports, began a program to increase the participation of domestic suppliers in the planned U.S. $6 billion expansion of public steelmaking capacity in the 1980s. By the terms of an agreement with the

National Economic Development Bank, the government agency that would provide supplemental finance, SIDERBRÁS signaled its intention to work more closely with domestic suppliers and local engineering concerns. This included redoubled efforts on the part of the holding company to standardize equipment purchases of its numerous steelmaking subsidiaries.

15. Data on annual output and exports are from CVRD reports. Iron ore market share is from unpublished data of the CVRD Department of Planning.

16. Raymond Vernon and Brian Levy, "State-owned Enterprises in the World Economy: The Case of Iron Ore," in Leroy P. Jones, ed., *Public Enterprise in Less-Developed Countries* (New York: Cambridge University Press, 1982).

17. CVRD, *Annual Report*, 1976.

18. TELEBRÁS, *Annual Reports*.

19. TELESP, *Annual Report*, 1979.

20. Centrais Eletricas Brasileiras (ELETROBRÁS), "The Brazilian Power Sector, 1980." But the bulk of the additional capacity targeted for construction lies in the Amazon region, far removed from the industrial Southeast.

21. ELETROBRÁS, *Annual Report*, 1979, p. 5.

22. But electricity investment began to taper off in real terms after 1979, a development with potentially major impacts on the pace of capital accumulation and economic growth in Brazil.

23. *O Estado de São Paulo*, January 17, 1978.

24. Instituto Brasileiro de Geografia e Estatística (IBGE), *Anuário Estatístico do Brasil*, 1979, p. 205.

25. The growth of real investment leveled off in 1978–9, however.

26. In 1981 Brazilian demand for imported crude oil fell very sharply. This reflected, in part, better energy pricing policies and improved conservation efforts but was mostly the consequence of the severe internal recession. GDP declined by 3.5% in 1981 after growing by nearly 8% in 1980.

27. Instituto Brasileiro de Geografia e Estatística (IBGE), *Anuário Estatístico do Brasil*, 1979, pp. 232–3.

28. *O Estado de São Paulo*, August 26, 1979.

6. Sources of growth and rates of return

1. The influence of trade unions on Mexican public enterprises is discussed in Thomas J. Trebat, "Public Enterprises in Brazil and Mexico: A Comparison of Origins and Performance," in Thomas C. Bruneau and Philippe Faucher, eds., *Authoritarian Capitalism* (Boulder, Colo.: Westview Press, 1981), pp. 41–58.

2. The development literature makes reference to an average COR of 2–3 for the economy as a whole. Werner Baer has reported these figures in his study of the Brazilian economy. See W. Baer, *Industrialization and Economic Development in Brazil* (Homewood, Ill.: Irwin, 1965), p. 130. See also James Land, "The Role of Public Enterprise in Turkish Economic Development," in Gustav Ranis, ed., *Government and Economic*

Development (New Haven and London: Yale University Press, 1973), pp. 80–1.

3. Reported in Constantino Lluch, "Employment, Earnings, and Income Distribution," in Peter Knight, ed., *Brazil: Human Resources Report* (Washington, D.C.: IBRD, 1979), Annex II, p. 19.

4. Wilson Suzigan, "As empresas do governo e o papel do estado," in Fernando Rezende et al., *Aspectos da participação do governo na economia*, IPEA Série Monográfica, no. 26 (Rio de Janeiro: IPEA/INPES, 1976), pp. 77–130.

5. For a discussion of these issues, see Alex Nove, *Efficiency Criteria for Nationalized Industries*, pp. 100–20; and E. J. Mishan, *Cost-Benefit Analysis* (New York: Praeger, 1976), pp. 119–224.

6. One possible estimate of the opportunity cost of public enterprise investment is the rate of profit on private sector investment that must be forgone. Turvey defines this opportunity cost as "the average risk-adjusted rate of return before tax expected on private investment projects which are just at the margin between acceptance and rejection." See Ralph Turvey, "The Second-Best Case for Marginal Cost Pricing," in J. Margolis and H. Guitton, eds., *Public Economics* (New York: St. Martin's Press, 1969), p. 336. He adds: "This, be it noted, has nothing whatsoever to do with accounting rates of return on the book value of existing assets." See ibid.

7. For estimates of the opportunity cost in Brazil, see Claudio Contador, "Custo de oportunidade de capital em condições de risco," *Pesquisa e Planejamento Econômico 5* (June 1975):163–218, especially Tables 2–4, pp. 197–9.

8. The decline in profitability after 1975 was continuous and not a result of special factors in 1979 that might have affected the economic environment for public firms.

9. This method was suggested to the author by Professor Samuel Morley of Vanderbilt University.

10. IBRD, *State Intervention in the Industrialization of Developing Countries: Selected Issues*, World Bank staff working paper no. 341 (Washington, D.C., July 1979), p. 12.

11. Ibid., p. 13.

12. John B. Sheahan, "Public Enterprises in Developing Countries," in W. G. Shepherd, ed., *Public Enterprise: Economic Analysis of Theory and Practice* (Lexington, Mass.: Heath, 1976).

13. L. P. Jones, *Public Enterprise and Economic Development: The Korean Case* (Seoul: Korea Development Institute, 1975).

14. Heba Ahmad Handoussa, "The Impact of Economic Liberalization on the Performance of Egypt's Public Sector Industry," paper presented to the Second B.A.P.E.G. Conference on Public Enterprise in Mixed Economy LDCs, Boston, April 2–5, 1980, p. 13.

15. John Sheahan, "Experience with Public Enterprise in France and Italy," in William G. Shepherd, ed., *Public Enterprise: Economic Analysis of Theory and Practice* (Lexington, Mass.: Heath, 1976), p. 144.

16. IBRD, *Mexico: Manufacturing Sector–Situation, Prospects, and Policies* (Washington, D.C.: IBRD, 1979), p. 71.
17. See discussion in Chapter 8 for more details.
18. E.V.K. Fitzgerald, *The Political Economy of Peru* (Cambridge University Press, 1979), p. 196.

7. Policies on pricing

1. See, e.g., the discussions of the matter in each of the following: William G. Shepherd, *Economic Performance Under Public Ownership: British Fuel and Power* (New Haven and London: Yale University Press, 1965); Richard Pryke, *Public Enterprise in Practice* (New York: St. Martin's Press, 1971); Alec Nove, *Efficiency Criteria for Nationalized Industries* (Toronto: University of Toronto Press, 1973); P. W. Reed, *The Economics of Public Enterprises* (London: Butterworth, 1973); Ralph Turvey, *Economic Analysis and Public Enterprises* (London: Allen & Unwin, 1971).

2. The assumptions include the following: (1) the total supply of labor is fixed; (2) no externalities in production or consumption; (3) diminishing marginal rates of substitution in factors; (4) diminishing marginal rate of transformation between commodities (production function concave to the origin); (5) consumer utility-maximization; producer profit-maximization; (6) all commodities and factors are perfectly divisible and saleable; (7) universal perfect competition; (8) unchanging technology.

3. The second-best situation is discussed in the references listed in note 1. An additional reference is the following: Ralph Turvey, "The Second-Best Case for Marginal Cost Pricing," in J. Margolis and H. Guitton, eds., *Public Economics* (New York: St. Martin's Press, 1969), pp. 336–42.

4. For a description of steel price controls in this earlier period, see Frank P. Sherwood, *O aumento do preço do aço da CSN: estudo de um caso*, Cadernos de Administração Pública, no. 61 (Rio de Janeiro: Fundação Getulio Vargas, 1966).

5. Corrective inflation was mentioned in a section on creation of public enterprise in 1964–7.

6. See Howard S. Ellis, "Corrective Inflation in Brazil, 1964–1966," in idem, ed., *The Economy of Brazil* (Berkeley and Los Angeles: University of California Press, 1969), pp. 177–212.

7. A review of basic legislation is available in Wilson Dutra and Vittoria Salles, "Padrões de Financiamento," pp. 14–71. Obviously, many important pricing matters, such as peak load problems, will not be discussed. For a full discussion, see P. W. Reed, *The Economics of Public Enterprise*, pp. 102–34. For a theoretical study of electricity pricing as well as an application to Brazil, the reader is referred to Paul R. Casperson, "Responsive pricing of Hydroelectricity in a Developing Region: The Case of Minas Gerais, Brazil," Ph.D. dissertation, Vanderbilt University, 1974.

8. Casperson points out that the static pricing model used in setting electricity rates is based primarily on the concept of recovering all financial obligations rather than on the intent to allocate resources efficiently. A

basic difference is that capacity costs for purposes of rate setting are the accountant's historical fixed costs rather than the economist's concept of fixed costs, which refer to the value of fixed resources (capital, land) in their best alternative uses and which, therefore, may vary over time. See Casperson, "Responsive Pricing."

9. See Reed, *The Economics of Public Enterprise*, pp. 106–8.

10. This is the impression of the author based upon interviews with officials at various electricity firms during 1975–6.

11. Judith Tendler suggests that the availability of external financing has been at times more important than size of the market in determining the construction of hydro facilities. See Judith Tendler, *Inside Foreign Aid* (Baltimore: Johns Hopkins University Press, 1975), pp. 63–72.

12. This abundance of hydro power made Brazil's multibillion dollar nuclear contract with West Germany controversial from the date of its signing in 1975. When the costs of the nuclear program then escalated far beyond original projections, the controversy in Brazil intensified and the original plan to build as many as 9 nuclear plants by 1990 was greatly scaled down.

13. Dutra and Salles, "Padrões de Financiamento," pp. 37–8.

14. This is based on unpublished information provided by ELETROBRÁS.

15. Baer, *The Development of the Brazilian Steel Industry*, pp. 127–9.

16. The results of this study are summarized in L. A. Correa do Lago et al., *A indústria brasileira de bens de capital* (Rio de Janeiro: Fundação Getulio Vargas, 1979) pp. 345–55.

17. Recall that a key objective of Brazilian steel policy has been to build sufficient steelmaking capacity for large-scale exports. Recent trends in the world steel market and financial constraints of the large state companies have caused these plans to be postponed.

18. Trebat, "Public Enterprises in Brazil and Mexico."

19. Horacio Boneo suggests interesting links between political regimes and public enterprise pricing policies. See "Political Regimes and Public Enterprises," paper presented to the Second B.A.P.E.G. Conference on Public Enterprise in Mixed Economy LDCs, Boston, April 3–5, 1980.

8. The financing of public enterprise investment

1. Webb expands on this point: "To support a self-financing policy is to prefer the results and effects of the resulting increase in indirect taxation (since in effect a unit sales tax would be in use) to the results and effect of the increases in taxation that might result from reliance on other ways of financing nationalized industries. This involves making decisions on the desired distribution of the tax bill and comparing the effects on resource use and factor supplies of the different types of taxes. Whether one form of taxation is to be preferred to another in this context is a question to which there is no simple answer." Michael G. Webb, *The Economics of Nationalized Industries* (London: Nelson, 1973), p. 145.

2. Malcom Gillis, Glenn P. Jenkins, Donald R. Lessard, "Public-Enterprise Finance: Toward a Synthesis," in Leroy P. Jones, ed., *Public Enterprise in Less-Developed Countries* (New York: Cambridge University Press, 1982).

3. This figure is a simple average of self-financing ratios reported for a large sample of industrial firms in 1973–4. See Fundação Getulio Vargas, "Investimentos na Indústria de Transformação," *Conjuntura Econômica* 29 (October 1975):70.

4. Andrew Gantt and Giuseppe Dutto, "Financial Performance of Government-owned Corporations in Less Developed Countries," *IMF Staff Papers* (March 1968):102–37.

5. SEST, *Empresas Estatais no Brasil*, p. 71.

6. The reader is referred back to the discussion of state-enterprise investment in Chapter 5.

7. SEST, *Fiscal Policy: Performance in 1980 and Guidelines for 1981*, Brasilia, 1981.

8. SEST, *Empresas Estatais no Brasil e o Côntrole da SEST: Antecedentes e Experiência de 1980* (Brasília, 1981), Anexo 18, p. 88.

Investment spending and treasury resources for
non-bank state enterprises, 1980 (Cr$ billion)

Enterprises	Total investment	Treasury resources	Treasury resources as % of investment
PETROBRÁS Group	112.0	1.9	2
SIDERBRÁS Group	108.4	14.7	14
ELETROBRÁS Group	122.3	16.4	13
TELEBRÁS Group	47.8	13.2	28
CVRD Group	34.5	0	0
RFFSA	40.7	45.1	111
ITAIPU BINACIONAL	47.1	0	0
All others	165.1	288.9	175
Totals	677.9	380.2	56

9. Anibal Villela, "As Empresas do Governo Federal," *Revista Brasileira de Economia* 16 (March 1962):98–113.

10. Ibid., p. 107.

11. Another common source of long-term finance is local stock market. In their study of daily trading and new issues among the 250 firms listed on the São Paulo exchange Graham and Mendonça found that five or six public firms dominated activity. For at least two reasons it is difficult to argue that these developments imply significant "crowding-out." First, the domestic stock market is a practically insignificant source of funds generally in Brazil and for public enterprises in particular. It was estimated that such financing accounts for less than 2% of investment needs. Second, as Graham and Mendonça point out, the dominant position of certain state-

enterprise issues in the stock market results from generally superior dividend policies and protection for minority stockholders. It would seem that by strengthening investor confidence in the reliability of financial assets, the public enterprises can contribute toward improving stock markets as a source of funds for all firms. See Douglas H. Graham and José Roberto Mendonça de Barros, "The Brazilian Economic Miracle Revisited: Private and Public Sector Initiative in a Market Economy," *Latin American Research Review* 13 (1978):19–22.

12. See Fundação Getulio Vargas, "BNDE–sua influencia no crescimento do pais," *Conjuntura Econômica* 27 (June 1973):98–104.

13. Banco Nacional de Desenvolvimento Econômico, "Operações do Sistema BNDE crescem 86% em 1975," *Conjuntura Econômica* 30 (May 1976):66–8.

14. Bank for International Settlements, "International Banking Developments–Second Quarter 1980" (November 19, 1980), Table 6.

15. On these points, see Lawrence J. Brainard and Thomas J. Trebat, "Commercial Banks and Balance of Payments Crises: The Cases of Peru and Poland," paper presented to the Conference on Multinationals in Eastern Europe and Latin America (Bloomington, Ind., March 1981).

16. David L. Scott, *Financing the Growth of Electric Utilities* (New York: Praeger 1976), p. 34.

17. Estimated on the basis of an examination of ELETROBRÁS annual reports from 1972 to 1975.

18. "A crise do setor siderúrgico estatal," *Gazeta Mercantil*, (May 21, 1981).

19. Wilson Dutra and Vittoria C. Salles, "Padrões de Financiamento em empresas estatais," FINEP Report, Rio de Janeiro, 1975, p. 34.

20. See Trebat, "Public Enterprises in Brazil and Mexico."

21. Andrew Gantt and Guiseppe Dutto, "Financial Performance of Government-owned Corporations," *IMF Staff Papers*, March 1968, p. 126.

Appendix B

1. For a sample of the type of information available in these files, see Centro de Estudos Fiscais, "Atividade empresarial dos governos federal e estadual," *Conjuntura Econômica* 27 (June 1973):66–96.

2. Other annual surveys of enterprises include "As 500 maiores sociedades anonimas do Brasil," published in the September issue of *Conjuntura Econômica* and the September issue of *Exame*, entitled "Os maiores e os melhores."

3. See the abundant information provided in the 1980 SEST report, *Empresas Estatais no Brasil e o Contrôle da SEST: Antecedentes e Experiência de 1980.*

4. It was not possible to obtain a breakdown of the share of each of these different labor expenditures in the total wage bill.

5. These are taxes paid by the firm, not the investment tax revenues that are gathered by the imposition of investment tax surcharges in sectors such as telecommunications and electricity.

6. Thomas J. Trebat, "An Evaluation of the Economic Performance of Public Enterprises in Brazil," Ph.D. dissertation, Vanderbilt University, 1978.

Selected bibliography

Official publications

Banco Nacional de Desenvolvimento Econômico (BNDE). *Relatório*, various issues.
Brazil. Conselho Nacional de Petróleo. *Relatório*, various issues.
Brazil. *Diário Oficial*, various issues.
Brazil. Ministerio da Industria e do Comercio. "Plano Siderúrgico Nacional." Rio de Janeiro, August 1969 (mimeograph).
Brazil. Ministério da Indústria e do Comércio. Conselho Nacional da Indústria Siderúrgica (CONSIDER). "O Programa Siderúrgico Nacional." Rio de Janeiro, October 1973 (mimeograph).
Brazil. Ministério da Indústria e do Comércio. *Relatório*, various issues.
Brazil. Ministério de Minas e Energiá. *Relatório de Atividades*, various issues.
Brazil. Ministério do Planejamento e Coordenação Econômica. *Plano Decenal de Desenvolvimento Económico e Social*. Brasília, March 1967.
Brazil. Ministério do Planejamento e Coordenação Geral. *Programa Estratégico de Desenvolvimento*. Brasília, January 1968.
Brazil. Presidencia da Republica. Secretaria de Planejamento. Instituto de Planejamento Econômico e Social (IPEA). "Programa Geral de Dispendios, 1976–78." Brasilia, 1975 (mimeograph).
Brazil. Presidência da República. Secretaria de Planejamento. Secretaria de Controle de Empresas Estatais (SEST). *Empresas Estatais no Brasil e o Controle da SEST: Antecedentes e Experiência de 1980*. Brasilia, 1981.
Brazil. Secretariat of Planning of the Presidency of the Republic. *Fiscal Policy: Performance in 1980 and Guidelines for 1981*. Brasilia, 1981.
Centrais Életricas Brasileiras, S.A. (ELETROBRÁS). *Orçamento Plurianual da Empresa, 1974–1979*. Rio de Janeiro: ELETROBRÁS, 1974.
Centrais Eletricas Brasileiras, S.A. (ELETROBRÁS). *Relatório*, various issues.
Centrais Electricas Brasileiras, S.A. (ELETROBRÁS). *The Brazilian Electric Power Sector*. Rio de Janeiro: ELETROBRÁS, 1980.
Centrais Eletricas de São Paulo, S.A. (CESP). "Tarifas de Energia Elétrica: Noções Básicas." São Paulo, 1975 (mimeograph).

275

Centrais Eletricas do Sul do Brasil, S.A. (ELETROSUL). "Salto Santiago Hydroelectric Project and Transmission System. Request for Financing from International Bank for Reconstruction and Development," 2 vols. Rio de Janeiro: ELETROSUL, 1975 (mimeograph).

Companhia Telefônica Brasileira (CTB). *Anuário Estatístico*. Rio de Janeiro, various issues.

Fundação Getulio Vargas. *Conjuntura Econômica*. Rio de Janeiro, various issues.

Fundação Getulio Vargas. Instituto Brasileiro de Economia. Centro de Estudos Fiscais. *O Setor Público Federal Descentralizado*. Rio de Janeiro: Fundação Getulio Vargas, 1967.

Fundação Getulio Vargas. "Dimensão e estrutura do setor público estadual," 2 vols. Rio de Janeiro, 1972 (mimeograph).

Instituto Brasileiro de Geografia e Estatística (IBGE). *Anuário Estatístico do Brasil*. Rio de Janeiro, various issues.

Instituto Brasileiro de Geografia e Estatistica (IBGE). Superintendência de Estatísticas Primárias. *Empresas Telefônicas*. Rio de Janeiro, various issues.

International Bank for Reconstruction and Development (IBRD), International Development Association. "Current Economic Position and Prospect of Brazil," 2 vols. Washington, D.C., 1971 (mimeograph).

International Bank for Reconstruction and Development (IBRD). *Mexico: Manufacturing Sector Situation, Prospects, and Policies*. Washington, D.C.: IBRD, 1979.

State Intervention in the Industrialization of Developing Countries: Selected Issues. Washington, D.C.: IBRD, 1979.

Siderúrgica Brasileira, S.A. (SIDERBRÁS). *Relatório da Diretoria*, various issues.

Telecomunicações Brasileiras, S.A. (TELEBRÁS). *Filosofia, Atos e Legislação*. Brasília: TELEBRÁS, 1973.

U.S. Congress. Senate. Committee on Foreign Relations. Subcommittee on Multinational Corporations. *Multinational Corporations in Brazil and Mexico: Structural Sources of Economic and Noneconomic Power*, by Richard S. Newfarmer and Willard F. Mueller. Washington, D.C.: Government Printing Office, 1975.

Secondary sources

Books

Baer, Werner. *The Development of the Brazilian Steel Industry*. Nashville, Tenn.: Vanderbilt University Press, 1969.

Baer, Werner. *Industrialization and Economic Development of Brazil*. Homewood, Ill.: Irwin, 1965.

Baldwin, John R. *The Regulatory Agency and the Public Corporation: The Canadian Air Transport Industry*. Cambridge, Mass.: Ballinger, 1975.

Bergsman, Joel. *Brazil, Industrialization and Trade Policies.* New York: Oxford University Press, 1971.

Boneo, Horacio. *Saber Ver Las Empresas Públicas.* San José, Costa Rica: EDUCA, 1979.

Bruneau, Thomas C., and Faucher, Philippe, eds. *Authoritarian Capitalism: Brazil's Contemporary Economic and Political Development.* Boulder, Colo.: Westview Press, 1981.

Capron, William M. *Technological Change in Regulated Industries.* Washington, D.C.: Brookings Institution, 1971.

Carvalho, Getulio. *Petrobrás: do monopólio aos contratos de risco.* Rio de Janeiro: Forense Universitária, 1976.

Chenery, Hollis B., and Syrquin, Moises. *Patterns of Development, 1950–1970.* London: Oxford University Press, 1975.

Correa do Lago, Luiz A., Lopes de Almeida, Fernando, and Lima, Beatriz M. F. de. *A Indústria Brasileira de Bens de Capital.* Rio de Janeiro: Fundação Getulio Vargas, 1979.

Diaz-Alejandro, Carlos. *Essays on the Economic History of the Argentine Republic.* New Haven, Ct.: Yale University Press, 1970.

Einaudi, Mario, Bye, Maurice, and Rossi, Ernesto. *Nationalization in France and Italy.* Ithaca, N.Y.: Cornell University Press, 1955.

Escobar, Janet Kelly. "Comparing State Enterprises Across International Boundaries: The Corporación Venezolana de Guayana and the Companhía Vale do Rio Doce." In Leroy P. Jones, ed., *Public Enterprise in Less-Developed Countries.* New York: Cambridge University Press, 1982.

Evans, Peter. *Dependent Development: The Alliance of Multinational, State, and Local Capital in Brazil.* Princeton, N.J.: Princeton University Press, 1979.

Fitzgerald, E.V.K. *The Political Economy of Peru, 1956–78.* Cambridge University Press, 1979.

Foster, C. D. *Politics, Finance, and the Role of Economics: An Essay on the Control of Public Ownership.* London: Allen & Unwin, 1971.

Franco Sobrinho, Manoel de Oliveira. *Empresas Públicas no Brasil: ação internacional.* São Paulo: Editora Resenha Universitária, 1975.

Furtado, Celso. *Análise do Modelo Brasileiro.* 2nd ed. Rio de Janeiro: Civilização Brasileira, 1972.

Glade, William P. *The Latin American Economies: A Study of Their Institutional Development.* New York: American Book, 1969.

Hanson, Albert H. *Public Enterprise and Economic Development.* 2nd ed. London: Routledge & Kegan Paul, 1965.

Hanson, Albert H., ed. *Nationalization, A Book of Readings.* University of Toronto Press, 1963.

Hirschman, Albert. *The Strategy of Economic Development.* New Haven and London: Yale University Press, 1958.

Holland, Stuart., ed. *The State as Entrepreneur.* London: Cox and Wyman, 1972.

Instituto Brasileiro de Siderúrgia (IBS). *Anais do II Congresso Brasileiro de Siderúrgia, 1972.* Rio de Janeiro, 1972.

Instituto Brasileiro de Siderúrgia. *Anuário Estatístico da Indústria Siderúrgica Brasileira, 1975.* Rio de Janeiro, 1976.

Johansen, Leif. *Public Economics.* Amsterdam and London: North-Holland, 1971.

Jones, L. P. *Public Enterprise and Economic Development: The Korean Case.* Seoul: Korea Development Institute, 1975.

Koontz, Harold, and Gable, Richard W. *Public Control of Economic Enterprise.* New York: McGraw-Hill, 1956.

Lafer, Celso. *O Sistema Político Brasileiro.* São Paulo: Editora Perspectiva, 1975.

Leff, Nathaniel H. *The Brazilian Capital Goods Industry, 1929–1964.* Cambridge, Mass.: Harvard University Press, 1968.

Luz, Nicia Vilela. *A luta pela industrialização do Brasil, 1908–1930.* São Paulo: Difusão Europeia do Livro, 1961.

Lyra, João F. *Regime e control das empresas públicas.* Rio de Janeiro: Pongetti, 1963.

Margolis, Julius, and Guitton, H., eds. *Public Economics.* New York: St. Martin's Press, 1969.

Martins, Carlos Estevam. *Capitalismo de Estado e Modelo Político no Brasil.* Rio de Janeiro: Edições Graal, 1977.

Martins, Carlos Estevam. *Estado e Capitalismo no Brasil.* São Paulo: Editora HUCITEC, 1977.

Musgrave, Richard. *Fiscal Systems.* New Haven and London: Yale University Press, 1969.

Newfarmer, Richard S. *Transnational Conglomerates and the Economics of Dependent Development: A Case Study of the International Electrical Oligopoly and Brazil's Electrical Industry.* Greenwich, Ct.: JAI Press, 1980.

Nove, Alex. *Efficiency Criteria for Nationalized Industries.* University of Toronto Press, 1973.

Nurkse, Ragnar. *Problems of Capital Formation in Underdeveloped Countries.* London: Oxford University Press, 1953.

Posner, N. V., and Woolf, S. J. *Italian Public Enterprise.* Cambridge, Mass.: Harvard University Press, 1967.

Pryke, Richard. *Public Enterprise in Practice.* New York: St. Martin's Press, 1971.

Ramanadham, V. V. *The Structure of Public Enterprise in India.* New York: Asia Publishing House, 1961.

Ranis, Gustav, ed. *Government and Economic Development.* New Haven, Ct.: Yale University Press, 1971.

Reed, P. W. *The Economics of Public Enterprise.* London: Butterworth, 1973.

Reid, Graham L., and Allen, Kevin. *Nationalized Industries.* London: Penguin Books, 1970.

Reynolds, Clark W. *The Mexican Economy: Twentieth-Century Structure and Growth.* New Haven, Ct.: Yale University Press, 1970.

Rezende da Silva, Fernando A. *Avaliação do setor publico na economia brasileira.* Coleção Relatórios de Pesquisa, no. 13. Rio de Janeiro: IPEA, 1973.

Rezende da Silva, Fernando, Monteiro, Jorge Vianna, Suzigan, Wilson, Carneiro, Dionisio, and Castelo Branco, Flavio P. *Aspectos da participação do governo na economia.* IPEA Série Monográfica, no. 26. Rio de Janeiro: IPEA/INPES, 1976.

Robson, William A. *Nationalized Industry and Public Ownership.* University of Toronto Press, 1960.

Roett, Riordan, ed. *Brazil in the Seventies.* Washington, D.C.: American Enterprise Institute, 1976.

Roett, Riordan, ed. *Brazil in the Sixties.* Nashville, Tenn.: Vanderbilt University Press, 1972.

Ruiz, Roberto. *O telefone.* Rio de Janeiro: Companhia Telefônica Brasileira, 1973.

Scherer, F. M. *Industrial Market Structure and Economic Performance.* Chicago: Rand McNally, 1971.

Scott, David L. *Financing the Growth of Electric Utilities.* New York: Praeger, 1976.

Shepherd, William G. *Economic Performance Under Public Ownership: British Fuel and Power.* New Haven and London: Yale University Press, 1965.

Shepherd, William G. *The Treatment of Market Power: Antitrust, Regulation, and Public Enterprise.* New York and London: Columbia University Press, 1975.

Shepherd, William G., ed. *Public Enterprise: Economic Analysis of Theory and Practice.* Lexington, Mass.: Heath, 1976.

Sherwood, Frank P. *O aumento do preço do aço da CSN: Estudo de um caso.* Cadernos de Administração Publica, no. 61. Rio de Janeiro: Fundação Getulio Vargas, 1966.

Skidmore, Thomas E. *Politics in Brazil, 1930–1964: An Experiment in Democracy.* New York: Oxford University Press, 1967.

Smith, Peter Seaborn. *Oil and Politics in Modern Brazil.* Toronto: Macmillan of Canada, 1976.

Stepan, Alfred. *The State and Society: Peru in Comparative Perspective.* Princeton, N.J.: Princeton University Press, 1978.

Suzigan, Wilson, Bonelli, Regis, Horta, Maria Helena, and Lodder, Celsius. *Crescimento Industrial no Brasil: Incentivos e Desempenho Recente.* Coleção Relatórios de Pesquisa, no. 26. Rio de Janeiro: IPEA, 1974.

Suzigan, Wilson. *Indústria: política, instituições, e desenvolvimento.* Série Monográfia, no. 28. Rio de Janeiro: IPEA/INPES, 1978.

Syvrud, Donald E. *Foundations of Brazilian Economic Growth.* Stanford, Calif.; Hoover Institution Press, 1974.

TECHNOMETAL. *Preços de Produtos Siderúrgicos.* 7 vols. Rio de Janeiro, 1972.

Tendler, Judith. *Electric Power in Brazil: Entrepreneurship in the Public Sector.* Cambridge, Mass.: Harvard University Press, 1968.

Tendler, Judith. *Inside Foreign Aid.* Baltimore: Johns Hopkins University Press, 1975.

Turvey, Ralph. *Economic Analysis and Public Enterprises.* London: Allen & Unwin, 1971.

Turvey, Ralph. *Optimal Pricing and Investment in Electricity Supply.* London: Allen & Unwin, 1968.

Turvey, Ralph, ed. *Public Enterprise.* London: Penguin Books, 1968.

Tyler, William G. *Manufactured Export Expansion and Industrialization in Brazil.* Tübingen: J.C.B. Mohr (Paul Siebeck), 1976.

Venancio Filho, Alberto. *A intervenção do estado no dominio econômico.* Rio de Janeiro: Fundação Getulio Vargas, 1968.

Vernon, Raymond., ed. *Big Business and the State: Changing Relations in Western Europe.* Cambridge, Mass.: Harvard University Press, 1974.

Vernon, Raymond, ed. *The Dilemma of Mexico's Development: The Roles of the Private and Public Sectors.* Cambridge, Mass.: Harvard University Press, 1965.

Vernon, Raymond, and Levy, Brian. "State-owned Enterprises in the World Economy: The Case of Iron Ore." In Leroy P. Jones, ed., *Public Enterprise in Less-Developed Countries.* New York: Cambridge University Press, 1982.

Villela, A., and Suzigan, W. *Política do governo e crescimento da economia brasileira, 1889–1945.* Rio de Janeiro: IPEA/INPES, 1975.

Villela, Annibal V., and Baer, Werner. *O setor privado nacional: problemas e políticas para seu fortalecimento.* Rio de Janeiro: IPEA/INPES, 1980.

Webb, Michael G. *The Economics of Nationalized Industries: A Theoretical Approach.* London: Nelson, 1973.

Wells Fargo Bank N.A. *Companhia Vale do Rio Doce.* San Francisco: Wells Fargo Bank, 1976.

Wilcox, Clair, and Shepherd, William G. *Public Policies Toward Business.* 5th ed. Homewood, Ill: Irwin, 1975.

Wirth, John D. *The Politics of Brazilian Development, 1930–1954.* Stanford, Calif.: Stanford University Press, 1970.

Articles

Abranches, Sergio H. "Empresa estatal e capitalismo: uma análise comparada." In Carlos Estervam Martins, ed., *Estado e Capitalismo no Brasil,* pp. 5–54. São Paulo: Editora HUCITEC, 1977.

"A questão da empresa estatal: economia, política, e interesse público." *Revista Brasileira de Administração de Empresas* 19 (Oct.–Dec. 1979):95–107.

"Análise da Empresa Estatal." *Visão*, May 26, 1975.

Bacha, Edmar Lisboa. "Hierarquia e remuneração gerencial." In *A controvérsia sobre distribuição de renda e desenvolvimento*, pp. 124–58. Ed. Ricardo Tolipan and Arthur Carlos Tinelli. Rio de Janeiro: Zahar, 1975.

Baer, Werner. "The Brazilian Boom, 1968–72: An Explanation and Interpretation." *World Development* 1 (August 1973):1–16.

Baer, Werner. "The Brazilian Growth and Development Experience, 1964–1975." In *Brazil in the Seventies*, pp. 41–62. Ed. Riordan Roett. Washington, D.C.: American Enterprise Institute, 1976.

Baer, Werner. "The Role of Government Enterprises in Latin America's Industrialization." In *Fiscal Policy for Industrialization and Development in Latin America*, pp. 263–81. Ed. David T. Geithman. Gainesville, Fla.: University Presses of Florida, 1974.

Baer, Werner, and Beckerman, Paul. "Indexing in Brazil." *World Development* 2 (Oct.–Dec. 1974):35–47.

Baer, Werner, Kerstenetzsky, Isaac, and Villela, Annibal. "The Changing Role of the State in the Brazilian Economy." *World Development* 1 (November 1973):23–34.

Baer, Werner, Newfarmer, Richard, and Trebat, Thomas. "On State Capitalism in Brazil: Some New Issues and Questions." *Inter-American Economic Affairs* 30 (Winter 1977):69–91.

Balassa, Bela. "Incentive Policies in Brasil." *World Development* 7 (Nov.–Dec. 1979):1023–42.

Banfield, Edward C. "Corruption as a Feature of Governmental Organization." *Journal of Law and Economics* 18 (December 1975):587–605.

Bergsman, Joel, and Candal, Arthur. "Industrialization: Past Success and Future Problems." In *The Economy of Brazil*, pp. 29–73. Ed. Howard S. Ellis. Berkeley and Los Angeles: University of California Press, 1969.

Blair, Calvin P. "Nacional Financeira: Entrepreneurship in a Mixed Economy." In *Public Policy and Private Enterprise in Mexico*, pp. 191–240. Ed. Raymond Vernon. Cambridge, Mass.: Harvard University Press, 1964.

Bonelli, Regis, and Facanha, L. O. "A indústria de bens de capital no Brasil: Desenvolvimento, problemas, e perspectivas." In *Indústria: politica, instituições, e desenvolvimento*. Ed. Wilson Suzigan. Rio de Janeiro: IPEA, 1978.

Bonelli, Regis, and Werneck, Dorothea F. F. "Desempenho industrial: auge e desaceleração nos anos 70." In *Indústria: politica, instituições, e desenvolvimento*, pp. 167–226. Ed. Wilson Suzigan. Rio De Janeiro: IPEA, 1978.

Cardoso, Fernando H. "Desenvolvimento capitalista e Estado: bases e alternativas." In *Estado e Capitalismo no Brasil*, pp. 205–20. Ed. Carlos Estevam Martins. São Paulo: Editora HUCITEC, 1977.

Cardoso, Fernando H. "Estatização e Autoritarismo Esclarecido: Tendencias e Limites." *Estudos CEBRAP* 15 (Feb.–March 1976).

Cardoso de Mello, J. M. "O Estado Brasileiro e os Limites da Estatização." *Ensaios de Opinião* 5 (1977).

Carvalho, Getulio. "PETROBRÁS: Duas Decadas e um Dilema." *Revista de Administração Pública* 9 (January 1975):14–39.

Cerqueira, Eli Diniz, and Boschi, Renato R. "Elite industrial e Estado: uma análise da ideologia do empresariado nacional nos anos 70." In *Estado e Capitalismo no Brasil*, pp. 167–204. Ed. Carlos Estevam Martins. São Paulo: Editora HUCITEC, 1977.

Contador, Claudio. "Custo de oportunidade de capital em condições de risco." *Pesquisa e Planejamento Econômico* 5 (June 1975):163–218.

Costa, Margareth Hanson. "A discutida ampliação da intervenção estatal." *Conjuntura Econômica* 33 (December 1979):90–2.

Coutinho, Luciano. "Política Econômica: 1974–1980." *Revista de Economia Política* 1 (Jan.–March 1981):77–100.

Coutinho, Luciano, and Reichstul, Henri-Philippe. "O setor produtivo estatal e o ciclo." In *Estado e Capitalismo no Brasil*, pp. 55–94. Ed. Carlos Estevam Martins. São Paulo: Editora HUCITEC, 1977.

Economic Commission for Latin America. "Public Enterprises: Their Present Significance and Their Potential in Development." *Economic Bulletin for Latin America* 16 (1971):1–70.

"Empresas estatais: acelera-se a estatização." *Visão*, August 29, 1980, pp. 421–3.

Erber, Fabio Stefano. "Desenvolvimento tecnológico e intervenção do Estado: um confronto entre a experiencia brasileira e a dos paises capitalistas centrais." *Revista de Administração Pública* 14 (Oct.–Dec. 1980):10–72.

Ferraz, Octavio Marcondes. "Política Realista para a ELETROBRÁS." *Revista Brasileira de Energia Elétrica* 2 (May–Oct. 1964):2–3.

"Filogenese das estatais." *Visão*, August 31, 1976, pp. 88–153.

Fishlow, Albert. "Some Reflections on Post-1964 Brazilian Economic Policy." In *Authoritarian Brazil*, pp. 69–118. Ed. Alfred Stepan. New Haven and London: Yale University Press, 1971.

Foxley, Alejandro, Aninat, Eduardo, and Arellano, José P. "Chile: The Role of Asset Redistribution in Poverty-Focused Development Strategies." *World Development* 5 (Jan.–Feb. 1977):69–88.

Frank, Charles R. "Public and Private Enterprise in Africa." In *Government and Economic Development*, pp. 88–123. Ed. Gustav Ranis. New Haven and London: Yale University Press, 1973.

Gantt, Andrew, and Dutto, Guiseppe. "Financial Performance of Government-Owned Corporations in Less Developed Countries." *IMF Staff Papers* (March 1968):102–37.

Gillis, Malcolm. "Allocative Efficiency and X-Efficiency in State-Owned Enterprises: Some Asian and Latin American Cases in the Mining Sector." *Technical Papers Series*, no. 13 (1978).

Glade, William P. "The Role of Public Sector Firms in the Integration of the Latin American Industrial Structure: Some Preliminary Observations." In *Economic Integration: Concepts, Theories, and Problems*, pp. 255–84. Ed. Hungarian Academy of Sciences. Budapest: Publishing House of the Hungarian Academy of Sciences, 1977.

Graham, Douglas H., and Mendonça de Barros, José Roberto. "The Brazilian Economic Miracle Revisited: Private and Public Sector Initiative in a Market Economy." *Latin American Research Review* 13 (1978):5–38.

"Guerra aos super-salarios." *Veja*, July 30, 1980.

Helena, Silvia. "A indústria de computadores: evolução das decisões governamentais." *Revista de Administração Pública* 14 (Oct.–Dec. 1980):73–109.

Holland, Stuart. "Europe's New Public Enterprises." In *Big Business and the State: Changing Relations in Western Europe*, pp. 25–44. Ed. Raymond Vernon. Cambridge, Mass.: Harvard University Press, 1974.

Hymer, S., and Resnick, S. "Interactions Between the Government and the Private Sector." In *Economic Development and Structural Change*, pp. 155–80. Ed. I. G. Stewart. Edinburgh: Edinburgh University Press, 1969.

Land, James W. "The Role of Public Enterprise in Turkish Economic Development." In *Government and Economic Development*, pp. 53–125. Ed. Gustav Ranis. New Haven and London: Yale University Press, 1973.

Lindsay, Cotton M. "A Theory of Government Enterprise." *Journal of Political Economy* 84 (July–Aug. 1976):1061–77.

Lluch, Constantino. "Employment, Earnings, and Income Distribution." *Brazil: Human Resources Report*, Annex II. pp. 1–74. Ed. Peter Knight. Washington, D.C.: World Bank, 1979.

Malan, Pedro, and Bonelli, Regis. "The Brazilian Economy in the Seventies: Old and New Developments." *World Development* 5 (Jan.–Feb. 1977):19–46.

Mamalakis, M. "An Analysis of the Financial and Investment Activities of the Chilean Development Corporation, 1939–1964." *Journal of Development Studies* 5 (January 1969):118–37.

Marglin, S. A. "The Opportunity Cost of Public Investment." *Quarterly Journal of Economics* 77 (May 1963):274–89.

Martins, Luciano. " 'Estatização' da Economia ou 'Privatização' do Estado?" *Ensaios de Opinião*, no. 9 (1978):30–7.

Monteiro, Jorge Vianna, and Cunha, Luiz Roberto Azevedo. "A organização do planejamento econômico." *Pesquisa e Planejamento* 4 (December 1973):1045–64.

Nelson, James R. "Public Enterprise: Pricing and Investment Criteria." In *Public Enterprise: Economic Analysis of Theory and Practice*, pp. 49–76. Ed. William G. Shepherd. Lexington, Mass.: Heath, 1976.

Niskanen, William A. "Bureaucrats and Politicians." *Journal of Law and Economics* 18 (December 1975):617–43.

Palatnik, Beny, and Orenstein, Luiz. "Perspectivas do Processo de Privatização no Brasil." *Encontros com a Civilização Brasileira* (September 1979), pp. 43–62.

Preston, Lee E. "Corporation and Society: The Search for a Paradigm." *Journal of Economic Literature* 13 (June 1975):434–53.

Quem é quem na economia brasileira, Visão, August 31, 1976.

Reynolds, Clark W., and Carpenter, Robert T. "Housing Finance in Brazil: Toward a New Distribution of Wealth." In *Latin American Urban Research,* vol. 5, pp. 147–74. Ed. Wayne E. Cornelius and Felicity W. Trueblood. Beverly Hills, Calif.: Sage, 1975.

Reynolds, Lloyd G. "Public Sector Saving and Capital Formation." In *Government and Economic Development,* pp. 516–52. Ed. Gustav Ranis. New Haven and London: Yale University Press, 1971.

Rezende, Fernando, and Castelo Branco, Flavio P. "O emprego público como instrumento de política economica." In *Aspectos da Participação do Governo na Economia,* pp. 35–76. Ed. Fernando Rezende et al. Rio de Janeiro: IPEA, 1976.

Sheahan, John B. "Experience with Public Enterprise in France and Italy." In *Public Enterprise: Economic Analysis of Theory and Practice,* pp. 123–84. Ed. William G. Shepherd. Lexington, Mass.: Heath, 1976.

Sheahan, John B. "Public Enterprise in Developing Countries." In *Public Enterprise: Economic Analysis of Theory and Practice,* pp. 205–34. Ed. William G. Shepherd. Lexington, Mass.: Heath, 1976.

Shepherd, William G. "Price Structure, Social Efficiency, and Equity." In *New Dimensions in Public Utility Pricing,* pp. 125–43. Ed. Harry M. Trebing. East Lansing, Mich.: Graduate School of Business Administration, 1976.

Sheperd, William G. "Regulation, Entry, and Public Enterprise." In *Regulation in Further Perspective,* pp. 5–25. Ed. William G. Shepherd and Thomas G. Gies. Cambridge, Mass.: Ballinger, 1974.

Suzigan, Wilson. "As empresas do governo e o papel do estado na economia brasileira." In Fernando Rezende da Silva, Jorge Vianna Monteiro, Wilson Suzigan, Dionisio Carneiro, and Flavio P. Castelo Branco, *Aspectos da participação do governo na economia,* pp. 77-134. Rio de Janeiro: IPEA/INPES, 1976.

Suzigan, Wilson. "Politica industrial no Brasil." In *Indústria: política, instituições, e desenvolvimento,* pp. 35–98. Ed. Wilson Suzigan. Rio de Janeiro: IPEA, 1978.

Tavares de Araujo Junior, José. "Escolha de Tecnicas e Rentabilidade das Empresas Governamentais." *Pesquisa e Planejamento Economico* 4 (June 1974):447–62.

Tavares de Araujo Junior, José, and Dick, Vera Maria. "Governo, empresas multinacionais e empresas nacionais: o caso da indústria petroquímica." *Pesquisa e Planejamento Econômico* 4 (December 1974): 629–54.

Thorp, Rosemary. "The Post-Import-Substitution Era: The Case of Peru." *World Development* 5 (Jan.–Feb. 1977):125–36.

Topik, Steven. "The Evolution of the Economic Role of the Brazilian State." *Journal of Latin American Studies* 11 (2):325–42.

Trebat, Thomas J. "Public Enterprises in Brazil and Mexico: A Comparison of Origins and Performance." In *Authoritarian Capitalism*, pp. 41–58. Ed. Thomas C. Bruneau and Philippe Faucher. Boulder, Colo.: Westview Press, 1981.

Turvey, Ralph. "The Second-Best Case for Marginal Cost Pricing." In *Public Economics*, pp. 336–42. Ed. J. Margolis and H. Guitton. New York: St. Martin's Press, 1969.

Villarreal, Rene, and Villarreal, Rocio R. de. "Las empresas públicas como instrumento de política económica en México." *Trimestre Económico* 45 (April–June 1978):213–46.

Villela, A. V. "As empresas do governo federal e sua importancia na economia nacional, 1956–60." *Revista Brasileira de Economia* 16 (March 1962):99–113.

Wahrlich, Beatriz. "Contrôle político das empresas estatais federais no Brasil: Uma contribuição ao seu estudo." *Revista de Administração Publica* 14 (April–June 1980):5–38.

Werneck, Arnaldo de Oliveira. "As atividades empresariais do governo federal no Brasil." *Revista Brasileira de Economia* 23 (July–Sept. 1969):84–110.

Unpublished Materials

Abranches, Sergio H. "The Divided Leviathan: State and Economic Policy Formation in Authoritarian Brazil." Ph.D. dissertation, Cornell University, 1978.

"Governo, Empresa Estatal, e Política Siderúrgica no Brasil." Rio de Janeiro: FINEP, 1977 (mimeograph).

Abranches, Sergio, and Dain, Sulamis. "A Empresas Estatal no Brasil: Padrões Estruturais e Estratégias de Ação." Rio de Janeiro: FINEP, 1978 (mimeograph).

Alves, Sergio, Ford, Ecila, and Dick, Vera. "O comportamento tecnológico das empresas estatais: A seleção das empresas de engenharia, a escolha de processos industriais, e a compra de bens de capital." Rio de Janeiro: FINEP, 1975 (mimeograph).

Bates, Lawrence W. "The Petroleum Industry in Brazil." Ph.D. dissertation, University of Texas at Austin, 1975.

Belen, Cihan. "The Role of the State Economic Enterprises in the Development of Turkey." Ph.D. dissertation, University of Connecticut, 1975.

Boneo, Horacio. "Political Regimes and Public Enterprises." Paper presented at the Second B.A.P.E.G. Conference on Public Enterprises in Mixed Economy LDCs, Boston, April 3–5, 1980.

Booz-Allen and Hamilton International, Management Consultants. "Pesquisa da Indústria Siderúrgica Brasileira." 4 vols. Rio de Janeiro: BNDE, 1966 (mimeograph).

Boschi, Renato R. "National Industrial Elites and the State in Post-1964 Brazil: Institutional Mediations and Political Change." Ph.D. dissertation, University of Michigan, 1978.

Carvalho, Getulio. "PETROBRÁS: A Case Study of Nationalism and Institution Building in Brazil." Ph.D. dissertation, University of Connecticut, 1975.

Casperson, Paul Richard. "Responsive Pricing of Hydroelectricity in a Developing Region: The Case of Minas Gerais, Brazil." Ph.D. dissertation, Vanderbilt University, 1974.

Coutinho, Luciano, and Reichstul, Henri-Philippe. "Tendencias recentes do investimento empresarial do Estado." São Paulo: FUNDAP/CLACSO, 1979 (mimeograph).

Dutra, Wilson, and Salles, Vitoria C. "Padrão de Financiamento em Empresas Estatais." Preliminary version. Rio de Janeiro: FINEP, 1975 (mimeograph).

Glade, William P. "The Study of State Enterprise in Economic Development." Paper presented at the Conference on Economic Relations Between Mexico and the United States, Austin, Texas, April 1973.

Guimarães, Cesar, ed. "Institucionalização do planejamento, colegiados governamentais, e intermediação de interesses." Rio de Janeiro: IUPERJ, 1977 (mimeograph).

"Perfil da Expansão do Estado Brasileiro na Esfera Econômica: 1945 –1975." Rio de Janeiro: IUPERJ, 1977 (mimeograph).

Holland, Joyce Elizabeth. "The Economics of Brazilian Transportation Policy, 1945–1970." Ph.D. dissertation, Vanderbilt University, 1972.

Kahl, Ary Barbosa Brito, Osorio de, and Botelho, Horacio. "Panorama da Telefonia no Brasil." Preliminary version. Brasilia: IPEA/IPLAN, 1973 (mimeograph).

Knight, Peter. "Brazilian Socioeconomic Development: Issues for the 1980s." Washington, D.C., 1981 (mimeograph).

Martins, Luciano. "Politique et Developement Economique: Structures de Pouvoir et Système de Decisions au Brésil." Ph.D. dissertation, University of Paris, 1973.

Martins, Luciano. "A expansão recente do Estado no Brasil." Rio de Janeiro: IUPERJ, 1976 (mimeograph).

Newfarmer, Richard S. "State Elites in Power: State Control of the Electric Power Industry in Latin America." Department of Economics, University of Notre Dame, April 1980 (mimeograph).

Reis, Leonidia G. dos, and Redinger, Myriam L. "Pesquisa tecnológica em empresas estatais." Rio de Janeiro: FINEP, 1975 (mimeograph).

Sercovich, Francisco Colman. "State-owned Enterprises and Dynamic Comparative Advantage in the World Petrochemical Industry: The Case of Commodity Olefins in Brazil." Development Discussion Paper no. 96, Harvard Institute for International Development, Cambridge, Mass., 1980.

Smith, Hadley Edwin. "An International Comparison of the Role of Government in Economic Development of Developed and Emerging Economies, With Particular Reference to Government Corporations." Preliminary draft, Pakistan Project, International Public Administration

Center, School of Public Administration, University of Southern California, June 1963 (mimeograph).

Trebat, Thomas J. "An Evaluation of the Economic Performance of Public Enterprises in Brazil." Ph.D. dissertation, Vanderbilt University, 1978.

Vianna, Dulce Maria Monteiro. "A pesquisa tecnologica na PETROBRÁS." Preliminary version. Rio de Janeiro: FINEP, 1975 (mimeograph).

Wernecke, William A., Jr. "The Mixed Corporation Model in Brazil: A Case Analysis of Three State Steel Firms, 1964–76." Undergraduate thesis, Stanford University, 1977 (mimeograph).

Index

Cambridge Latin American Studies

293